Whitewater
OUTLAW
Confessions of a Serial Offender

Ken Baysinger

Whitewater OUTLAW
Confessions of a Serial Offender

Whitewater Outlaw *Confessions of a serial Offender*

ISBN 979-8-218-56099-7

Copyright © 2024 by Ken Baysinger
All Rights Reserved

No part of this publication may be reproduced, stored in a retrieval system or transmitted in any way by any means, electronic, mechanical, photocopy, recording, or otherwise, without the prior permission of the author, except as provided by USA copyright law.

This is a work of fiction. Unless otherwise indicated, all the names, characters, businesses, places, events and incidents in this book are either the product of the author's imagination or used in a fictitious manner. Any resemblance to actual persons, living or dead, or actual events is purely coincidental. Opinions expressed by the author or the characters are not necessarily those of the publisher.

Published by Ken Baysinger

December 2024

Book design copyright © 2024 by Ken Baysinger. All rights reserved.

Cover design copyright © 2024 by Ken Baysinger. All rights reserved.

Cover Image
Tamara Baysinger in Wild Sheep Rapid
Photo by JP Baysinger

Published in the United States of America

Prologue

2021

The first thing I must say is that this story is fiction. The great adventure described here never happened. But bear in mind that even if every word of this story were true, I would still have to *say* that it is fiction. The alternative is that my own words could potentially be used to prosecute me for the multitude of legal infractions described here. So, be assured, this story never happened.

However, while the main storyline is fiction, that doesn't mean that the details of the grand adventure are made up. On the contrary, I am trying my best to describe, with minimal self-aggrandizement and exaggeration, some of the things that I have experienced in floating the rivers of the west, and which you might experience if you were to attempt to make the grand circuit of whitewater rivers.

I say that with an additional caveat. This is not a guidebook. The fact that I have had specific successes or failures in the course of my many river trips does not suggest that you would experience the same outcome if you were to treat my narrative as an instruction manual.

But just for the sake of entertainment, let's all pretend that this story is actually 100% true, and take it from there. Unless you are in law enforcement, in which case, please refer to the opening sentence.

It has been suggested that the idea of becoming a serial offender was born out of cabin fever resulting from the Great COVID-19 Lockdown of 2020. That theory is not without merit, even though it is not the way things happened. In reality, the idea had been percolating for many years. It is only the coincidence of timing that creates the illusion of cause and effect.

Back in 1966, while I was aboard USS Enterprise performing my miniscule role in the fiasco known as the Vietnam War, there was a movie called *Endless Summer*. It was a documentary about two surfers who followed the weather around the world to catch the waves at all of the best surfing destinations on earth. Warren Miller has famously done the same thing with skiing, producing a new movie every year.

So, in hours of daydreaming during the ensuing decades, I've idly pondered the attraction a similar adventure, but on whitewater rivers instead of ocean waves or ski slopes. Maybe I could become the Warren Miller of rafting, except for the part about movie-making talent.

However, there's a problem. Surfers can go to any beach, at any time, and paddle out to catch a wave. Warren Miller can go anyplace in the world to make his great ski movies. But you can't do that with river trips. You first need to obtain severely rationed government-issued permits to go rafting. Without those permits, you are breaking the law the instant you climb into your boat and start downriver.

Still, the "Whitewater Summer" daydream persisted. It did so despite the understanding that after more than half a century of whitewater rafting, there is good reason to question whether I actually would be physically *capable* of living the dream. And proving to myself, if not to the skeptical world, that I *am* is pretty good motivation in itself.

My wife, Linda, is the leader of the skeptical world, and is quick to remind me that I am three-quarters of a century old. Not that I needed a reminder. All I have to do is look in a mirror—something that I avoid doing as much as possible.

But a couple of years ago, Linda's younger son, Kevin, announced that he was going to hike the full length of the Pacific Crest Trail, from the Mexican border to the Canadian border. I used to do some backpacking, but had never undertaken a journey of that magnitude. My longest backpacking adventure was the 50-mile, six-day "Fosseen Trek" on Mt. Spokane when I was a Boy Scout.

Photo by Author
Boy Scout badge from my 1960 adventure, backpacking on Mt. Spokane

Kevin is in his early forties, rapidly approaching the age I was when I last strapped-on a pack for even a one-night outing. I can't deny that I felt some stabs of envy as he prepared for the big hike. Instead of just *dreaming*, Kevin was *doing*. So, it is fair to say that his Pacific Crest Trail adventure was a motivating factor in my Whitewater Summer.

We all have something to prove. And in this post-COVID-19 era, there is a palpable need to demonstrate that we are not the pathetic wimps that we've shown ourselves to be as a result of the virus created in the virology lab in Wuhan, China. We dutifully obeyed the sometimes-absurd and often contradictory dictates of politicians who know no more about the virus than we do, even though their personal conduct defied the rules they made for the rest of us. And we wore our masks of shame in the pitiable hope that they would keep us safe.

Photo by Jackie L. Baysinger
Backpacking with my family and dog in 1986

The Great Pandemic was a war. It had to be fought, because the alternative was losing by default. And we fight wars knowing that there will be casualties. We accept the casualties as the price we pay for our pride. COVID has stripped us of our pride. We've proven ourselves to be so fearful of catching the virus that we've spent most of a year cowering in quarantine, and we've deservedly lost our self-respect as a result.

Imagine George Washington cancelling his crossing of the Delaware River out of fear that some of his men would get frostbite. Imagine General Meade retreating from Cemetery Ridge out of fear that he might lose 5,000 men turning back Pickett's Charge. Imagine the Americans in the Higgins Boats approaching Omaha Beach deciding to turn back out of fear that the Germans might kill them.

They did what they had to do in order to complete the task that history had given them, while we, in the twenty-first year of the twenty-first century cling to the fanciful belief that we can live life without risk. All we need to do is cloak ourselves in the bubble-wrap belief that if we hide from it long enough, it'll go away and leave us happy and overweight.

And we have proven ourselves willing to sacrifice our jobs, our businesses, our ability to support ourselves, and worse, we knowingly do that to our neighbors and fellow citizens. We do it out of fear, carefully and deliberately cultivated by politicians and their accomplices in the propaganda ministry of the dominant media.

While I will not claim that COVID is not a serious thing, I am utterly unconvinced that it is the catastrophe that it is portrayed to be. For decades, we have accepted the reality that the ordinary flu kills an average of 60,000 Americans a year, despite the existence of flu vaccines that are available to anyone who wants them. During 2020, 335,000 deaths in the U.S. were attributed to COVID, making it six times as deadly as influenza.

But throughout the year, we heard stories like that of the Florida man who died in a motorcycle accident and was subsequently counted as a COVID death. There have been many thousands of similar reports, where people who died *with* COVID were counted as having died *from* COVID. How can that happen, and what does it mean?

My doctor, who is an actual physician, not someone with a PhD in education, explained it to me. The medical community in its entirety was ordered by the government to perform a COVID test on every person who died. That was not an unreasonable thing to do, since there was the possibility that antibodies present might help in the development of treatments or vaccines. However, the statistics were deliberately misused, creating the illusion of a far greater than actual lethality for COVID.

Medical institutions did it to improve their qualifications for financial assistance from the government. Establishment politicians used the higher number to legitimize their abuse of authority and to denigrate their opposition. "News" media love the higher number, not only because it makes for more sensational copy, they also love the establishment politicians.

So, the current 600,000 deaths narrative just might be false. My doctor says that the medical journals he reads estimate that the actual number of deaths *from* COVID is about 40% of those who die *with* COVID, or about 240,000.

Now, I don't take that number lightly. It is still more than triple the annual death count for flu. But we do not feel the need to alter our lifestyle in any significant way to keep from getting flu. We need to stop allowing ourselves to be made into helpless wimps, and lead our lives with the certain knowledge that we are all going to die. Accept that.

Cross the Delaware. Stand your ground on Cemetery Ridge. Storm the beach at Normandy. Face the enemies who want to take your life. And then make the most of the life you have.

And maybe doing that takes the form of an endless summer of whitewater rafting.

June 16, 2021

Chapter One

A Surprise Opportunity

For many years, I have followed a website called Mountain Buzz. It is a forum for everything related to whitewater boating. I read it mainly for tidbits about new equipment, trip reports, and information about significant changes in the rivers themselves.

But it is also one of several websites that serve as clearing houses for participation on float trips. Sometimes, it is a group that needs a boatman to fill a spot because of a cancellation. Other times, it is an inexperienced group looking for an experienced trip leader. Mostly, it is groups wanting to fill vacant spaces on their permits and get additional wallets to share the cost of the trip.

Within the whitewater community, it is considered bad form to have a coveted float permit and use it for fewer than the prescribed number allowed. The vacant seats are seen as lost opportunity to all who were not so fortunate as to win a permit in the annual lotteries, where the chances of winning are slim to none.

I am speaking specifically about the permits that are most difficult to get—the Selway River, the Middle Fork of the Salmon, and most of all, the Grand Canyon. Every year, tens of thousands of people apply for the few hundred permits that are issued. In the hundreds of permit lotteries I've entered over the years, I've won only four that I can recall. Except for those, I've always gone on somebody else's permit.

This goes a long way toward explaining why solo boating is a rare thing on whitewater rivers. You need to be part of a group, simply to improve the chances that you'll be able to go at all—assuming that you are disinclined to break the law and risk the consequences of getting caught without a permit.

About 25 or 30 years ago, a Portland river runner who was well-known for writing newspaper articles and guidebooks decided to break the law and float the Rogue River without a permit. His goal was to challenge the constitutionality of the permit system. Since his objective was to get caught, in order to take his case to court, he publicly announced his intentions.

The result was that he was caught and ticketed. In the end, he quietly paid the fine, after his attorneys assured him that he could not win in court. Potentially, his equipment could have been confiscated, and he could have been finger-printed, booked, and lodged in a county lock-up. So, he got off easy and gave up any further notion of publicly defying the system.

So, rafting has become almost exclusively a group activity, except on the few rivers that still do not limit public access through a permit system.

In my early days of whitewater rafting, I was still able to run the Rogue River whenever I wanted to, without anybody's permission—well, except for my wife's. You *always* need your wife's permission. All of my early multi-day river trips were just my wife and me on a raft outfitted with a wooden frame that I built in the garage. And except for day-trips, we encountered only a few other people on the river.

But as more and more people took up whitewater sports, the sense of solitude that had been an integral part of rafting started to diminish. For a while, we had to anticipate the days when we were more likely to encounter the unwashed masses, and schedule our trips on other days. Obviously, that didn't last.

The whitewater community as a whole had to make a decision. Was it better to forego solitude and enjoy the river simply for the action, or to forcibly restrict access to the rivers? Limited access won, and those in charge of the most popular rivers created lotteries to determine who would be allowed to use the rivers. So, those who wanted to go rafting started forming groups in order to put more entries into the permit lotteries.

I will tell you, forming a rafting group can be an extremely difficult thing to do. The first thing you discover is that in January *everybody* wants to go on your July raft trip. But most of them don't have rafts, and they don't want to buy or rent one.

So, if you are serious about forming a rafting group, you're probably going to have to provide rafts for at least some of your participants. At times over the years, I've had—much to my wife's dismay—as many as half a dozen rafts that I could make available to people I wanted to take along on river trips.

And then there's the people who love the *idea* of going on a multi-day river trip, but who are unable to make the mental commitment to actually *do* it. They say they want to go. They play along through the weeks or months of planning and preparation, and then, a week before the trip, announce that they have to stay home and tend to the u-pickers in their peach orchard.

Imagine it. We'd been planning the river trip for six months, talked about it at least once a week throughout that period, and *never once* did they remember that they owned a peach orchard! So, I had to re-calculate my shopping lists, re-distribute all of the group gear that those people were supposed to carry, make new transportation and shuttle plans, and (the biggest insult of all) I had to go to their place to retrieve the gear that I'd lent them—after picking a basket of peaches.

Recruiting people to go on raft trips is an ongoing task. I've found that most people are good for three or four raft trips, and then they switch their annual vacation plans back to things like Carnival cruises, European tours, tropical beaches, and other such activities.

They have either tired of rafting, or they've tired of me, though the latter seems quite unlikely, especially in the face of such endlessly amusing touches as the use of peanut butter in squeeze tubes that make sandwiches look like puppy accidents, or my jokes, which never fail to bring tears of laughter to the eyes of all present.

But regardless of the reason, they're finished, and I need to find someone else to help lug the heavy gear to and from the rafts every day, and to help pad the odds of winning a permit lottery. Lately, I've employed the tactic of finding new relatives through DNA websites and recruiting them before anyone gets to them and talks them out of it.

The result of all this was that, except for a couple of Rogue River lodge trips, I hadn't done a one-raft river trip since the very earliest days of my rafting obsession. And I really had no plans to do another. Nor did I have any plan or desire to become a serial violator of river permit laws. So, the idea of a whitewater version of *Endless Summer* seemed destined to remain an idle pipedream.

All of that changed on the last day of March, when someone on Mountain Buzz using the name "Hydro-Maniac" posted a plea for an experienced Grand Canyon boatman to lead their group of first-timers down the river. They had a small group (eight-person) permit, but with only nine weeks until their launch date, two members of the group had dropped out. And they were the only members of the party who had ever floated The Canyon. To make matters worse, one of them, while not the permit holder, was the main organizer and leader of the group.

So, they were looking for someone with Grand Canyon experience, who would be able and willing to lead a group of strangers on their float trip, launching May 23, and who could actually work such a thing into his personal schedule on short notice. I met all but one of those requirements. I'd previously led two Grand Canyon trips, and being retired, I didn't need to worry about scheduling. But I was pretty cautious about joining a group of people I didn't know. There are way too many things that can go bad on a three-week-long blind date.

I was just about to click to a different post, when I noticed that Hydro-Maniac was from Canby, Oregon, just seven miles from my home. Canby's a small town. I go there fairly often. I might even know the guy, even though I was pretty sure that I'd never been on a raft trip with anyone from Canby. So, I paused.

There was nothing to lose by at least talking to the guy. What the hell. He might even turn out to be someone I could recruit into my rafting group to fill the vacancy that resulted from the pending heart surgery that forced one long-time member to retire from rafting. Some people quit for any little thing.

So, I answered the post. I pointed out that we were almost neighbors, and that I had the experience he was looking for. Within five minutes I had a personal message back from Hydro-Maniac, who expressed his excitement about my having volunteered to lead his raft group. I answered back, suggesting that we get together, maybe have a beer or two, and see if we really wanted to bind ourselves together for three weeks on an adventure where there is no escape option until you reach the takeout.

He agreed that I had a point, and asked if I could meet him at his place in Canby, because he had a car posted for sale on Craigslist, and some people were on their way to see it. We settled on 3:30, that being close enough to cocktail hour to justify guilt-free consumption of beer.

I have to say that I was rather uneasy about going rafting with someone who calls himself Hydro-Maniac. The name implied a lot of things. A maniac is a crazy person—an out-of-control nut-case thrill-seeker, someone with more machismo than brainpower. On the other hand, my own user-name is "The Mogur," a name familiar to the readers of Jean Auel novels, meaning the wise all-knowing one with supernatural abilities. And, by the way, I did not give the name to myself. Members of my rafting group dubbed me The Mogur during my one and only Selway River trip, long before Mountain Buzz existed.

In spite of my better sense, I entered Hydro-Maniac's address into the GPS navigator in my classic (meaning "old beater") Ford pickup and headed toward Canby. As I pulled into the driveway, I realized that I'd been there before. Next to the house on the semi-rural property was a large pole building that housed a metal shop. Fourteen years earlier, in preparation for my first Grand Canyon trip, I'd had some welding done in this shop. It was hard for me to reconcile "Hydro-Maniac" with welder.

I turned away from the flash of an arc welder that greeted me as I approached the shop. Looking at a welding arc can blind you. I even close my eyes when watching arc welding on YouTube videos.

"Are you The Mogur?" asked a lady who had emerged from the house and was approaching me.

She looked to be in her fifties, was a bit heavy but far from obese. Her smile revealed that she had all of her teeth. That was a promising sign.

"Yeah. I'm The Mogur. Ken is my name."

"I'm Charlene—Hydro-Maniac."

I must have let my surprise show, because she immediately added, "Actually, that's my son's user-name on Mountain Buzz. But I'm the one who posted the message. Let's go see if we can pry my husband away from his welding."

I'm not very good at remembering faces, and worse at remembering names. But just in case he remembered me, I said, "You may not remember me, but you did some welding for me a few years back."

He said, "I meet so many people, after a while, the faces and names all blend together. I'm Ray Johnson."

"Should I call you Jay?" I asked.

"Oh, you can call me Ray, or you can call me Jay, but you doesn't has to call me Johnson." He actually got my obscure joke. And if you didn't, google it.

"You welded-up an aluminum raft frame that I was modifying to fit a different raft, back when I was getting ready for my first Canyon trip. That was about a dozen years ago."

Charlene said, "I looked at some of your old posts on Mountain Buzz."

"I have no secrets."

Ray said, "Let's go sit on the porch with a beer and talk about this Grand Canyon trip."

I said, "My first question is about the composition of the group."

"Well, there's the two of us, our son and his wife, and a couple of their friends. They're all in their thirties."

"What about whitewater experience?"

"They're all experienced—we are too." He nodded toward Charlene and continued, "We've run the Deschutes, Rogue, Snake, and several other rivers."

"So, you have your own boats?"

"Yeah. We all have rafts and kayaks."

Ouch. Kayaks? The last thing I wanted to do was row a support boat for a group of kayakers.

But before I could voice my concern, Ray said, "For this trip, we're going to be renting rafts from Canyon REO."

I relaxed and asked, "So, are you buying the whole package from them—food and all?"

"Well, we weren't planning to. But the folks who canceled-out were going to do all of the meal planning, so now we're having to re-think the whole thing. I mean, none of us have ever planned meals for a trip of more than three or four days."

"Okay," I said cautiously, "We'll come back to the question of food. But I have to say right off that I'm not interested in rowing a rented raft. If I go, I'll be taking my own raft. And it comes with a complete kitchen setup that is far better than anything you could rent."

Photo by Author
My custom-built SuperStove camp kitchen. When closed down, it occupies a standard-size dry box bay on the raft.

Charlene said, "I saw the pictures of your camp kitchen on Mountain Buzz, and it looks pretty nice."

"Thanks. It's ideal for a group of six to fourteen people."

Ray said, "Well, that would save us from having to rent a kitchen set or throw one together from what we have. I like the idea that yours is already done."

"It includes the four-burner propane cook top, all of the pots, pans, dishes and silverware, plus a big crab-cooker for boiling dishwater, a couple of Dutch ovens, dish pans, a table, and a water purification system; and it's all ready to go."

"That sounds great. So, what about meal planning? Should we have Canyon REO take care of that?"

"It would be the easiest thing to do, but you'll pay a pretty hefty price for the convenience," I commented.

Ray said, "Yeah, but I don't know how we'd do all of it by ourselves, especially on such short notice."

"I get that. But we're getting a bit ahead of ourselves. I want to meet the other people in the group before I commit to doing this. If we can all get together, and agree that we're probably not going to kill each other half-way down the river, then we can work out the details, including what to do about food."

This whole conversation took place two days after my wife's son started his 2,700-mile hike on the Pacific Crest Trail—following his dream.

Chapter Two

My Rafting Resumé

After a few day-trips on rivers around Portland with a friend who had a beat-up yellow "six-man" raft, a couple of badly weathered wooden paddles, and a few pitifully inadequate life vests, I decided to get my own raft. The place to go in those days was Andy & Bax, on Portland's east side.

I went home with a brand-new version of my friend's raft and a pair of puffy orange Type I life jackets. I was taking this whole rafting thing far more seriously than my friend ever had, and I opted to make my raft an oar-raft, rather than a paddle-raft, because that's what serious rafters do.

Photo by Author

I built a simple four-board plywood frame with oarlocks mounted on wooden blocks, and got some row-boat oars—a pair plus a spare. Meanwhile, I'd been collecting newspaper and magazine articles about rafting, including a few that purported to be guides for floating various rivers in and around Oregon. I was thereby becoming an expert even before the varnish on my frame was dry.

One article I had was written by that previously-mentioned Portland river runner who tried to challenge the permit system on the Rogue River. The article was about rafting the Rogue, and it inspired me to take my wife down the Rogue on our new raft.

By the time we set-out for the Rogue, I had accumulated two afternoons of whitewater rowing experience, one on the Sandy River, and one on the North Santiam. And, of course, I had the newspaper article.

Photo by Jackie Baysinger
Our riverside camps were very basic. Cooking over a fire, sleeping bags rolled out on a plastic tarp, and a kitchen table made of rock or driftwood.

The details of my first Rogue River trip are included in Chapter 25. In some ways it was a comedy, but I learned a lot about rafting, and when it was all over, I was totally hooked on the sport.

Back home, I started telling all of my friends what a great time we had, and a few months later, in the dead of winter, one of my co-workers asked if I'd be interested in buying a raft that he had.

It was a nearly new 14-foot raft that he'd bought to use as a fishing boat that he could carry in the trunk of his car. The first time he took it fishing, it took over an hour to pump it up, and then when he went out onto the lake, a slight breeze blew him to the far shore, and it took the rest of the day to fight his way back to his car. He never used the raft again.

Based on a similar raft for sale at Andy & Bax, I figured the raft was worth about $500. As much as I wanted the raft, I told my friend that I couldn't pay him what it was worth.

Photo by Author
The World Famous "twelve-man" raft was a Japanese imitation of the military ten-man rafts that were becoming hard to find.

He said, "Well, how much *can* you give me?"

I said, "Come on, Chuck. I don't want to insult you."

"Nothing you say will hurt my feelings. How much?"

"Hell, I don't know. Okay, a hundred bucks is about all…"

"Sold," he said.

And that was the day I became a World Famous rafter. Later, Chuck confided that he was going to just give me the raft if I hadn't named a price. But at $100, it was probably the best deal anyone ever got buying a raft.

This is not to say that the raft was without its issues. It had absolutely no upturn on the ends, although the 22-inch-diameter of the perimeter tubes did a fairly good job of keeping water from splashing into the raft. It had four air chambers, which, like the *Titanic's* watertight compartmentation, made it unsinkable.

But the inflation valves were tiny, made to thread onto a pair of crappy hand-pumps that came with the raft. And the raft was heat-seeker black, so in the sun, it would quickly become too hot to touch. We always had to keep a scoop close by to water it down before sitting on it.

My culturally insensitive friends named the raft *Sambo* (after the children's book and restaurant chain), but we shall call it *Mariah* here, to keep our publisher out of trouble with the ever-vigilant language police.

My first order of business was to build the ultimate touring frame for my new raft. It had to be built of wood, because that was the only material I knew how to work with. Loosely based on a frame

Photo by Author

With this frame *Miria*h became a stable and versatile touring raft.

Photo by Author

Mariah's first expedition, with wife and dog on the Rogue River in 1976. For the record, Norwegian Elkhounds are not fond of getting wet.

design that I saw in Bill McGinnis's great book, *Whitewater Rafting*, I spent the rest of the winter building my masterpiece.

It consists of five components: the center "box" structure, the front and rear decks, and the left and right decks. Disassembled, it fit neatly inside my van for convenient transport. It was assembled using 29 bolts. For 40 years, I believed that this frame made the raft impossible to flip, but in 2008, my brother-in-law proved me wrong at Wild Sheep rapid in Hells Canyon.

Photo by Author

Miriah and *Silver Sieve* at Foster Bar on the Rogue, 1985.

Mariah was my flagship for the next ten years. I did a trip in 1980 with some guys who were using a rented Riken *River Rider* raft that came with something I'd never seen on a raft before—a folding table! Up to then, I believed that kitchen tables had to be made from driftwood and flat rocks.

That innovation, together with the availability of a newly invented material called aluminum inspired me to build a new frame for *Mariah*. It had exactly the same dimensions as the wooden frame, but the front and rear platforms lifted off the frame and unfolded into tables. No more squatting in the sand to cook!

Photo by Author

My fleet on the John Day River in 1984: *Silver Sieve*, my 8-year-old son's 2-man raft the 6-man Campways, and *Mariah*. Note the kitchen, with two tables that were part of Mariah's frame.

One day, while browsing the Oregonian Classifieds, I ran across another World Famous 12-Man raft for $100 OBO. I had to go take a look at it, since I already had a perfectly good frame for it. I drove to Mt. Angel and found the old raft sitting on the lawn, half-deflated.

It was a pitiful sight. I could see about a dozen small patches, and the raft had been covered with silver Gacoflex rubber paint, in an effort to repair the deteriorated neoprene surface. The seller assured me that she'd hold air "all day, with maybe a top-off at lunch time." He accepted $50 for it, so I took it home and named it *Silver Sieve*. I then had *two* expedition rafts, along with the old *Campways* 6-man raft, and that meant I could entice a broader group to join my raft trips. No raft? No problem!

My sister and her family joined us for a week-long float on the John Day River in 1984, and that made it official: I had my very own rafting group.

Then, in 1986 I walked into Andy & Bax and found a raft better than anything I'd ever hoped to own—A 15-foot Riken *Cheyenne*, a self-bailing raft with a regular price of $5,500.

Photo by Jerry Baysinger

Cheyenne at Tappan Falls on the Middle Fork, with my cousin Judy up front. Note the extreme taper of the front and rear tubes.

But this one was a year old and priced at $2,300. It was actually one of two *Cheyenne* prototypes designed by Vladimir Kovalik and hand-built for Dan Baxter. This very raft had been featured on the front-cover of *River Runner* magazine a year earlier.

Its unique design feature was the extreme taper of the perimeter tubes, down to nine inches, on the front and rear ends of the raft. The idea was that the extreme rise in the inflated floor of the raft would lift the boat up and over normal waves, but the tapered tube would punch through larger ones. It would take-on a lot of water, but that was okay, because it was a self-bailing raft. And it was bomb-proof.

I put down a deposit, and then went home to get *Mariah's* aluminum frame, to see if it would work on *Cheyenne*. I assembled it on the showroom floor in the basement of Andy & Bax, and satisfied myself that it would work. All I had to do was figure out how to pay for the raft. I stretched some truths and told some lies, and somehow came up with the money. I had a raft that I was certain would last the rest of my life. And so far, it has.

I used *Cheyenne* a few times with *Mariah's* frame, but it wasn't a perfect fit. So, I designed and built a new aluminum frame for *Cheyenne*, returned my original aluminum frame to *Mariah*, and the old wooden frame to *Silver Sieve*.

Now that I had *Cheyenne*, a raft that was truly suitable to run the Grand Canyon, I put my name on the notorious wait list. My original number was 12,780, so, 12,779 groups would go down the river before I did.

It was somewhere in this general timeframe that my wife became convinced that I was crazy. I guess you could make that argument, but *she* was the one joining a cult-like band of born-again fundamentalists.

On the other hand, I was the one quitting my job as a corporate advertising manager to buy a big whitewater rafting company, so she may have had a point. But I wanted to make a living doing the thing that I loved doing—whitewater rafting.

The company I bought was Oregon River Experiences, which had built their business around row-yourself guided trips (as opposed to the paddle-raft or ride-with-guide trips offered by traditional outfitters). This concept appealed to a more active, hands-on clientele, and gave ORE what we advertising people call a "unique selling proposition." We offered what no other company at the time did.

Photo by Author

An O.R.E. group on the Lower Salmon—five guest rafts and two guide rafts.

I have been repeatedly reminded that the late Ken Warren was also doing row-yourself trips. That's true, as far as it goes. The difference between his trips and ours was that Warren did very little actual guiding. He provided rafts for his guest to row, and he provided meals for them. But on the river, Warren's guests were mostly left to their own devices. He was more outfitter than guide. We were both.

We had a fleet of nearly sixty rafts, including forty twelve-foot Riken *Pioneers* rigged with frames and oars, and my guides would assign two guests to each raft, and lead them, follow-the-leader style, down the river. Guests could simply watch and imitate what the lead guide did, exactly as I had done on my first Rogue River trip, when I shadowed a guided group and learned by watching. On our company trips, every third or fourth boat in line was another guide raft, to refresh the line and coach the guests.

In my first season as an outfitter, I learned more about rafting than I'd learned in fifteen years as an amateur. And it went way beyond boatmanship, encompassing all aspects of planning and executing group river trips. With about two-dozen guides, and four sets of equipment, I had as many as four groups out on the ten rivers where we operated, on any given day from May through September.

Spending 50 to 60 days on the oars every season made me a damn good boatman—certainly not the greatest of all time, but definitely in the top tier. And in leading row-yourself groups, it is necessary to tell the guests what they're approaching before it comes into sight. That means memorizing every rock, every chute, and every hole in every rapid. Being a great boatman doesn't in itself require that, and that's what made row-yourself trip leaders an elite group.

Throughout the 1980s, and unbeknownst to me (I've always wanted to use that phrase), a slime-ball named Charles Keating was systematically looting the assets of Lincoln Savings and Loan, committing crimes for which he was eventually sent to prison, and triggering sweeping changes in federal banking regulations.

In 1992 I was finally making a respectable profit as an outfitter, when my banker called to inform me that her bank could no longer back my company. The new regulations severely reduced the amount of every bank's portfolio that could be invested in small business. Without financing, my only options were to sell-out, shut down, or find a sugar daddy. Every other small business in the country faced the same issue, all because of Charles Keating and his cronies, known as "the Keating Five."

That illustrates how history happens, and explains why I sold my rafting business in 1993 to an energetic young river guide whose father could bankroll the purchase. I swallowed the bitter pill and went back into the world of corporate advertising and publishing.

But I'd formed many friendships while running the rafting business, including a group that had booked at least three trips with me. They contacted me early in 1993 to say that they'd won a permit to float the Selway River. This is the most tightly restricted river in the country, with only one party a day allowed to launch.

Tom, the group's leader invited me to join them and lead the trip in the same way as the row-yourself trips they'd booked with my company. I might be crazy, but I knew better than to pass-up a chance to float the Selway.

It was during that trip that Tom dubbed me "the Mogur," the wise, all-knowing one—and a major character in Jean Auel's popular *Clan of the Cave Bear* novels. He had previously nicknamed one of my guides Ayla, the tough blonde who tames horses and lions in the same series. From there, it was a small step to start calling our group "The Clan of the Nose Hair." My apologies to Jean Auel.

Since then, we've done at least one major expedition every year, including trips on the Middle Fork, the Main Salmon, the Lower Salmon, the Snake, the Owyhee, the Grande Ronde, the John Day, the Rogue, and two spectacular trips through Grand Canyon.

Photo by Jerry Baysinger
Madonna on the Middle Fork at Tappan Falls. JP Baysinger rowing.

In 1996, while preparing for a Clan trip down the Rogue, I made the sad discovery that mice had chewed a hole big enough to pass a basketball through in one of the main tubes on *Silver Sieve*. Unable to convince myself that I could repair it and make it safe to use, I retired the old raft. That left somebody without a raft for the upcoming Rogue trip, so I took a trip to Andy & Bax to see if they had anything that would solve the problem.

The answer turned out to be a pair of Momentum cataraft tubes. It was easy to rationalize the expenditure, since I already had a frame that would work with the tubes—the aluminum frame that I built for *Maria*h in 1983. That gave me the cataraft that was to become known as *Madonna*. I reunited *Maria*h with her original wooden frame, so I ended up with the same total number of rafts.

Shortly before Christmas in 1996, I met my future second wife, Linda. In the course of a three-hour "meet for a quick cup of coffee" conversation, I determined, among many other things, that we shared a lot of recreational interests. Still, it took four years to convince her to run off to the Caribbean and get married. During that time, we rafted together on the

Photo by Author
Linda hiking up Cherry Creek on the Snake River in Hells Canyon, 1998.

Owyhee, Snake Main Salmon, and the Rogue.

During that Rogue trip, we stopped at the Helfrich Tree, an attraction that is well-known to river guides, but not to most private boaters. In the morning that day, I had told Linda to try to find a heart-shaped rock, which she would need later. It's all part of the guides' build-up to a stop at Winkle Bar.

But Linda, knowing nothing of the Helfrich Tree, got the idea that it was a build-up to a marriage proposal. In a state of mental panic all morning, she tried to figure out what to do. Upon arrival at the Helfrich Tree, I explained that if you place a heart-shaped rock at the base of the tree, it will cure a broken heart. That's the old tradition.

Photo by JP Baysinger
Heart-shaped rocks under the Helfrich Tree

Two months later, following the real marriage proposal, Linda admitted that in the anti-climactic moment when I explained the tradition of the Helfrich Tree, she learned something. After having braced herself to tell me that she wasn't ready to get married, when I didn't ask, she realized that she was. Although I knew none of it at the time, it was the big turning point. So, heart-shaped rocks and the Helfrich Tree at Winkle Bar will always have a very special meaning to me.

2006 turned out to be a pivotal year in the evolution of the Clan of the Nose Hair. Early in the year, I received my Grand Canyon Wait List "continuing interest form," which stated that my position on the list was now a three-digit number—a huge milestone.

Then, a couple of months later, the Park Service announced that they were scrapping the wait-list system and moving to a "weighted lottery" system. I'd been on the wait list for seventeen years, and just when I was within sight of a permit, they ditched the system!

After a twenty-minute tirade about the absurdity and unfairness of the abrupt rule change, I started reading the details. First, more private permits would be available—not for more people, but for more groups. All permits had previously been for groups of up to sixteen people. In the new system, about a quarter of those permits were split into two eight-person groups.

The other golden egg in the Easter basket of changes was summed up in the word "weighted" in defining the new lottery. Everyone who had been on the now defunct wait list was given an extra lottery entry for every year we had been on the list. That meant that in the October lottery, for the 2007 season, I would get *eighteen* entries.

Of course, I entered the lottery. I went for a small group permit, because, number one, I didn't know sixteen people who could do a Grand Canyon trip, and number two, I really didn't want to lead a group that big. The bigger the group, the more challenging it is to lead.

When the lottery results were released, I was shocked (and thrilled) to learn that I'd won. I was finally going to float the mighty Colorado River. All I needed was a group to take along.

And one other thing. I kind-of needed a new raft. My "forever raft," was showing her age. Over the years, *Cheyenne's* floor had taken a beating. In one event, on the Upper Clackamas River, I'd run across a barbed wire fence lying just below the surface of the water. It cut a three-foot gash in the floor.

I had it professionally repaired, but nobody took the time to thoroughly dry out the inside of the tubes. The lingering moisture began breaking-down the adhesive that held the internal I-beams in place, and one day, the I-beams pulled loose, making the floor look more like a pillow than an air mattress. No bueno.

By then, the Riken company had stopped making rafts, and the only replacement floor I could find came from the Hyside company. The "factory refurbished" floor that I bought fit fairly well, but it didn't last. Within a year, its I-beams started to separate, so I sent it back to the broker who sold it to me for a *second* refurbishment.

But I'd lost confidence. It had held up okay for our Middle Fork trip in 2006, but I questioned how it would hold up in Grand Canyon. So, I started researching new rafts, to see if any would work with my very personalized frame. I found two, both sixteen-foot rafts—from Aire and Vanguard.

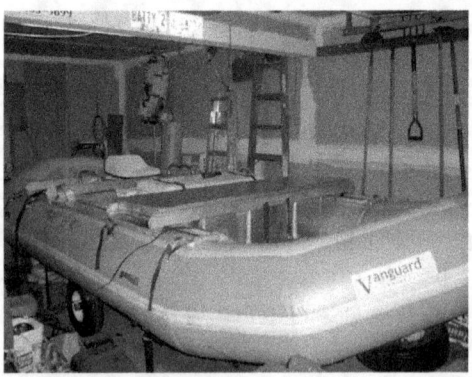

Photo by Author
My custom aluminum frame is a perfect fit.

In a stroke pure luck, I found an off-season bargain price on a yellow, year-old Vanguard that had been used only three times and was in perfect condition. As expected, my frame fit perfectly. So, the next question was what to do with *Cheyenne*.

My daughter Tamara had been rafting all her life, and had been a participant on many of my Clan trips. But her little twelve-foot raft, *Bright Star*, had barely survived the Middle Fork. *Cheyenne* still had some life, so I offered it to her.

Within days of that, an ad for two new-old-stock Riken floors for *Cheyenne* popped up on Craigslist. I sent her the ad, and she jumped on it. Meanwhile, I took *Madonna's* frame (which originally had been built for *Mariah*) and had it cut down the middle and widened nine inches to properly fit *Cheyenne*.

Photo by Linda Baysinger

Rigging *Cheyenne* and *Vanguard* at Lee's Ferry the day before our launch.

So, now Tamara had a Grand Canyon raft. She and her husband signed on. So did my sister Jan and her husband Chris, who had a great little Riken *Miwok*. At thirteen-and-a-half feet, *Miwok* was a bit small, but Chris was a superb boatman who could make it work.

The remaining two places on my Grand Canyon permit were claimed by two of my brothers, Jerry and Jim, who were regulars on Clan trips. Neither had a raft capable of making the trip, so Jim bought a sixteen-foot Aire, and Jerry a fifteen-foot Star. They spent the weeks preceding the trip building frames for their new rafts. And Jim also did all of the welding on a new tandem-axle trailer for my raft.

The preparations for a Grand Canyon trip are astronomical—especially if it is your first. Jerry and I spent two or three weekends at Jim's place working on the equipment, and I spent many, many hours working out the menus, shopping lists, and packing lists.

We did a lot of things right and a few things wrong. One of my mistakes was yielding to the "urgent need" of two members of the party to get back home within two weeks. But on the whole, it was the trip of a lifetime.

Six years later, I entered another Grand Canyon permit lottery, and astoundingly, I won again. Most of the same group came back (but not Linda, who kind-of burnt out on river camping). By this time, Jan and Chris had also retired from rafting and sold *Miwok* to our youngest sister, Joni and her husband, Other Chris. On this trip, we corrected the mistakes we made on the first, and it was a nearly perfect trip.

In succeeding years, Jim and I built a new frame for *Madonna*, out of steel EMT conduit. This "loaner" raft has been on many Clan of the Nose Hair river trips, and has more in her future.

This entire chapter has been true, with barely a trace of exaggeration. There will be plenty of that in the rest of this story.

Chapter Three

Meeting the Millennials

Ray and Charlene were fine. I felt quite comfortable about going on a raft trip with them—even one of nearly three weeks duration. But I harbor an instinctive skepticism about people born after 1990. They grew up in a foreign world, and many have never assimilated into the adult culture. In short, they are Millennials, and as such, are not to be trusted.

With COVID protocols still firmly in place, our meeting was illegal. There were seven of us, and the Oregon governor had decreed that no more than six people could gather in a private home, and that was only if they were all of the same family. So, right off the bat, we were breaking two laws when we gathered at Ray's place the day after our first meeting.

Charlene introduced me to her son, Joseph, and his wife, Sophia. Now, in my world, if your name is Joseph, everyone calls you Joe. But in the Millennial world, only the formal name would do. So, until we could find an appropriately disparaging nickname, we'd all have to call him Joseph.

His friends were named Steven (not Steve) and Krystal—with a K. We were all sitting in a circle on Ray's porch, having decided to take a chance on being seen and ratted-out by some random busybody driving past and observing our flagrant defiance of the COVID quarantine. What's more, thrill-seekers that we all were, we'd agreed to forgo the compulsory surgical masks. It didn't worry me. I'd been vaccinated, and I'm sophisticated—meaning that I was immune (according to a former President, who was explaining in 2020 why the rules didn't apply to him).

The conversation started as you would expect in a group made up of three old people and four Millennials.

Pointing at my Vietnam Veteran hat, Krystal asked, "So, did you, like, fight in Vietnam?"

I said, "I didn't actually do much fighting. But I was there."

Steven said, "So, I know a guy who went to Afghanistan. Or maybe it was Iraq. One of those places."

Enough of that. I asked the key question, "Right now, there's seven of us. Do you have anyone lined-up for the eighth spot? From an organizational standpoint, eight is better than seven."

Charlene said, "About a dozen people besides you answered my post on the Mountain Buzz. We haven't made any promises to any of them. Were you planning to bring someone?"

"Probably not. My wife has retired from rafting. I've talked with the others in my group, but so far, nobody's been able to figure out how to get that much time off work on such short notice."

"Should we pick somebody from the others who answered the post?"

I said, "I'd like to have some input on that decision. I'll take a lot of things into account. Experience, equipment, age, personality."

Everyone was nodding in agreement, so I addressed the group. "Ray and Charlene said that you're renting rafts. Who's going to row them?"

Ray said, "I'll row one. Steven and Joseph will trade-off rowing the other."

"And those are the eighteen-foot rafts?" I asked.

"Yeah. Sixteen or eighteen. Something like that."

The vague answer was worrisome. "An eighteen-foot boat is a whole lot bigger than a sixteen. Do you have experience rowing big rafts?"

Ray said, "Mine's a fifteen. Joseph has rowed it quite a bit, so I don't see any problem from that standpoint. Steven, what's your rowing experience?"

Steven said, "Like, I've rowed quite a few different rafts, you know? I think the biggest was like a fifteen-footer."

"Well, here's what I'm getting at," I said. "The first thing you need to keep in mind about rafting Grand Canyon is that the rapids are like nothing you've ever rafted before. On a May trip, the river flow is going to fluctuate between 9,000 and 14,000 cubic feet per second. That'll be three or four times the flow on the Deschutes. Five to eight times the Rogue. The nature of the water is completely different.

"And there's more to it than just the flow. On both of my prior trips, the river was carrying a heavy silt load. The muddy water is a whole lot heavier than clear water. It makes the river very pushy and very difficult to read. On top of that, the rapids themselves are unlike anything you've seen on the rivers around here. They are steeper, faster, longer, and even the easy ones are capable of flipping you if you hit it wrong."

"So, are you trying to talk us out of going?" asked Charlene.

"Definitely not," I explained. "I'm just saying that there's a real need for thorough preparation. Starting with the raft size. With three or four people on each of your boats, you need to be sure that you're getting eighteen-footers. Sixteens are good for two, but are very questionable for three, what with all the gear you'll need to carry."

Joseph said, "Sure. But like, with the kayaks, there'll never be more than two on either of the rafts anyways."

Uh-oh.

"Kayaks?" I asked, nearly choking on the word.

"So, yeah. We're bringing, like, a couple of them, ya know, and like, there'll never have to be more than two people on either of the rafts."

My gut reaction was to end the discussion right there. I had no desire to play the role of porter for kayakers. It is almost impossible for kayakers to carry their own gear. Besides, I've often found kayakers to be elitist snobs, and some are arrogant asses. Kayakers tend to believe themselves to be superior beings.

Ray said, "We figure it'll be handy to have a couple of kayaks along as safety boats, in case one of the rafts gets in trouble."

I've heard that argument many times, but I've never seen it play out in reality. I'm not saying it never happens. It just means that I've never seen it. There is no question that a kayak can make maneuvers that are impossible for a raft, so, though skeptical, I let Ray's point stand.

But from a trip leader's point of view, mixing rafts and kayaks has the inherent problem that kayaks go downstream faster than rafts. In general, you control a raft by rowing against the current, and you control a kayak by paddling into the current. Maintaining group integrity means that the kayaks are going to have to frequently stop and wait for the rafts to catch up.

It means that a trip leader on a raft may often not be in the lead. And you can't lead from behind. The trip leader is deciding which rapids should be scouted, where to stop to do the scouting, and where to stop for sightseeing, lunch, and overnight camp. How does that work if you have a couple of kayaks a quarter-mile out front? The question is rhetorical. It *doesn't* work.

Some Basic Whitewater Boating Principles

For the benefit of readers who are not conversant in the language of whitewater boating, here are some of the basics. The first is the question of controlling a boat in moving water.

You control a boat by making it move at a different speed than the water on which it is floating. This is true of all boats in any kind of moving water. Power boats nearly always do that by moving faster than the current. The same is true of kayaks. Oar rafts and drift boats, on the other hand, are controlled by moving *slower* than the current.

Kayakers paddle downstream, always moving faster than the current, and that's what makes them able to maneuver. Rafters in flat moving water may do the same, using easy push strokes on the oars. However, in fast-moving, broken water, those push strokes are not strong enough to make hard maneuvers.

The objective is to move the boat from an unfavorable position relative to whatever obstacle lies ahead, to a position where the current will carry the boat safely past the obstacle. The more critical the maneuver, the more power will be needed. When rowing, the pull stroke is at least three times more powerful than a push stroke.

Hence the mantra, "Pivot and pull."

For paddlers, the pull stroke is the stronger stroke. That's true for paddle-rafting as well as kayaking. The result is that paddlers accelerate into rapids, while rowers decelerate. In an undisciplined situation, the boats can become tangled with each other, resulting in a loss of control for one or both.

Another major difference between kayaks and rafts is their mass. Kayaks are small and light. Rafts are large and heavy. More mass means more friction and more inertia, so it takes more power to achieve a change of direction.

There is no value judgement here. Nobody can say that one craft is inherently better or worse than the other. Each has its own merits and deficiencies.

But for a long expedition, such as a 300-mile float through the Grand Canyon, the ability to carry a heavy load of supplies and equipment gives rafts the commanding advantage. Sure, lots of people run the canyon in Kayaks. But nearly all of them depend on having a support craft—either a drift boat or a raft—to carry the heavy gear.

In effect, the oarsman becomes the servant of the paddler, and for some people that is acceptable. For me, it is not.

Not wishing to be any more obnoxious than usual, I said, "Well, it'll require some discipline to make that work. And you'll still need the larger rafts, because your rafts will have to carry all of the gear and supplies for the people in the kayaks."

Because I damn sure won't carry any of their gear.

Throughout the conversation, Charlene had been leafing through a pile of papers that she'd pulled from a large manila envelope. She finally found the one she was looking for and said, "They are eighteen-foot rafts. That's what we reserved."

I said, "Good. Then we should be able to figure out how to carry everything."

Well, crap. Without intending to, I'd just agreed to lead a mixed group—rafts and kayaks. I'd have to lay down some pretty strict rules. And I should make an appointment to have my head examined.

"Now, for the kayaks, you'll probably need to have drysuits. And you'll definitely need to have a strong brace and a solid roll. Otherwise, the river will chew you up and spit you out."

"Drysuits?" asked Steven. "So, we heard that it'll be like a hundred degrees every day."

"It probably will be. But the water will still be fifty-four degrees. Sitting in a kayak, you'll lose body heat even without getting wet. And you'll be wet all the time. Do consider drysuits."

"We have good paddling jackets. They'll keep us plenty warm."

"The Park Service personnel at Lee's Ferry might not even let you start down the river without drysuits. Buy 'em. Borrow 'em. Rent 'em. Steal 'em, for all I care. But don't try to go without them."

I faked a grin, in an effort to make my words seem less harsh.

"The next big question is food."

"Grant—the guy who was going to be our trip leader—was going to plan our meals. Now that he's not going, we're probably going to have Canyon REO take care of all that. They're the ones we're renting the rafts from."

"Have they quoted you a price?" I asked.

"We haven't picked a specific meal package, but they gave us a ballpark price estimate. I think they said $50 a day per person."

I did some quick arithmetic. "So, for the float to Pearce Ferry, you'd be talking something like $1,000 each."

"Well, it won't actually be quite that much. We're going to get out at Diamond Creek."

"Okay, so knock off maybe $150," I said, "So, you're looking at about $850 per person, right?"

"That sounds about right."

"I have a computerized meal-planning system that I've used for about 300 river trips, both private and commercial. I can cut your food costs in half. So, if you're figuring $850, I can do it for around $400. But it will involve some pre-trip work by everyone."

Charlene said, "Wow, that certainly sounds good. But what kind of food are we talking about? I mean, Canyon REO has some pretty high-class meals."

"Mine are better. We can sit down an choose what we want from a list of about 250 meal options. They're the same meals that you'd get on a full-service guided trip. No granola bar breakfasts. No beans and franks."

"You mean Frank can't come along?" Ray asked.

"That's right," I said. "And that was supposed to be *my* lame joke."

I pulled out my visual aids folder containing individual meal sheets and shopping lists from a prior trip, and spread them out on the table.

I said, "Here are some examples. They'll give you an idea how things will be done."

"Oh, hey, these look pretty good," Sophia said. What do you think, Joseph?"

"Um, yeah, sure. It all sounds good to me."

The rest were nodding their heads in agreement.

"Okay. Next meeting, we'll pick our meals, and from that, I'll make the shopping lists. Next item is transportation and shuttle. What're your plans?"

"All six of us can ride comfortably in our Suburban. I have a good enclosed cargo trailer—like a U-Haul—that'll carry our gear."

I said, "Great. I'll drive my pickup, with my raft on its trailer, all set up and ready to launch. I suggest that we shuttle both rigs and divide the cost equally among all of us, since everyone benefits from the gear we're bringing. Agreed?"

Everyone murmured something that sounded like approval, so I moved to the next item. "Your rental rafts will come with dry boxes and ice chests. The ice chests will come with solid ice already in them. They'll be delivered to Lee's Ferry the day before launch. But we'll need to have some way to carry all of our food from the grocery store to Lee's Ferry, and then we'll transfer it into the rented dry boxes and coolers."

"How's that going to work?" Steven asked.

"I'll separate the shopping lists so that one set will be for food that doesn't require refrigeration, and the other set will be for the stuff that goes into the coolers. All of the non-cooler shopping will be done at home, before we leave. Then we'll do the shopping for perishables in Cedar City, Utah, two days before launch."

"How're we going to do that? We won't have our ice chests until the next day."

"That's correct. You'll have to bring along coolers to use in the interim. If you don't have enough of them, I have a few that you can use. Then we'll transfer the food into REO's ice chests first thing in the morning on launch day."

"That sounds, um, really complicated," said Krystal. "Like, how're we going to keep track of everything?"

"It is complicated, but it isn't difficult, as long as we pay close attention to the lists and work methodically."

"I guess we'll have to trust you on that, since you've done all this before," Ray said. "So, what's next?"

I said, "Duty Teams. We'll have four teams. Two people to a team." Then, I added, "Assuming that we find someone to fill that eighth spot. If we don't, I'll be a one-man team."

Charlene said, "I'll go to work on screening people for that last spot. Does it matter if it's a guy or a gal?"

"Life at home will be easier if it's a guy. Or if it has to be a gal, make sure she's fat and homely and has a guy's name, like Chris or Mel," I said.

"Seriously?"

"No. That was a joke. But the ideal situation would be someone who'll bring another raft, so that we'll have more ice chest and dry box space."

"Okay," Charlene agreed. "I can see that."

"And it would be ideal if it's someone from around here, so we can meet him in person before the trip. I've never liked going on blind dates."

"Anything else?" Ray asked.

"Can we all get back together on Saturday? I'll bring a tentative float plan, duty schedule, and a complete meal list. Each duty team will select the meals they want to prepare—and that'll include everything from shopping and packing, to cooking and serving."

Steven asked, "So, can I trade-off cooking for dishwashing or something? Like, I'm no good at cooking."

"That's why we work in teams. You can work it out with Krystal as to who does what, as long as everything gets done. It's all about teamwork, okay?"

Everyone was nodding in agreement, so I gathered my papers and stood up. On my way home, I noted that it was April Fool's Day. Great.

Chapter Four

Hammering Out the Details

Our Saturday meeting started with a discussion about the float plan. The question of whether to takeout at Diamond Creek or Pearce Ferry was already decided. The group was going to takeout at Diamond Creek. That's where Canyon REO would meet them, load up their rafts, and transport the people up to Hualapai Lodge on the canyon rim.

I said, "That's fine, but I think I'll go on down to Pearce Ferry."

I didn't elaborate on my reasons, but if anyone had asked, I'd have said that I did not want to pay the Hualapai tribe's predatory fees for using the Diamond Creek takeout and shuttle, and I didn't want my pickup subjected to the notoriously atrocious road leading down Diamond Creek.

The tentative float plan that I showed the group called for arriving at Diamond Creek on the sixteenth float day. That was not an arbitrary choice. Sixteen days is the maximum time the National Park Service allows boaters to spend in this section of river in prime season. And in my mind, it didn't make sense to rush down the river any faster than necessary. We'd spend a lot of effort and money getting our rafts and equipment to the river. It made no sense to cut the trip unnecessarily short and force ourselves to hurry.

"Oh," Charlene said. "Sixteen days? What's that make it—June eighth? We're sort of counting on getting out on June fourth."

"Wait. You want to do it in *twelve* days?" I asked, making no effort to conceal my incredulity."

"Well, yeah. A lot of the non-motorized guided trips do the run in twelve days," Ray explained.

I said, "That's a *really* aggressive schedule for a private trip. You have to remember that the guides who do the trip in twelve days have tons of experience. For the most part, they don't even need to scout the rapids."

"The thing is, some of us have to be back at work on Monday. Your plan doesn't even get us off the river until Tuesday. We *have to* takeout on Friday."

I took a deep breath.

"I've done this trip twice. The first time, we got to Diamond Creek on the fourteenth day. That was specifically so that a couple of people in our group could get to Las Vegas and fly home that day. That schedule ended up making for a fairly stressful trip. We felt the time pressure almost every day."

"Yeah, but we just can't get the extra time off work," Krystal objected.

"Here's the deal," I said. "If you have to do the trip in twelve days, then you're going to have to find someone else to do it. I can't enjoy a trip with that kind of time-pressure built into it. You'll need to average over twenty miles a day, and that's a real challenge."

"So, twenty miles doesn't seem like so much," Joseph said. "We ought to be able to do that in like four or five hours, no problem."

Trying my best to sound agreeable, I explained, "That's four or five hours of actual float time. It doesn't include any sight-seeing stops. It doesn't include scouting time, or lunch stops. It doesn't allow for emergency stops—like catching a flipped raft, turning it upright, and all that goes along with that."

"We can do our sight-seeing from the rafts, can't we? We don't need to stop for lunches. We can just eat on the fly."

"Let's look at a typical river day. With everyone's cooperation, we might get out of camp at 9:00. You think you can cover your twenty miles by 3:00 in the afternoon. My experience says that it'll be closer to 5:00. You'll be hard pressed to get dinner dishes done before dark. And there'll be almost no time at all to just sit-back and relax."

Ray said, "The guy who was going to lead the trip said we could do it."

"I'm not saying it can't be done. I'm just saying that I can't guarantee you a pleasant, enjoyable trip on that schedule. It's your once-a-year vacation. It may be a *once-in-a-lifetime* adventure. Does it really make sense to turn it into a race against the clock?"

Charlene was the first to break. "Yeah, that's a good point. But if they can do it on the guided trips…"

"On a guided trip, there's a paid staff to do all of the work. The camp is all set up before the guests arrive. They can enjoy cocktails while the staff makes dinner and cleans up afterward. But a private trip doesn't have a paid staff. We have to do everything ourselves. We can have just as much fun, but we need to allow time to do the work that has to be done."

"Could we *pay you* to do that stuff? And maybe get a paid helper to fill the last space on our trip?"

I said, "Forget that idea. Paying me would make it a commercial trip, and that would be a federal crime. The permit holder and I could face substantial fines and even jail time."

"Yeah. That's no good," Ray said, looking at Charlene. "A couple of extra days is not a problem for us."

He turned to the others and asked, "Is there any way you can get a few extra days off?"

The Millennials looked at each other and simultaneously shrugged their shoulders.

"I *might* be able to work something out," Joseph said.

"Well, *maybe*," said Steven.

Krystal and Sophia rocked their heads back and forth in what looked like a choreographed movement.

Sophia said, "Um, I guess so. Like, maybe."

Ray finally turned to me and asked, "Can we get off the river on Sunday? That way, if anyone really *has* to be at work on Monday, they can catch a plane home from Las Vegas."

I said, "Fourteen days is still aggressive, but not impossible. But like I said before, it'll take everybody's cooperation to stay on schedule."

"Everybody okay with that?" Ray asked.

I still didn't like it, but everyone else agreed to the Sunday takeout. It would require us to make sixteen miles a day.

I asked, "Have you had any luck finding someone for the eighth seat?"

Charlene said, "I have two people interested. But both are in Colorado. I haven't heard from anybody who lives around here."

Steven spoke up. "I was talking to a dude who might be able to go. He's like checking on it."

"Is he experienced?" I asked.

"So, I've done a couple of trips with him."

"When will he know if he can do it?"

Steven shrugged. "Like, maybe a couple of days. I don't know."

We all agreed to keep working on filling the vacancy, and moved on to meal selection. I showed a duty rotation chart that broke down the trip according to camp stops—fourteen camps, including the put-in camp at Lee's Ferry.

"We'll have four teams. The biggest task is always meal preparation. We'll divide that up by river camps. One team will have the cooking duty at each camp. So, you'll cook dinner in the evening and breakfast in the morning. And you'll also be in charge of organizing supplies for the next lunch. Those not on cook duty will do the dishwashing and other things."

Steven studied my duty roster example and said, "Like, does it have to be so complicated? I mean, we always just share the work, and it all gets done. Why does it have to be like the army or something?"

"You've been in the military?" I asked.

"No, but like, you know what I mean."

"I've been in the military. Believe me, it is nothing like this."

"Yeah, so, it still seems awfully strict. Like, why do we have to say who's supposed to wash dishes, and who's supposed to set up the toilet? I mean, can't we just *do* it?"

"Just do it, huh? Like Michael Jordan and Nike. But what if someone in the group turns out to be a slacker—is that still a word? I'm talking about someone who'll let others do the work, while he does as little as possible. Haven't you ever known somebody like that?"

"Maybe, but it never, like, caused any problem, or anything."

"We're going to be on the river for two weeks. If we don't get the work done efficiently, we'll find ourselves slipping behind our schedule. That puts everyone under pressure. Doing things this way helps us be efficient. Everybody knows exactly what he is expected to do. No thinking about it, no overlooked duties."

"Yeah, but…"

"You understand my point. It might look like excessive organization now, but on the river, it makes everything easier."

"So, it looks like a good idea to me. Like, it's just a chart," Krystal said to Steven. "I mean, what's wrong with having a chart?"

"Let's figure out what to do about the meals," I said. "Two teams will have three camps, and two teams will have four. I'll take four. Anyone else?"

Charlene said, "We can take four."

Mothers always want to make things easier for the kids—even when the kids are thirty-some years old.

I said, "That makes me Team One, and you Team Two. Joseph and Sophia will be Team Three. Steven and Krystal, Team Four. Now, let's start by choosing which dinners we each want to cook. I've already made my choices."

I pulled out a menu planning sheet with my meal choices already penciled in. Everyone passed around the list of dinner options, and one by one, selected things that sounded good to them. I moderated the discussion, pointing out which meals were more work, which ones had to be done early in the trip—seafood, for example—and which ones don't require refrigeration and should be saved for the last few days of the trip, when we might be out of ice.

It took about an hour to fill-in all of the blanks on the form. I'd take it home, feed the data to my spreadsheet, and like magic, we'd have complete shopping lists and a preparation sheet for every meal.

"Next time we get together, I'll have your shopping lists and meal sheets. Then we'll talk about how the shopping and packing will be done. What we're going to end up with is two food packs for each meal—one for the dry box and one for the ice chest. They'll be sealed in large Zip-Loc bags, and they'll be clearly labeled, so nobody will have to dig around looking for things. Digging around in the ice chests on a 110-degree day is one of the fastest ways to melt your ice. And in Grand Canyon, ice equals happiness."

I couldn't tell how much of this they understood, but we'd go through the whole process a step at a time, and it'd end up being relatively painless.

When we got back together week later, I had everything calculated for eight people, based on Charlene's assertion that the final spot would be filled, even though she still didn't have anyone firmly committed. Steven's friend seemed the most likely prospect.

Before this meeting, I'd already done my shopping for non-perishable items. For visual aid, I took along the box of supplies for my first camp, which would be at Lee's Ferry. I explained that when I went to the store, I'd carried four shopping bags—one for each of my camps. I arranged them in a shopping cart, with the meal sheets for each camp in one of the bags. Then as I made a round of the store, I put each item in the appropriate bag.

Getting through the check-stand without scrambling the contents of the bags required paying close attention to every move the checker made. The checkers have their own system, and this isn't it. Everything from Bag A had to go back into Bag A, and so on.

When I got home, I dealt with one bag at a time. First step was to get rid of bulky packaging. If, for example, a meal called for five cups of pancake mix, I measured five cups into a Zip-Loc bag and discarded the box. I used a Sharpie to label each ingredient. When I'd made everything as compact as possible, I transferred it into a two-gallon Zip-Loc marked with the camp number, placing canned goods in the bottom.

After I'd showed all of this to everyone, they all agreed that it wasn't actually as hard as it sounded. I had bags for camps one, five, nine, and thirteen. The four bags would fit comfortably in my main dry box, along with the supplies for my extended run to Pearce Ferry.

Six weeks to Launch Day. I got to thinking more about my plan to continue my trip past Diamond Creek after the rest of the group left the river. The biggest thing wrong with the idea was that I'd have to trailer my raft without help when I got to Pearce Ferry. Years ago, on some of my family trips, I had to get my raft off and back onto my flatbed trailer without help, so I knew it could be done. But I also knew that it could be difficult or impossible if the boat ramp wouldn't let me back the trailer all of the way into the water. And that was far from a sure thing at Pearce Ferry.

Two modifications to the trailer might solve that problem—a full-width roller across the back edge of the deck and a winch on the tongue. I did a little bit of engineering and made a short supply list. I showed my sketches to Ray, and he said he could do the welding whenever I was ready.

The winch cable could not connect to the D-ring on the bow of the raft, because it probably would rip right off, the first time I tried to load a fully rigged raft. Instead, I planned to connect the cable to the front of the raft frame. This way, the pulling force would be attached directly to the heaviest part of the load—the frame and everything attached to it.

A key to this design was that the cable had to be above the bow tube on the raft, meaning that I needed to mount a winch post on the trailer tongue. While searching for a hand-crank boat trailer winch, I ran across an electric one and upgraded my plan. The winch would be mounted on a plate at the base of the post. The cable would be routed over a pully on top of the post, and then to the raft frame. This would apply a slight lift as it pulled the raft onto the trailer.

I took the trailer out to Ray's welding shop, where he made the modifications. With these improvements, I was sure I could get the raft on and off the trailer without help, in just about any situation

It was right after this that things started to spiral into what would become my Whitewater Summer.

Chapter Five

The Temperamental Owyhee River

The Owyhee River is in the southeast corner of Oregon. It originates in the high desert country of Nevada and Idaho, and that can be a very dry part of the country. The flow of the Owyhee is dictated entirely by each winter's snowpack. Most years, the optimum season for rafting the Owyhee is no more than two or three weeks long. Some years, there's no rafting season at all.

As I did every year, throughout February and March, I'd been monitoring the snowpack in the river basins where I might want to do a raft trip, and this included the Owyhee. I always watch the Owyhee, because it is one of the rivers that doesn't have a permit lottery—at least for the time being (knock on a carbon-fiber oar shaft).

In mid-February, a series of winter storms came through the Pacific Northwest, giving new optimism to the possibility of doing an Owyhee trip. Another succession of storms came through in March, and prospects started looking pretty good. By that time, I already knew that nobody in my regular rafting group, The Clan of the Nose Hair, had scored a permit in the Recreation.gov lotteries, despite a total of at least 84 entries in five lotteries.

As I posted the possibility of an Owyhee trip, Clan members started weighing-in on the idea. But the temperamental nature of the Owyhee makes it difficult for those who have real jobs. Most are simply not able to drop everything and head-out on a moment's notice, when the flow is right.

Nevertheless, prior to Charlene's post on Mountain Buzz, I'd done some preliminary work on that hypothetical Owyhee trip, just in case the weather and river flow came together. Later, even as I was getting things together for the Grand Canyon trip, it was looking more and more like an Owyhee trip would be possible around the end of April.

And I really did *want* to go back to the Owyhee. I'd done it only once, and that was in the 1990s. So, despite having made the commitment to lead the Grand Canyon trip, I continued pursuing my plan for a Clan trip on the Owyhee. I rationalized that it would be good conditioning in preparation for The Canyon. Besides, there's no rule that says I must do only *one* trip a year.

Conditioning really *is* important. And I was in pretty darn good shape, for an old fart. In reality, though, working-out on a rowing machine cannot, by itself, put you completely in shape for rowing the Grand Canyon.

This is a good time to mention my lurking discomfort with the ravages of age. When I was at my best, I was a damn good boatman—among the best in tight, technical situations, and better than passable in the big water. *Way* better. But I couldn't help wondering if I'd lost my edge.

Last time I went down Grand Canyon, I had to have my son row my raft through Lava Falls, because I was experiencing debilitating back spasms. On a recent Lower Salmon trip, I completely lost the line in China Rapid and drove head-long into an easily avoidable hole, barely averting, by sheer luck, a Maytag job, or possibly even a flip. And last time I rowed Hells Canyon, I misjudged the entry at Granite Falls and dove straight into the "green room," burying the raft, but again avoiding disaster by the slimmest margin. It would be irresponsible to gloss over the question of whether my skills were still up to the task.

A week on the Owyhee would help a lot. It would give me a chance to test my skills and reflexes. *Rationalize. Rationalize.* And if I had any physical issues on the trip, I'd be able to bag the longer trip. That would be bad for Ray and Charlene, but not as bad as having their trip leader crap-out halfway through the trip.

By mid-April, I was mentally locked-in for running the Owyhee, even though I hadn't yet said so to myself. If the water was right, I was going, even as the number of Clan participants went from nine to seven, seven to four, and four to two. And then when that last person dropped out, I found myself forced to decide whether or not I wanted to do a solo trip.

In all my rafting, I'd done only *one* solo trip. It was on the Rogue River in 1989, when I owned the rafting company and ran commercial trips. In July, I had scheduled myself to guide three consecutive Rogue trips almost back-to-back. And because two sets of the company gear were committed to trips in Idaho, I was spread pretty thin for the Oregon trips—so much so that I was using my personal raft and pickup to supplement the company gear on the Rogue.

The first of the three trips had been a rare three-day paddle trip, at the end of which I sent the other guides and all of the company gear straight from Foster Bar to Happy Camp, California for a paddle trip on the Klamath River. My next two trips would be row-yourself trips, using a whole different set of rafts, and a different guide team. They'd arrive two days later.

Instead of going home between the trips, only to turn around and come right back, I chose to hang-out at Almeda Bar. I arrived back there in the middle of the afternoon, and found a vacant campsite close to the boat ramp, where some guys with drift boats were preparing to start downriver.

One of them spotted me and hurried over to ask if I could give him a ride to the Galice Store to buy some coffee. He explained that they'd already sent their vehicles away with the shuttle driver and had no way to get there, and they certainly couldn't do the trip without coffee.

I pulled a two-pound can of Folgers from the bottom of my food box, where it had resided for several years, in anticipation of exactly this kind of emergency. The guy offered to pay, but I told him it wasn't necessary. Nevertheless, he offered me a pint of Black Velvet, which seemed like a favorable exchange.

I followed him down to the boat ramp to complete the trade, while the others in his group puttered around getting their boats ready to go. With nothing better to do, I hung around and joined their chatter.

They were old guys, though probably at least ten years younger than I am now, and as old guys tend to do, they were talking about the old days. The oldest among them was telling what it was like to be a guide thirty years earlier. He said that back then, the final test of whether you could be a Rogue River guide was to make the run from Grave Creek to Foster Bar in one day. That would prove that you knew the river and were a strong, competent boatman. Oregon has long-since dispensed with the notion that river guides need to be licensed, so the "final exam" is no longer needed.

After the guys left, I thought that over. I had an extra day to burn. And this was a chance to prove to myself that I was as good as any guide from the old days. I was sure that I could do in one day the thirty-four-mile trip that I'd just finished doing in three.

So, I walked over to the permit office, a half-mile away, and asked if there were any no-shows that day. And there were. Next, I drove to the Galice Store and arranged to have my rig shuttled to Foster Bar the next day.

At 5:30 in the morning, I slid my raft off the trailer at Grave Creek. Snacking on leftovers from my previous trip, I pushed my way downstream. My raft was light and nimble, because I was carrying no gear or supplies. After bumping my way down the lining chute at Rainie Falls, I passed the old guys at Whiskey Creek, enjoying their coffee. The best part of waking up is Folger's in your cup. I waved but didn't stop. In fact, the only times I stopped all day were when bladder capacity forced me to. I arrived at Foster Bar at 6:45 that evening.

It was a satisfying adventure. I enjoyed the solitude, and I especially enjoyed the fact that I was able to do something that none of my company guides had ever done. That mattered, because it was my first year owning the company, and a couple of my guides were vocal in questioning my rafting skills—and/or overly smug about their own.

So, in 2021, I was thirty-two years older, and the idea of doing another solo trip had a perverse appeal. I was finished with my part of the advance preparation for the Grand Canyon trip, and my big yellow raft sat in the garage on its trailer, all ready to go.

The problem was that in order to take that rig on an Owyhee trip, I'd have to unload a lot of things that were already packed, and then re-pack them before the Grand. Not to mention the fact that a lot of my equipment simply wasn't suited for a solo trip. For example, my "SuperStove" camp kitchen was awesome for a group of a dozen people. But it was all but impossible for one person to manage. Like most of my gear, it was designed for medium-sized group trips.

I called my sister—the one who owns a nicely-rigged "fourteen-foot" Riken *Miwok* self-bailer, which is actually closer to thirteen feet long, but was in like-new condition despite being twenty-some years old. My sister had claimed it in her divorce, even though she had no intention of ever rowing it. I asked if I could use it for my Owyhee trip, and she said yes.

Photo by Jerry Baysinger
The Riken *Miwok* is ideal for small rivers.

I towed my freshly-improved trailer to Spokane and loaded the *Miwok* onto it. The raft was rigged with a top-of-the-line Recretec aluminum frame, a pair of high-quality dry boxes and a Yeti ice chest. The *Miwok* was far more suitable for a solo trip than was my sixteen-foot *Vanguard*.

Back home, I pulled out my sister's front-seat dry box and replaced it with a pair of half-sized boxes that I'd bought back in the days when my wife and I were doing occasional trips by ourselves. Being five-foot-nothing and proportionately muscular, Linda was not the best choice for carrying the other end of a heavy, full-size dry box.

So, I got two half-size boxes, which fit nicely into the front dry box bay, and each was easily manageable by one person. I ordered one of the boxes with sockets for legs on one side, and no hinge on the lid. I installed a reversed piano hinge that allowed the lid to flip open a full 270 degrees, and then attached a two-burner Partner stove to it, making a mini-SuperStove.

Photo edited by Author
The mini Superstove was never builtt. But I did *think* about it.

Unfortunately, Linda broke her leg a few years ago, while pulling weeds (don't even ask), and even though it healed nicely with the help of a ten-inch titanium rod, she lost confidence in regards to undertaking any strenuous adventures. So, my two-person rafting outfit had gone largely unused ever since.

The half-size utility box held an LED lantern, dish pans, a hatchet and folding shovel, so about the only things that I had to borrow from the Grand Canyon rig were the first-aid kit, a pair of three-gallon water jugs, and my ceramic water filter. I strapped a folding table on top of the two half-size dry boxes and strapped my dry bag on top of that, where a front-seat passenger would have sat.

My old ScatPacker toilet system was built around a heavy-duty five-gallon plastic bucket with a screw-on lid and most importantly, a watertight seal. It had served well on all of my raft trips for fifteen years, until we made our first trip in Grand Canyon, where regulations prohibit the use of plastic buckets for waste containment.

Photo by Jan Brandvold
Old but still functional ScatPacker Toilet.

Photo by Jan Brandvold
The Grand Canyon approved EcoSafe. Yes, my sister takes pictures of toilets.

But it was fine for my Owyhee trip, and one bucket would have more than adequate capacity for a solo trip. And it weighed a lot less than the rocket box EcoSafe toilets that we got for The Canyon.

In the back of the *Miwok* was a small stern frame with a plywood floor where I could strap a propane tank and the ScatPacker toilet, with reasonable assurance that it would stay upright—at least as long as the raft did. My firepan (Page 170), which was the body of my kids' old Radio Flyer wagon, nested upside-down on top of the toilet, with my folding chair on top of that, all secured under a cargo net.

I also packed an item that had been part of my standard equipment for fifteen years—my AED (Automated External Defibrillator). I had acquired it because so many in my group were, as I was, getting old. If someone was going to go into cardiac arrest, I wanted to be able to deal with it. But it didn't really make much sense on a solo trip, because you can't use an AED on yourself.

The oarsman's seat is a padded full-size dry box, where I would pack all of my food and whatever else I might want easy access to during the day. Everything needed to be as simple as possible for a solo trip, especially the food. I wasn't about to go hungry, and I didn't want to go with trail food, which is compact, lightweight and easy, but expensive.

For breakfasts, I stayed with traditional eggs, bacon and toast—and maybe change-up occasionally with sausage or Spam, or pancakes. Breakfasts were easy, no matter what. Lunches would be mostly snacks—like those pretzel balls filled with peanut butter, mixed nuts, crackers and cheese, Payday Bars. Yeah, health food.

Cooking dinner for one has always been a problem. I could spend as much time on a meal for myself as I would for a group of ten. That was out of the question. So, entrees mainly came from cans—beef stew, chili, enchiladas—or very easy things like mac and cheese, some canned vegetables, a few bags of salad—all very simple, with minimal cookware to wash. For dessert, a glass of fine wine from a box.

As for shelter, I decided that my dome tent was not the best choice for the trip. Sure, I could set it up by myself—I'd done it many times. But a Timberline tent was better. Freestanding, quick and easy to set up—and it gives the option of setting up just the frame and rainfly, without the tent itself. That is ideal for nights when I'd want shelter from dew or even light rain, but didn't need the full protection of the tent. I got the "four-person" size, so that there'd be room to set up a very simplified kitchen under it if I had to. For good measure, I also carried a ten by twelve tarp.

Photo by Author
Timberline Tent.

More details would come up, but my basic plan was in place. I had my Spot II satellite messenger so that I could send out daily messages giving my location when all was well, or call for help in case of an emergency. As always, I carried a twelve-volt garden tractor battery in a six-pack cooler. It would run a pump for the air bed that I would not go without, and it would power an inverter from which I could recharge my phone, camera and tablet batteries.

Five weeks before my departure date for Grand Canyon, the weather and water conditions fell into place for the Owyhee trip. I made a final call to my Clan boaters, but nobody could join me. I packed my Owyhee guidebooks and a couple of paperback novels into an ammo box, and as an afterthought, added the guidebooks for the John Day River. If, for any reason, I got to the Owyhee and couldn't float that river, I'd have an alternate trip to do—not that I expected anything to prevent me from floating the Owyhee.

I made a call to Ray and Charlene, and they assured me that preparations were going smoothly, and they'd just received confirmation that Steven's friend, whose name was Jason or Jeremy—one of those J names—would be filling the final slot on the trip. He wouldn't need to do anything regarding food, because he'd be my duty team partner, and I'd already taken care of it. The next morning, I headed out for the Owyhee.

Ever supportive, Linda said, "I think you've lost your mind," as I climbed into my pickup.

Chapter Six

All Roads Lead to Rome

Rome Oregon sits a couple of miles from the Idaho state line, a full day's drive from Oregon City, nearly all of which is on two-lane highways. My twenty-seven-year-old F-150 might not be exactly what collectors covet as a "survivor," but despite the quarter-million miles showing on the odometer, it was still respectable in its appearance and as dependable as when I bought it.

It is, however, ruthless in its consumption of fuel. After stopping for a fill-up in Bend, and heading out toward Rome, I spied a fiberglass pickup canopy for sale alongside the highway. The thing about it that caught my eye was that it was exactly the same color as the trim on my pickup. The sign said $100 or best offer, but the $100 was crossed out and replaced by $75.

I don't necessarily believe in providence or destiny, but that canopy seemed to have been put there just for me. I made a loop and went back for a second look. I found it to be in excellent condition, despite having been on a pickup almost identical to mine that had been totaled in a head-on collision with a Toyota whose driver fell asleep at the wheel. The seller was so excited at the

Photo by Jan Brandvold

Color-keyed canopy on my classic Ford F150 gas hog.

sight of my truck that he immediately discounted the price to $50, and offered to help me install it.

Half an hour later, I resumed my drive to Rome. The canopy would be handy for the drive to and from the Grand Canyon, providing a measure of security for things in my pickup bed. And though I was carrying nothing back there on this trip, it relieved me of having to decide whether or not to set up a tent at the put-in.

The overcast that had stayed with me from the time I left home cleared off as I drove eastward, and the blue skies made me optimistic. I've gone rafting in all kinds of weather, and the only thing that ever drove me off the river was wind—well, lightning once, but it was accompanied by heavy wind gusts. Rain and even snow can be dealt with, but wind can render you helpless.

Arriving at Rome in the early evening, I found that the launch site had changed little in the two decades since I'd last seen it. The "boat ramp" was a steep, rutted dirt grade that I wouldn't even consider backing down without the assurance of four-wheel drive to get myself back up.

There were four or five primitive campsites with well-weathered picnic tables, an outhouse, and a lever-action pump for good water. Anyway, the sign said it was good, although the well's proximity to the outhouse was something I had to avoid thinking about.

On the tailgate of my pickup, I heated a can of "genuine Italian" raviolis, something I hadn't eaten since I was a kid. The label said, "serves four." It actually meant one, and I washed it down with a can of cold beer.

As soon as the sun set, the temperature plummeted, and left me with no desire to sit outside and enjoy the evening. I inflated my air bed and rolled out my sleeping bag under my new old canopy, and crawled into my cocoon to stay warm and listen to the river.

There was a heavy layer of frost covering the ground, my pickup, and my raft when I got up in the morning. I dressed in layers, including Gortex raingear—not because I expected rain. It was a clear, bright morning. The raingear was insurance against the inevitable splashing I'd get when the river became choppy. My footwear consisted of Teva sandals over thin neoprene wetsuit boots.

I once did an October Rogue River trip with a group of fishermen from the office where I worked. Our weather was decent, but cool. One fisherman had dispensed with my advice on what to wear and dressed as he would if he'd been going out to cut firewood in the Oregon forest—cotton long johns, blue jeans, and a thick flannel shirt, a denim jacket, over which he wore a rubberized nylon rain suit. To keep his feet warm, he chose felt-lined pack boots.

"Glenn, if you get dumped off the raft, you're going to float like a bag of sand," I said.

"No, I'm a strong swimmer. Besides, I'm not going to get dumped," he assured me. He looked to the guy who was rowing the raft he'd be on.

"I've never dumped a raft yet," the boatman assured me.

"Do me a favor," I said to Glenn. "Keep your lifejacket on whenever you're on the raft. It'll make it easier to find your body."

He wore it, and probably would have done so without my telling him to. But by mid-afternoon, after we'd gone through a dozen good rapids, I noticed a change in his posture. He was hunched over his fishing rod, with his elbows tucked in tight. I should have said something then, but the sky had cleared, the sun was out, and I was quite comfortable.

An hour later, I pulled in to the little campsite at Kelsey Creek, and the other rafts followed. When Glenn tried to get off the raft, he was shivering so hard he could barely walk. All of his cotton clothing had become damp, mostly from his own perspiration, which was trapped in his non-breathable raingear, and his boots were filled with cold water.

We had to build a big fire to warm him up, and the next day I made him wear borrowed clothes more suitable to the occasion. It was in the day when polypropylene was still considered to be an exotic material and wasn't widely available—at least not at an affordable price. I personally found that my 1970s plaid polyester slacks and Technicolor nylon-polyester shirts worked pretty well, even though I had disco music ringing in my ears. Of course, all the old-timers all still swore by wool.

After breaking a thin layer of ice from the pan of water I'd left overnight on the picnic table, I made coffee and a quick breakfast of fried eggs and grilled English muffins.

I packed up my gear and loaded everything onto my raft before backing down the boat ramp and sliding the raft into the river. I parked my rig where the shuttle driver from Jordan Valley would pick it up later in the day.

Sun was breaking over the hills to the east as I pushed off and rowed out into the current. The river was flowing at something around 2,300 cfs (cubic feet per second), which I consider to be the optimum flow for floating the Owyhee. The water was a translucent pale green—far from clear, but even further from the thick, muddy soup I'd experienced on my Grand Canyon trips.

The current carried me under the Highway 95 bridge while I adjusted the oarlocks and settled into my seat. I inhaled deeply to savor the pure morning air, and nearly gagged on the aroma of a freshly mucked cattle barn. The first few miles of this run are in farm and ranch land, but the eroded chalk-looking bluffs in the distance hinted at the scenery ahead.

Alone with my thoughts, I once again contemplated why I was there. Was it really to get in shape for the Grand Canyon trip, or was there something else? Did I have something to prove with this solo raft trip? And to whom was I proving it?

There was no wind, and enough current to keep the raft moving easily downstream. As nearly all river rafters do, I sat facing forward, using push-strokes on the oars to control and move the raft downstream. At least ninety percent of the rowing on a raft trip is done with push-strokes. But it is the pull-strokes that get you through the rapids, because a good pull-stroke is two to three times as powerful as a push-stroke.

This is a fact that escapes most novice boaters. We all face downstream because we want to see where we're going; and because we're facing downstream, we nearly always use easy, relaxed push-strokes. That's fine is calm water, but when you *really* need to make a hard maneuver, you have to use a pull stroke. That's Rafting 101. Thousands of times, when coaching rookie boaters, I've shouted, "Pivot and pull!"

Knowing the importance of strength in my pull stroke, for most of the last quarter-century, I've spent thirty minutes a day on a good rowing machine, and I have complete confidence in my ability to pull my raft around obstacles and into clear channels. But the rowing machine does nothing at all for the muscles that are needed for pushing the raft downstream in easy water.

For most of the fifty years I've been running rivers, I never had any reason to even think about the strength of my push stroke. But in the past few years, I've noticed that about three days into a river trip, I have felt signs of cumulative fatigue in the muscles I use for my push stroke. It hasn't been a big deal on the five to seven-day trips I've been doing; but what would happen on a twenty-day trip?

This Owyhee trip would give me the opportunity to get these muscles into condition for the Grand Canyon trip. I wanted to take six days to do this trip. That meant averaging twelve miles a day before arriving at the reservoir behind the Owyhee Dam. From there, it is a seven-mile slog on still water to the Leslie Gulch boat ramp.

It would be easy to average fifteen miles a day, and still have a leisurely trip, but I was in no hurry. I could sit back and simply go with the flow. Contradicting that desire was the need to exercise my push stroke, and that meant that I had to keep pushing downstream.

I set an easy pace, rowing downstream in the calm water of the first few miles of the trip. After passing Jordan Creek, I spotted the gauging station at Mile Four. A quarter-mile east of the gauging station there is an old stagecoach stop, but I believe that it is on private land, and I don't know if public access is allowed.

Another mile downstream, the ranch land gave way to the first canyon section of the trip. The river narrowed and the current moved more quickly. I was nine miles from the put-in when I started encountering some actual rapids. The morning chill had given way to a comfortable afternoon, with clear skies and a temperature around 70. Layer by layer, I removed excess clothing, and by this time I was in shorts and a polypro knit shirt.

I stopped for lunch at a place called Lower Fletcher, where I made a couple of deli sandwiches and washed them down with a beer. I remembered from my previous Owyhee trip that for the next three or four miles there were no campsites. That had kept Linda and me on the water for an hour after we were ready to stop, because we'd gotten a later start than I had on this trip. If I had to go another five miles, it would still be a comfortable day's travel.

The government map shows two Class III rapids and a Class IV rapid in the next couple of miles. But the map also said that the ratings were for a low-water run. At the moderate level I had, the rapids were straightforward and easy. It was only an hour after lunch that I pulled into a decent camp at Mile 14.

The map calls it Hike-Out Camp, though I can't imagine who would want to do that. I've been told that the trail out of this camp leads back to Rome. Having no particular desire to hike back to Rome, I contemplated my leisure-time options. My primary rationale for doing this trip was the need to get in shape for the Grand Canyon trip. But was simply rowing enough?

No. In a spasm of irrational good intentions, I resolved to do something about my figure. Yes, that. I've worn 34-inch Levi's for at least twenty-five years. But lately, it has become increasingly difficult to fasten them. And photography somehow causes the embarrassing illusion that my gut hangs out. To be honest, I'd noticed that a couple of decades ago, but cameras seem to be getting worse in that respect.

So, I resolved to force myself to do sit-ups in camp every day. That first night, I did as many sit-ups as I possibly could, to set a baseline for improvement. The first of my incremental goals was to attain double-digits.

Chapter Seven

Owyhee Adventures

Over the years, I've learned that the most important time of any day on the river is the time you get out of camp in the morning. It sets the pace for the entire day. If you're slow getting out of camp, you'll feel pressured all day and still arrive late at your next camp—if it isn't already occupied.

My ten o'clock rule is based on the assumption that you have a limited time on the river, meaning that you must get to the takeout by a specific day and time. This is true on nearly all river trips, whether because the government limits the number of days you can spend in the river corridor, or because you have a job that you need to get back to. So, my rule is that if you aren't out of camp by ten, you're late. On all river trips, the group leader sets the pace, first by example, and then by good management—meaning that there are several sub-paragraphs to the ten o'clock rule.

One of the challenges I experienced in leading commercial river trips was motivating the guests to stay on track without causing them to lose their sense of relaxation. As previously discussed, my company specialized in row-yourself trips. But another component of our "hands-on" approach to rafting was that my company did not use swampers (underpaid lackeys), meaning that the guests had to put up and take down their own tents and pack their own dry bags. So, while other companies promoted their highly-catered experience, we offered the sense of independence and personal accomplishment, and a lower price.

Our guides always had to be careful not to make the work feel like drudgery. Story-telling and cheerleading are big parts of being a river guide. Keep it fun, but never forget the ten o'clock rule. As Tom Hanks said in Castaway, "We live and we die by time, and we must never commit the sin of turning our backs on time."

That applies to private raft trips as well. I call it the FedEx rule. My "Clan" group has become very efficient with morning chores. The designated "bull cook" gets up and starts the stoves, heating water for coffee and dishwashing. Then, while the breakfast team works on food, everyone else rolls sleeping bags, takes down tents, and packs bags. The breakfast team will do theirs while others do dishes and break down the kitchen. In this way, we often get out of camp before 9:00.

That gives us an extra hour for leisure activities in the afternoon and evening. And a side-benefit is that we usually get first shot at the best campsites, except when we're sharing the river with outfitters who employ camp-runners—swampers who break away from their groups in the morning and race downstream to claim the premium camps. There are few greater joys than beating the camp-runners to the most coveted camps.

So, there I was, on the Owyhee River, all by myself, and the first thought I had in the morning of my second river day was the ten o'clock rule. And the second thought was where I was relative to my twelve-mile-a-day float plan. I was two miles ahead of schedule.

While lingering in the warmth of my sleeping bag, I pulled out my map and looked to see what camps were in the area of Trip Mile 24. What I found was Ryegrass Hot Spring. One of the great pleasures on a river trip is soaking in a natural hot spring. This one was ten miles ahead.

One thing about doing a solo trip is that a ten o'clock departure is exceptionally easy to accomplish. My entire camp setup was far simpler than what is needed for a group. I could easily be underway by eight. But since it was a chilly morning, and I hadn't seen another boat on the river, I decided to dawdle around, drink an extra cup of coffee, and maybe go for a 9:30 departure.

The sun reached my side of the river at 7:30, and by 9:00 I was comfortable in shorts and a light wind-breaker, as I climbed aboard my raft. A little over an hour later, I arrived at the Weeping Wall, where hundreds of small springs burst from the cliff on the left side of the river, sparkling in the morning sun. I stopped and filled my water bottles with the cold, pure spring water.

A few miles further, I came to the first of two significant rapids. The map rates them as Class III+, but I remembered them as being pretty easy. But again, the ratings are for lower water levels, where the channels are narrower and there are more obstacles to dodge. As on my previous trip, these two rapids were straightforward read-and-run rapids.

If I'd been leading a group with people who hadn't seen it before, I'd have stopped at the "Rustler's Cabin" above the east bank a mile after the second rapid. But I'd explored it before, and interesting though it was, I didn't need to see it again.

Two miles further downstream, I spotted Ryegrass Hot Spring and pulled ashore. A few yards up the bank, the near-boiling mineral water bubbles from the earth in a steaming pool about eight feet in diameter, and way too hot for soaking. The pool overflows in a small stream that runs ten feet down into the river, where someone had moved rocks around to form a sort of a soaking tub at the point where the hot and cold waters mix. You can adjust the temperature to your liking by moving a few rocks around to let in or divert hot or cold water.

I dug out some snacks and a beer and settled into the soaking tub. Two fishermen in a drift boat came by, and I told them that they were welcome to stop and use the hot spring, but they said no thanks and went on past. For the rest of the afternoon, I alternated between reading and soaking, keeping myself hydrated with IPA from Deschutes Brewery.

As dinnertime approached, I put a can of beef stew and a small can of applesauce in the hot spring pool. That was about it for meal prep. After about an hour, I fished them out with a pair of long tongs. I routinely heat canned foods by placing them in a pan full of water and bringing it to a gentle boil. Several people who have seen me doing that have taken cover, certain that the can would explode. It won't. As long as the can is fully immersed and not leaking, the contents cannot boil (high school physics).

The only risk comes when you first squeeze the can opener and puncture the top of the can. At that moment, the release of pressure, like opening a bottle of Champagne, can cause a momentary geyser of hot stew. I generally let the can cool for a few minutes before opening it, and have never experienced explosive decompression of my dinner.

Beef stew and hot, spiced applesauce made a satisfying meal, followed by a sunset soak in the hot spring. As I'd done the night before, I set up my tent frame and rain fly (without the tent) in case of frost or dew. I woke up sometime during the night to find a pair of antelope grazing a few feet away.

The next morning, even after a soak in the hot spring and a French toast breakfast, I got underway before eight. A mile downstream was Pruitt's Castle, which is a prominent geological feature on the west side of the river. Years ago, I watched a TV show featuring an Owyhee raft trip, where the guide led a hike up to Pruitt's Castle. Linda and I tried to make that hike, but were unable to find the trail, because we'd landed at the wrong beach. My goal for the morning was to find the trail and hike it.

Pruitt's Castle is a tall mound of heavily eroded rock that has formed towers and spires banded in shades of yellow, orange, and brown. The mile-long trail leads up a steep gully to a flat mesa with a stunning view of the river canyon. It took me an hour to make the climb, with frequent stops to catch my breath and ponder the consequences of having a heart attack out there, alone in the Owyhee wilderness, with my Spot II messenger safely stowed on my raft.

The scramble back down was quicker and maybe less strenuous, but felt more treacherous. The round trip probably took about ninety minutes. Back at the raft I pulled out the little thermos that I'd filled with coffee during breakfast.

Photo by Linda
Pruitt's Castle, as seen from river level.

I had four miles of easy floating before I came to Dog Leg Rapid, which, like the two Class III rapids that I ran the day before, was easy and fun. At that point, I was approaching Whistling Bird Canyon, where one of the two most challenging rapids of the trip is located. Rated Class IV, Whistling Bird Rapid features a steep drop over a wide rock bar in a sharp left turn. At the bottom of the drop, the current drives hard toward the right bank, where a massive slab of rock has slid from the cliff, coming to rest vertically, with a portion of the current flowing behind it. Getting caught in there would ruin your day.

Photo by Linda
Approaching Whistling Bird Canyon.

After a short scouting hike, I picked my way down the rapid, staying left as much as the rocks would allow, and passed easily along the safe side of the slab. Not far after that, I found a similar slab on the left, but without the rapid. I poked the raft into the shaded grotto behind the slab and paused to snack on crackers and sardines.

I floated two more easy rapids that are rated Class III

for low water runs, and then arrived at Montgomery Rapid, which is rated Class IV at all levels. I scouted it from the right bank, identifying a well-defined chute near mid-stream. Near the bottom of the rapid, the river makes a right turn and pushes hard toward the left wall, where three large boulders sit right where the current wants to take you. There's a narrow chute between two of the boulders, but it looked to me like the better route would be to work to the right, and stay away from the boulders.

Having made my choice, I turned to walk back up to my raft, when I saw a three-raft group come around the bend and approach the rapid without scouting. I figured they must know the river better than I did—a reasonable assumption, since I'd been there only once before, and that was over twenty years ago.

They started into the rapid to the left of a mid-stream boulder, exactly as I planned to do. But at the point where I would have started working to the right, away from the left wall, they allowed the current to carry them left. The boatman in the first of the rafts caught a steep, narrow chute between the boulders, and then pulled hard right to avoid a boulder that lay against the left shore. The second boatman did the same.

On the third boat, the oarsman approached the left chute with his bow toward the wall, countering the current's leftward push. But he got himself a few feet too far from the wall. Recognizing that, he tried to correct his position by pushing on the oars, but he ran out of time and space.

His raft went sideways and broached on the larger of the two boulders. His left oar was ripped out of his hand. Instinctively, he lunged toward the oar, shifting his weight to the left side of the raft. Instantly, the left side went under water, and the other side rode up onto the rock. In a fraction of a second, the raft filled with water as the force of the current wrapped the raft around the rock. The oarsman, still in the raft, made a desperate attempt to grab

Photo by Jan Brandvold
Raft pinned and boatman helpless.

anything within reach to pull himself up. He managed to get one hand on the right-hand side rail of his frame, but seemed unable to pull himself up. All of this took about three seconds.

I scrambled upstream to find a better vantage point, and I could hear the oarsman shouting. I couldn't make out his words over the noise of the rapid, but I'm pretty sure that one of them was "Help!" From my position on the right shore, there was nothing I could do. He was far beyond the reach of a throw-bag, even if I'd carried one along on my scouting hike.

I tried shouting for him to pull himself up, but of course, he couldn't hear me. Meanwhile the other two guys in his group rowed over to the right bank, tied-up, and hurried back up the shoreline, carrying throw-bags and a coil of rock-climbing rope.

"What's he doing?" the first guy asked.

I said, "It looks like he's stuck where he is—like maybe his foot is wedged, or something."

"Damn! We need to get over there!"

The other boatman asked, "Yeah, but how are we going to do that?"

"I don't know! I don't know! Maybe I can go upstream and try to swim to him."

"That sounds pretty risky. And what if you can't grab hold of the raft?"

"Someone will have to be downstream to pick me up in case that happens," he said, looking at me.

I said, "I don't like the idea of trying to swim to him. Look how fast the current is over there. Even if you got hold of something, you probably wouldn't be able to hold on."

"But what else can we do?"

I didn't answer immediately. I walked back and forth, studying the situation. There were two smaller exposed rocks in the river just downstream from the one where the raft was wrapped. One was on the left, close by the chute the other rafts had taken, and within three feet of the wrap-rock. The other was closer to our side and further downstream, leaving a miniscule eddy just below the wrap-rock.

"I think I can get my raft into that little eddy. One of you can ride on my raft and try to get onto the rock. It'll be a touchy move, because if I miss the eddy, I'll probably end up hitting that other rock."

"Shit, man. That doesn't even look possible. You really think you can do it?"

"Right now, it looks like our best shot. Your friend is hanging on by one hand. He can't do that for very long."

"If you're willing to try it, I'll go with you." He turned to his buddy and said, "Go back to the rafts and be ready to pick us up if either of us ends up in the water."

He and I started scrambling back up toward my raft, frequently looking back to identify any nuances in the current that would affect our approach to the eddy.

"I'm Ken," I said.

"Chad. That's Lee out there."

"Okay, Chad. You have a good knife?"

"Shit! I left it on my raft. Should I go back for it?"

"No. I have one you can use. If Lee has a foot wedged between the raft and the frame, you might have to puncture the raft to free him."

When we got back to my raft, I gave Chad my pathetically dull scuba diving knife in its scabbard, which he strapped to his lower leg. I instructed him to climb onto the back of my raft. I quickly put on my life jacket, and untied the raft.

I worked my way out to mid-current, and pointed the raft downstream. I rowed against the current to slow myself down, angling left or right to adjust my position. When we got within fifty yards of the wrapped raft, I told Chad to be ready to climb onto the rock the instant I got into the eddy.

The current was accelerating, and I had to pull hard to slow down. At the last possible instant, I pivoted the raft, placing the stern to pass within inches of the boulder. The instant it was clear, I gave a quick pull on both oars, followed by two sharp pulls on my right oar. The back of the raft broke the eddy line, and the current swept the bow in an arc to the left.

"Now!" I shouted to Chad, as I pulled the raft up beneath the wrap-rock. There was no room to work my left oar, so it was impossible to hold my position there.

Behind me, Chad found handholds on the rock, and boosted himself off my raft. That pushed me out of the eddy, but I was able to catch the larger eddy beneath the boulder to my right. I looked over my shoulder and saw that Chad had made it onto the rock. He motioned unnecessarily for me to hold my position, and then worked his way over to where I hoped Lee was still hanging on.

He apparently found footing somewhere in the wrapped raft, and he ducked down out of my sight. Seconds ticked by. I had to keep working my oars in order to keep the raft up against the rock at the head of the eddy, working mostly by feel, since the raft was still pointed downstream. Seconds turned to minutes that felt like hours.

"Ken!" Chad shouted. "Can you catch a line?"

I looked over my shoulder to see him standing on the rock, with Lee next to him, sitting on the side of his raft, looking dazed and exhausted. Chad had a throw-bag in his hand.

"Hook your end to the front corner of the raft frame," I shouted. "When you throw it, try to put it right in my lap."

A few seconds later, he shouted, "Okay! I'm hooked up. Are you ready?"

"I'll swing the raft. As soon as you have a clear shot, make the throw."

I doubted that he'd get a second chance if he missed, because I wouldn't be able to hold my raft in the eddy while I caught the line. But I was only twenty feet away, so it should be an easy toss. I tucked my right oar handle under my knee, to free my hand to make the catch, and made two short pulls on the left oar.

"Now!"

Chad under-handed the throw bag, which uncoiled its line as it sailed in a rainbow arc toward me. I caught it with my right hand, dropped the left oar, and stood up. Letting both oars trail in the water, I got both hands on the line and pulled it tight. My raft continued its pivot to the left, until it faced upstream. I pulled myself upstream, back into the lower eddy, while climbing over my ice chest to the front of the raft. I threw an overhand loop in the line and used a carabiner to attach it to front crossbar on my frame.

That took care of Step One. The situation was stabilized, and everyone was safe. Next, we had to get Lee from the boulder into my raft. I could see that he was too exhausted to help free the raft.

I got his attention and shouted, "I need you to swim over here."

He shook his head adamantly.

"I'll toss you a line, and pull you over. You won't be in the water for two seconds."

With Chad's help, Lee reluctantly worked his way down the steep downstream face to the boulder. I tossed a line to Chad, who handed it to Lee. He let go of the rock and I reeled him in. He was dead weight as I dragged him up into my raft. Step Two finished.

Lee sat down on the floor in the middle of my raft and lay back against the side tube. "I had a big folding knife on a cord attached to my PFD. It got wedged between my seat and the frame, and I couldn't get it loose. It was holding me down."

Now we had to figure out how to salvage the raft. From where I was, it appeared to be evenly pinned against the boulder. The line holding my raft in the eddy was attached to the front of the wrapped raft's frame. I hoped that might help drag the raft around the left side of the rock, into the chute the other two rafts had taken.

"Chad! Can you see if it wants to go one way or the other?"

"I can't really tell, but what I can see is that most of the load is in the back. I think that's the direction it'll want to go," he said.

The back of the raft was to my left, as I looked upstream. I wasn't excited about bringing the raft around that way, because it would run straight onto the next rock down.

"Can you unload some of the gear in back?"

"Give me a minute," he said. He climbed over the rock and again ducked out of my sight.

"There's a couple of water jugs, a big dry bag, and a rocket box. And there's some small dry bags, too."

"Can you untie any of that stuff"

"Yeah, I think so."

"Okay. Here's the plan, then. I'll throw you a line. You tie it to one of those things, and let it float down to me. I'll pull it in. Empty-out the water jugs. If we can make the back of the raft light enough, it just might come free."

"Sounds good," he said.

So, I tossed my throw line to him, and a few minutes later pulled in an empty water jug. Next came a five-gallon propane tank, followed by the other water jug. Chad sent the two small dry bags together, and I added them to the growing pile in the front of my raft. The big dry bag turned out to be really heavy. I suspect that it'd leaked and soaked everything inside. Either that, or Lee was carrying a bag full of lead shot.

"I think it's starting to move," Chad shouted, while climbing over the high side.

He sat on the boulder, with both feet against the raft, and pushed. I could see nothing happening, but Chad kept on pushing. Then he established a rhythm, pushing and releasing, and little by little, the jostling started to shift the raft in the direction of the chute between the boulders.

"Here we go!" Chad shouted.

The raft came free and started down the chute. Chad climbed on and held fast through the steep drop. My raft started to move as well, because the two were still tied together. I hastily reached over and unclipped the carabiner, while Chad scrambled to get Lee's spare oar unstrapped. The raft was pushed against the rocks on the left bank and then rebounded back into the current.

"Lee!" I shouted. "Take the oars and stay with Chad."

He climbed up out of the foot well into the oarsman's seat, and started rowing. In a few seconds, we ran out of the tail waves into smooth water, and Lee was able to row to shore where the third guy was still standing by with his raft. He grabbed my raft and pulled it to shore, and a moment later Chad brought Lee's raft in.

"Everybody okay? I asked.

"No shit, man! That was one slick move you made, getting in below that boulder," Chad said.

"It was pretty tight. For a second there, I wasn't sure we were going to make it," I said.

But Chad was right. It was a *really* slick move. But I can't honestly say whether it was skill or luck. I guess it's skill if you make it, and bad luck if you don't.

I started unloading Lee's gear from the front of my raft and stacking it on shore. When I hefted the waterlogged dry bag over the side, I suggested, "You need to find a place to camp as soon as you can, while the sun's still up. You'll have to spread everything out to dry."

Lee shook his head. "I don't think I can row any more right now."

I could see that Lee was shaking, maybe from being in the cold water, but more likely from post-adrenaline shock. I told him to lie down and let his friends re-load his raft.

I said, "My map shows two campsites less than half a mile ahead, and there is only smooth water between here and there."

Chad nodded and suggested, "As long as there aren't any rapids, I can tow the raft half a mile."

"Okay then. If you have everything under control, I think I'll be on my way," I said.

"Yeah, no problem," Chad said. "And thanks for the help. I don't know what we could have done by ourselves."

I pushed off and started downstream, feeling suddenly fatigued from the stress and exertion of the rescue. I'm sure any medical expert would tell you that under these circumstances, the one thing you should *not* do is drink a beer. Mine was a Black Butte Porter.

Exerting the bare minimum effort, I drifted downstream past the campsites I'd suggested to Chad. I made about two more miles before coming to a campsite at the foot of a wave train called Tanager Rapid, near Mile 36. When I checked the time, I was surprised to see that it was 4:30. I would have guessed that it was around 3:00.

The next morning, I slept-in until 6:30. My plan was to float past Birch Creek and camp a couple of miles short of the slack water of Lake Owyhee. In no particular rush to get underway, I took off after breakfast, and hiked a couple of miles up a dry wash to the remains of an abandoned homestead. I got back to my raft and started downstream at 10:30, in violation of my ten o'clock rule.

Nuisance Rapid, about two miles downstream from my camp shows as Class IV on my map, so I took a few minutes to do a cursory scout. Finding nothing to warrant a Class IV rating at my water level, I went back to my raft and made an uneventful run. A few minutes later, I ran Morcum Dam Rapid without scouting.

In mid-afternoon, as I arrived at Greeley Hot Spring, I found the camp unoccupied, so I stopped to enjoy a brief soak. I considered staying for the night, but that would leave me with 23 miles to cover the next day. So, I held to my plan and spent the night at a place called Basque Camp, 15 miles from Leslie Gulch.

Photo by Linda

The remains of an old water wheel along the right bank tell you that you are approaching the flat water of Lake Owyhee.

I got out of camp before 8:30, but a couple of miles downstream I started to feel the wind blowing in my face. It was a warm day, and at first, the breeze felt good. Many groups either bring a small outboard motor for the twelve-mile run down the slack water of Lake Owyhee to Leslie Gulch, or meet someone with a power boat to pull or push them down. But I'd gambled on not having to fight the wind.

At Mile 58, the river makes a sweeping ninety-degree right turn, and that's where the wind really kicked up. Before long I was rowing like a galley slave. After four hours of that, I gave up on the idea of going all the way to Leslie Gulch, and pulled ashore at Black Rocks. It is the location of the only mapped campsite on the lake, and is four miles from the Leslie Gulch boat ramp.

From the campsite, I took a short walk to a nice hot spring, where a plastic pipe carries the warm water to a pleasant shower on the lakeshore. Traditionally, the last night on a river trip is time for a farewell party, but on a solo trip, the concept of a farewell party seems kind of ominous. Sitting in camp watching the sunset, I was thinking ahead to my takeout the next day.

I got out of camp early the next morning, but almost immediately found myself rowing against the wind. It wasn't as strong as it had been the previous afternoon, but the clock was working against me. The standard anxiety about the vehicle shuttle leads to the question of what if my rig isn't there. But assuming that it was, as nearly always is the case, what was my plan? I knew from my previous Owyhee trip that the drive out of the canyon and then all the way home would take all of twelve hours.

Originally, I'd intended to get to Leslie Gulch late the previous afternoon, trailer the raft, and "camp" in the back of my pickup. From there, I'd have been able to get home in the evening of April 29th. That was important, because Linda and I had already made travel plans for the 30th.

For years, Linda had wanted to tour the Painted Hills and the John Day Fossil Beds in central Oregon, so we had reservations to spend three nights at the historic Condon Hotel, starting on April 30th. That set up an absurd itinerary for me, driving clear across the state on the 29th, just to turn around and drive half-way back on the 30th. But with my delayed takeout, I would have to drive past midnight to get home. That made a ridiculous situation untenable.

I had a better idea, but first things first. I arrived at Leslie Gulch at 10:30, and easily loaded the raft, using my new power winch setup. My drive out from Leslie Gulch to US-95 took me east, into Idaho. My phone started beeping when it found service somewhere outside of Homedale. I pulled into a gas station to see who'd been trying to call me.

As expected, there had been about a dozen calls from Charlene and Ray, and even more from helpful people with the alarming news that the warranty on my twenty-seven-year-old pickup was about to expire. I'd missed those calls, so now I'm screwed.

My first call was to Linda. I told her about my delay and suggested that it would make more sense for me to meet her in Condon instead driving all the way home. It meant that she'd have to drive to Condon on Friday and back home on Monday. She was surprisingly agreeable, probably because she'd get to drive her convertible on a sunny road trip.

With that settled, we exchanged reports on the events of the past week, and she gave me a progress report on Kevin's trek. In a month on the trail, he'd hiked over 500 miles.

I commented that although my experience was refreshing, I was a bit fatigued from my long row down the lake against the damnable headwind.

"I'll tell you all about it this evening," I said in closing.

Next, I listened to all of the voice mails from Charlene. It was pretty much as I'd expected.

"What should we do when the list calls for 2.33 tomatoes?"

My answer was, "Sometimes the fractional amounts don't make logical sense. Use your best judgement. In this case, maybe you buy two large tomatoes, or maybe you buy three small ones. Don't cut tomatoes in the store. They won't like it."

"What does KB mean on the shopping list?"

"It means Kitchen Box. As your instructions state, the kitchen box is on my raft, and I will take care of everything on the KB list. Don't buy anything that says KB."

"My son doesn't like broccoli. Should I buy less than the shopping list calls for?"

"Once we start trying to adjust for individual tastes in food, there is no end to it. It will completely defeat the purpose of using the computer to calculate our shopping lists. The quantities that the computer specifies are based on years of real-life experience. Don't try to second-guess the software."

"I have a really good recipe for Lasagna. Can I use that instead?"

"Yes, but I don't recommend it. A month from now, when you're on a beach next to the Colorado River, will you remember your recipe? You will have my recipe in your hand."

And then she dropped was the big bomb: "Jeremy—the guy who's taking the last spot on our permit—he's a vegan. How are we going to accommodate him?"

Oh, shit. My cook team partner is a vegan? My only answer to that was that he's on his own. I have no vegan recipes in my menu system. Nor do I make any special accommodations for diabetics, transexuals, psychotics, neurotics, Land Rover drivers, or otherwise flawed individuals. As a group, we decided what meals we wanted. If the guy wants to join the group, he has to accept what we've already done. A lot of the shopping is already done. We're not going to change everything to accommodate him. Being a vegan is a matter of choice, not a medical necessity.

I had these conversations and others with Charlene that afternoon in the shade next to the gas station in Homedale. By the time I was done talking, I was exhausted and hungry. I sat down for an old-fashioned diner-style hamburger (definitely *not* fast food).

It was early evening when I arrived in Condon and located the Condon Hotel. I parked at the curb behind Linda's convertible and found her in our room with our Yorkie, Rolo.

Chapter Eight

What's Next?

During my long drive from Leslie Gulch to Condon, my thoughts were dominated by my upcoming Grand Canyon trip. First it was kayakers, and now I had to deal with somebody's aberrant dietary choices.

So, initially, the idea of floating the John Day River was just a ploy to purge my mind of my growing negativity about the Grand Canyon trip. As long as I could avoid thinking about kayaks and vegans, I could defer my stress and feel at peace. On the face of it, it was an absurd idea.

But I had to continue the mental exercise. First off, would it even be *possible* to float the John Day in the time remaining before the Grand Canyon trip? In my mind, I built a calendar of the next month, starting with my weekend in Condon with Linda.

I could easily drive from Condon to the launch site at Service Creek on May 3rd, and if I floated from there to Cottonwood Bridge, it might take ten days. That would still leave eleven days before the permit date for the Grand Canyon trip. Three of those days would be spent on the road to Lee's Ferry. Would the remaining eight days leave enough time to get everything ready for the big trip? Actually, for the most part, I *was* ready, so…

For Linda and me, the long weekend touring the fossil beds and painted hills was our first real escape from the year-long COVID quarantine. Things still were far from normal, but a growing number of people were rebelling against the seemingly ineffective, and on that basis, unnecessary restrictions.

Friday evening, during dinner at a sidewalk café across from the hotel, Linda saw me rubbing the muscles at the back of my neck, and asked, "Do you really think you're in shape to do this Grand Canyon trip?"

I said, "Of course. But I've been thinking about floating the John Day, to get a little more conditioning. The water level is perfect, so why not, right?"

"How long is that trip?"

As I answered, I actually ducked my head as if anticipating some kind of projectile being thrown in my direction.

"Depending where I put-in and takeout, it could be as short as four days or as long as ten."

"Are there mental health checkpoints along the way?"

I sensed a trace of sarcasm.

"I always carry a copy of *I'm OK, You're OK* in my library box, just in case."

That wasn't true. But I did have a copy of the *John Day River Drift and Historical Guide,* which would be far more useful.

"I think you're out of your mind," she said.

"That's nothing new," I reminded her.

"So, what about your Grand Canyon trip? Does this insanity of yours leave enough time to get that organized?"

"Even if I do the whole ten-day run, I'll still have a week before we leave for The Canyon. That will be plenty of time."

"Sounds like you've been thinking about this for a while."

"It was a long drive back from the Owyhee. But it still isn't a sure thing," I said. "I'll need to see what I can do about a permit."

Back at the hotel, I searched the internet for information about that. I don't know when the Bureau of Land Management began limiting access to the John Day River, and I'd never attempted to get a permit under whatever system they had created for issuing them. So first, I went to the BLM website.

Then I closed the Black Lives Matter website and went to the Bureau of Land Management website, where I found a convoluted mess of rules and instructions that were so byzantine that I was tempted to go back to the other BLM site.

I ended up on the infamous Recreation.gov website, where I found that I'd need not *one*, but *two* permits to float the river—one for the section from Service Creek to Clarno, and another for the section from Clarno to Cottonwood Bridge.

I went through the motions of checking for available launch dates, and learned that half of the allocated permits had been released on March 1st, and the other half would be made available the next morning, May 1st at 7:00—accidentally perfect timing on my part.

I considered just ignoring the permit system and taking my chances on getting caught. Instead, I got up early to see if I could actually get the permits. At exactly 7:00, I searched for available launch dates, and I found that several permits were available. *So why did I have to go through all of this rigamarole?* The answer, as most government-related issues are, was money. Each permit carried a fee of $20, plus a $6 processing fee. I'd need two permits: one for the section from Service Creek to Clarno, and the other from Clarno to Cottonwood Bridge.

I'm just (barely) old enough to remember when $52 was a lot of money, and emotionally, it still registers that way, even though I'd just spent $350 for three nights lodging and $50 for a microwaved dinner.

The $52 tax to go rafting was pure theft. My righteous indignation over the fee nearly motivated me to become a criminal. Nearly, but not quite. That would come later. I went ahead and booked the permits.

On Monday. After Linda headed home, I went to Condon's only grocery store to replenish my food, beer, ice, and supplies. I also drove to the Condon city RV park and used the RV dump station to clean-out my ScatPacker toilet bucket—something I'd almost forgotten about until I was re-packing the raft. Generally, it's not a good idea to save last week's shit for next week's raft trip.

Photo by Author
John Day River near Clarno Bridge. in 1984

It was a one-hour drive to Service Creek, and I arrived there shortly before noon. There had been a pretty hard rain on Saturday, and the surrounding desert hills were green with new grass. At the Service Creek Stage Stop, I arranged to have my rig shuttled to Cottonwood, and noted a small blackboard that said the flow that morning was 4,500 cfs. That's a very comfortable level for boating, and there'd be good current through even the flattest parts of the river.

It was a quarter mile down to the launch site, where there's not an actual boat ramp, but I was able to back the trailer down to the river's edge and push the raft into the water. I parked my rig, noting that there was only one other rig in the parking lot, and nobody else anywhere in the park. Nobody came along to check my float permit, so in that sense, I had wasted the $52.

Several decades ago, when I first floated the John Day, I had approached it with low expectations. From the way it was described in the guidebook I had at the time, I expected to find an uninspiring float through farm and ranch land with occasional stretches of bland scenery. I'd chosen the John Day only because most of its rapids were mild enough to be safe for little children.

The 117-mile John Day float from Service Creek to Cottonwood Bridge has exactly *one* Class III rapid. All of the other rapids are Class II or less. Just about anyone in just about any kind of boat could float the John Day. But what the John Day lacks in thrills, it makes up for in solitude. Between Clarno and Cottonwood on my 1984 trip, I saw two parties during my entire eight days on the river. The real surprise, though, was the scenery, which was always pleasant and, in some places, borderline spectacular.

If you're floating the John Day, I urge you to try to find a copy of Arthur Campbell's book, *John Day River Drift and Historical Guide*. It contains a wealth of interesting historical information in a mile-by-mile guide. But it's been out of print for many years, and is very hard to find. A few people on Amazon offer copies at stupidly high prices, based on the notion that if it's out of print, it must be valuable. But occasionally a copy comes up at a price that is more in line with the fee I paid for my unnecessary but required permit.

Photo by Author
One of the many Class II rapids in the John Day River Canyon, 1984.

I've had my copy since the 1980s, when I bought it for ten bucks. And no, you can't have it. Well, maybe, but only if you're willing to pay a stupidly high price.

Once away from the launch site for my new adventure, I pushed downstream at a leisurely pace, listening to a John Grisham audiobook on my tablet, which I kept charged by a solar panel. Because of my late launch, I managed to float only about seven miles, stopping at Deer Creek, just below Russo Rapid, which was a simple wave train at this water level.

As a general rule, I like to camp near rapids, because the sound blots out the noises that tend to interrupt my sleep—including everything from bears raiding the ice chest to grasshoppers farting.

When I awoke sometime between midnight and dawn, it took my brain a few seconds to sort out what was different. The sound of the rapid seemed to have changed. No, wait. What I was hearing was something else, on top of the sound of the rapid. Rain drops were pattering on my rainfly.

When I realized that, I switched on my light to see if any part of my sleeping bag was poking out from under the fly, since I hadn't thought a tent would be necessary when I set up camp. Fortunately, the rain was not accompanied by wind, and most of my things were still dry. This validated my decision to buy the 4-person size tent, which has an eight-and-a-half by seven-foot footprint, so even with just the rainfly set up, the protected area was adequate for me and all of my stuff. But I would *never* try to put four people in it.

After stuffing my clothes and things into my dry bag, I satisfied myself that I was safe from the rain and went back to sleep. It was still raining when I got up in the morning, and as I scanned the sky, I could see nothing to suggest that the storm was passing, so I dressed for a day in the rain. Before abandoning my shelter, I packed up my air bed, sleeping bag, and clothes, making room under the rain fly to prepare breakfast.

I put my fire pan upside down in the middle of the shelter, and set up my mini-kitchen (minus legs) on top of that. Once I had water on the stove for coffee, I made a quick foray into the rain to gather supplies for a decent breakfast. Breakfasts are important to me—even more so when it's raining.

My ingenious idea of using my tent fly as a kitchen shelter quickly devolved into a goat rodeo. First and foremost, the low height of the rain fly meant that the only way I could move about was on my hands and knees. That's okay for sleeping, but it doesn't work very well for cooking. It didn't take long to discover that whatever I needed at any given moment was always out of reach, so I was constantly scooting around on my butt. In the confined area, that often resulted in things getting knocked over or pushed out into the rain.

Somehow, I managed to finish breakfast without setting anything on fire, and then I started packing up. But the whole process had been a pain in the ass. And making things worse, I've always hated having to break down camp in the rain. No matter how hard you try to keep things dry, the rain always finds a way to get into your drybag and kitchen box while you're packing up. You have to just hope that the rain will stop before you have to set up your next camp. It *could* happen.

After leaving camp, I floated on easy water enjoying the look of the hillsides with their fresh carpet of green grass. There was no wind, and with gentle rowing, I kept moving at about three miles an hour. I passed occasional stretches of farm land before coming to a big horseshoe bend to the left, immediately followed by two hard bends back to the right.

It was noon and still raining, as I approached the Twickenham bridge. It was here, in 1979, that I ended an overnight trip from Service Creek—our first experiment in taking small children on a river trip. As of 2021, I still had never floated the section from Twickenham to Clarno, so most of what I knew about it came from my guidebook.

Farms and ranches became more frequent after passing Twickenham, and I found the scenery pretty mundane for the next few miles. Rowing downstream in the persistent rain, I had plenty of time to contemplate how to set up a better shelter for cooking.

Kitchen shelters had always been a problem for me. Number one, they are very tedious to set up, usually requiring at least three people. Number two, they are very vulnerable to wind. A couple of decades ago, following a debacle with a cheap "picnic canopy" that tore to pieces in the wind while six of us tried to set it up, I bought an expensive new product called a Moss Parawing.

Photo by Author
Scenery in the lower canyon.

The Parawing is a great shelter. It is extremely well made, very durable, and able to withstand moderately strong wind gusts. But it is virtually impossible for one person to set it up. That's why I hadn't brought it along. Instead, I had the big old PVC tarp and a bunch of parachute cord. Honestly, I'd probably have been better off with the Parawing. But I still couldn't have set it up by myself.

In mid-afternoon, I pulled ashore on the left bank, at the foot of Homestead Rapid. There isn't really a camping beach there, at least not one capable of supporting a group, but it had the one feature I needed: lots of anchor-points for putting up the tarp, which I spread-out on the gravel next to a ten-foot-tall basalt boulder.

I strung a line from one corner of the tarp over the top of the boulder, and tied it off to an exposed root on the other side. At two of the other three corners, I tied lines to the thickest branches on the scrubby willows that surrounded the gravel bar. But it seems that there's always one corner where there's no anchor. For this, I had to dig a hole and find the biggest rock I could carry. I wrapped a line securely around the rock, which I placed in the hole and covered with gravel. Old timers call that a dead man. Most people would be horrified if I told them that I'd buried a dead man on the beach.

With all four corners tied, I then used my oars to raise the tarp above my head. I got out my chair and a beer, and sat down to enjoy being out of the rain for the first time all day. It had taken almost an hour to set up the tarp, and considerably less time to drain the beer. After that, I set up my kitchen and tent. I spread out all of my damp things under the shelter to dry as much as possible. It drizzled all evening and into the night, but I awoke at some point to the sound of silence. The rain had finally stopped.

Everything that was damp in the evening was still damp in the morning, and I had no choice but to pack it up that way, thus ensuring that anything that was still dry would share the moisture from the things that weren't.

A couple of miles after leaving camp, I passed the Priest Hole Recreation Site, where in 1989, a teenage boy on a church outing drowned while trying to swim across the river. He and a friend made it to the far shore, but only the friend made it back. Church groups are notorious for having poor leadership on outdoor activities.

The victim's body was pulled from the river three days later, eight miles downstream, by one of my guides conducting a raft trip for my biggest customer, the Elderhostel Corporation. Unable to transport a dead body down river for two days in ninety-degree weather, the guides wrapped the victim in a tarp and left him in the tenuous shade of a juniper tree. One of the guides stopped at the next ranch and called the county sheriff, who completed the recovery.

I'd been counting on camping at one of the campsites that showed on my map in the Big Bend area, but one was occupied by what looked like a Boy Scout troop, and the other by the drift boat fishermen I'd seen at Russo Rapid. So, I continued two more miles to a very nice little camp under a cluster of pine trees on the left bank, upstream from Cathedral Rock.

By then, the sky had cleared and the sun was out, so by the time I had my raft unloaded, the temperature was in the upper seventies. I

Photo by Author

spread out everything I owned to dry before the sun dropped behind the hills in the west.

The morning sky was clear, and I started downstream under blue sky and sunshine. The scenery improved markedly after I passed the Burnt Ranch area. Burnt Ranch Rapid was straight-forward and fun, as were two more riffles downstream. With rugged hillsides on my right and intermittent farmland on my left, I floated almost due north for most of the next four miles.

I started my fourth day on the river with an early departure and almost no whitewater all day. Around noon, I passed Big Muddy Creek, the site where Bhagwan Shree Rajneesh established his notorious commune in the 1980s. After the arrests of several of his key followers, "Osho," as they called him, fled the country and Rancho Rajneesh was razed.

In the afternoon, just when I was starting to look for a place to camp, I spotted the Clarno bridge ahead. I hadn't been paying close attention to where I was, and had already passed the good camping areas. I went under the bridge and another three miles before finding a nice little camp on the left bank, below prominent red bluffs. In four days, I had floated 52 miles.

Photo by Jackie L. Baysinger
Author taking *Mariah* through Clarno Rapid at medium-low flow.in 1984.

With an early start the next morning, I went only a mile before pulling in to scout Clarno Rapid from a high bluff above the left bank. Clarno Rapid has wrecked many boats and taken several lives, so scouting is recommended. As on my 1984 trip, I found it to be an easy read-and-run rapid; but it's long, and definitely has many rocks and holes to avoid.

At this point, just about all vestiges of civilization disappear, as the river drops into scenic gorges and frequent easy riffles. In the middle of the afternoon, I passed through Basalt Rapid and entered the spectacular canyon called

The Narrows. I found a small beach with a good spring on the right bank shortly below a large island, and called it a day.

Before leaving in the morning, I filled my water jugs with fresh spring water. The river turned sharply to the right, and for a couple of miles flowed in a southeasterly direction. At a place called Arch Rocks, the river made a horseshoe bend to the left, and resumed its northward flow.

Thirtymile Creek at River Mile 84 was an unmistakable landmark. I could see several structures on the bluffs above the river, and cattle were grazing on the hillside. I camped for the night at Beef Hollow, on a beach sheltered by a big black rock. In the evening, I reviewed my notes, and realized that I was a day ahead of schedule. If I continued at this pace, I'd get to the takeout at Cottonwood Bridge a day before the shuttle service was scheduled to deliver my pickup and trailer.

The campsite I was in was a whole lot more desirable than what I'd find at Cottonwood, so I did a layover. This gave me the opportunity to add many more details to my river notes, which eventually would become this narrative.

Photo by Author

The old wagons have deteriorated significantly since this photo was taken in 1984.

Underway the next morning, I looked forward to easy floating and several good sightseeing opportunities. At River Mile 76.3, the river makes an abrupt 90 degree left turn, and a deep eddy on the right marks the location of three old wagons that were left there in the 1920s. They had been used in the making of a silent movie, and then were abandoned. When I visited them in 1984, they were still more or less intact. But the years have taken their toll.

A few miles further, I located petroglyphs at Potlatch Canyon. They are unprotected, and some recent visitor had painted them, presumably to make an imprint on cloth. I place a curse on the shirt made from that cloth.

In 1984, on our third night after launching from Clarno, we camped on the left, between River Miles 70 and 69. The kids called it "Sagebrush Camp." I'm pretty sure that's the same place I stayed after my eighth day on the river, four of which were spent above Clarno.

Photo by Author
Typical John Day River Camp, circa 1984. Under those juniper trees, watch out for rattlesnakes and ticks.

I continued my leisurely pace, averaging twelve to thirteen miles a day, noting landmarks on the map as I floated by. I passed Fern Hollow, Bull Basin, and Stair Step Palisades in my first two hours. I stopped for lunch opposite Citadel Rock, and camped that afternoon on a sandbar near Piano Box Canyon.

My last full day on the river took me to a beach on the right bank, less than four miles from the Cottonwood Bridge. After ten easy restful days on the John Day, I felt that my soul had been renewed.

The four-mile run down to the takeout was easy, but filled with triumph and trepidation. I had reached the conclusion of my physical training. The next trip would be the real thing.

Photo by Author

Chapter Nine

Canyon Countdown

Back home late in the day on May 13th, eleven days before our Grand Canyon launch date, I felt stronger and more energized than I'd felt in at least ten years. During the drive home from the John Day, I talked on the phone with Charlene, and she said that everything was on track, but there were some more questions regarding the shopping and packing. I suggested that we get together on Saturday to get everyone onto the same page.

Friday morning, I got started on my final preparations for the Grand Canyon. I emptied-out my dry bags and ran my towels and smelly clothes through the laundry. My gritty sleeping bag had to go to the laundromat, because it was too big for our washer at home. By evening, I had everything re-packed in my dry bags, ready to go.

I drove out to Ray's place the next morning, and that was when I first met Jeremy, my kayaking vegan cook team partner. I try not to be judgmental, but sometimes I just can't help it. Jeremy had a ring in his nose, and his ear lobes were stretched around hoops that were close to an inch in diameter. And I remember when only ex-cons had facial tattoos.

I resolved to be cordial. "Hi. I'm Ken."

He mumbled something that was either "Hey" or "Hi."

"Glad you could join us. Ever run the Grand Canyon before?"

"Um, like this'll be my first time, ya know? But I done lots of rivers, like, around here?"

"I think Charlene told me that you're bringing a kayak. Have you ever rowed a raft?"

"A raft? Not really. Like, I prefer to be one with the river, ya know? Like, that's what kayaking is all about."

"Do you have first-aid or CPR certification? Whitewater rescue?"

"Uh, like I know a lot about that stuff, but nobody said I had to, like, have any cards 'n stuff."

"You don't. I just wanted to know what you're bringing to the table."

"So, I can do all that kind of stuff, ya know? I'm just not into paperwork."

I felt it best to change the subject. "I understand you're vegan."

"Uh huh. I don't eat anything that, like, has a mother?"

Oh, for God's sake!

"I guess you've seen the menu we've adopted for this trip…"

"Yeah, like Steven showed me? And I'm down with it? Like, I can just skip the animal parts, ya know?"

From experience, I knew that it wasn't really that simple.

I asked, "Will you get enough to eat that way?"

He gave a moronic laugh. "Like, I'm used to living in a meat-eater's world, ya know, so I know what it takes? I'll just, like, bring my own food."

I wondered if this was the right time to ask if he expected the rest of us to cook his "special" food for him, and if everyone was okay with having to do that. It was a question that was certain to come up. Vegans on other river trips that I'd led had fended for themselves, and that's what I'd expect from Jeremy.

"That's fine," I said. "We'll have to see about making enough stove space for you to work with."

Implication: You're on your own, buddy.

I addressed the whole group. "Does anyone have any questions?"

"Um, I've noticed that a lot of the things on my recipe sheets are like not on my shopping lists? So, I'm like doing my shopping from the recipe sheets?" said Krystal.

I asked, "Can you show me an example?"

"Sure."

She then pulled out the menu sheet for Team Four's first meal and pointed to things she had circled.

I took a couple of deep cleansing breaths.

"Look at the right-hand column. What does it say?"

"I never paid any attention to that column. What does it mean?"

Very patiently, and without prefacing my answer with "as I have explained on multiple occasions in the past," I said, "For the most part, that column indicates where you'll find the item in the grocery store. It's the aisle number."

She interrupted, "Wait. Like, won't the aisle numbers be different from one store to the next?"

Another deep breath. "Yes, but the specific aisle number is irrelevant. The point is that all grocery stores group similar items in the same locations—you'll always find peanut butter in the same aisle as jam, and you'll always find pickles in the same aisle as olives, mayo, and mustard. Your shopping list is sorted so that all of the things that are likely to be in the same part of the store are grouped together on the shopping list. That will keep you from having to go back to any particular part of the store over and over as you go down your list."

"Oh! I get it! I guess I didn't notice that when I was shopping. But what about the things that weren't on the list?"

"What do you see instead of an aisle number?"

She looked over two pages of her shopping list. "It looks like most of them have KB in that column."

"And what does that mean?" I asked, perhaps a bit patronizingly.

"Uh. I don't know."

"Kitchen Box. It means it is an item that is stored in the kitchen box on my raft, for use in multiple recipes. So, I put all of the KB items on *my* shopping list, to assure that the kitchen box is fully stocked, and to keep us from buying a new shaker of salt for every meal."

I hadn't previously explained that more than five or ten times.

"Oh. So, I shouldn't buy things that are marked KB?"

"Shop from your shopping lists, *not* the meal sheets. Trust your shopping lists and buy what they call for. Nothing else."

"But there are some things missing from the shopping list that *aren't* marked KB."

She pointed to an example. "My breakfast recipe calls for maple syrup, but it isn't on my shopping list. There are several things like that, and they aren't marked KB either."

I explained, "That's a matter of economy. Sometimes, when we're going to use a particular item—like syrup, or butter, or coffee—in several meals, it is more cost-effective to buy a single large package than half a dozen small packages. I put the 'grouped' quantity on the shopping list where it is first used on the trip."

"Uh, okay, but how am I supposed to know that?"

"Just buy what your shopping list says. Then, when we're on the river and you're fetching the supplies for that breakfast you will probably be able to recall who first served syrup. If not, just ask."

"Syrup isn't the only thing…"

"No, but I'll guarantee that whatever else you think you're missing is on someone else's shopping list, and will be stored in that team's dry box or cooler."

"What if someone forgets to get something?"

"The penalty for forgetting to buy something that is on your list can range from social ostracism to summary execution, depending whether it is, for example, mustard or coffee."

"Um, I guess I bought some things that I, like, shouldn't have," Krystal admitted.

"At this point, don't worry about it. We'll just have extra. It's more trouble than it's worth to try to sort out and return the stuff we don't need."

"Really? I mean, I can do it—I don't want to run-up our costs."

"If you think it's a significant amount of money, and you have the time, go ahead. That's your call," I said.

I looked around and asked, "Anything else?"

Sophia said, "Um, I had that same question."

"But now you understand it?"

She nodded. "I was also wondering about the shopping in Utah. Why can't we just do all of the shopping at home before we leave?"

I had explained all of this too, a month before. A part of me wanted to say, "Because I said so, and you asked me to be the trip leader."

Instead, I repeated what I'd said before, "Most of what we're buying in Utah is fresh produce and bakery products. We're counting on having that stuff last for up to two weeks after we leave Lee's Ferry. We need everything to be as fresh as possible when we start down river."

She elected to argue the point. "Yeah, but it's only a couple of extra days."

I answered, "When you do your normal shopping at home, how often do you buy your perishables two weeks before you plan to use them?"

"Uh, I don't know. It probably happens sometimes."

"And if something goes bad, you just zip over to Safeway and replace it, right? Problem is, there are no grocery stores in Grand Canyon. That's why we're shopping in Cedar City. Any other questions?"

I said that with a big smile, which I hoped Krystal would interpret as a friendly way of settling the debate, but which actually was my way of laughing at her obstinance. No passive aggression here. Nope.

Then, I asked, "Do all of you have motel reservations for Saturday night in Cedar City?"

"Well, actually, our plan is to leave here early on Saturday, and spend the night in Salt Lake City. Then we'll drive to Cedar City Sunday morning and do the shopping, on our way to Lee's Ferry." said Ray.

"That's not a good idea. It's way too far from Salt Lake to Lee's Ferry, and shopping will take a lot longer than you think. You wouldn't get to Lee's Ferry in time to rig your rafts."

"Oh, we don't have to rig them. The rental company said they'd deliver them already set up," he explained.

I said, "You will still need to pack all of your food, supplies and personal equipment, and then secure it all. It will surprise you how much time that'll take. Leaving Cedar City early Sunday morning gets us to Lee's Ferry before noon. From Salt Lake with a shopping stop along the way, you'd be lucky to get there before dark."

Charlene turned to Ray and said, "So, maybe we should leave home on Friday instead of Saturday, and spend Friday night in Boise or Twin Falls, and then, like Ken says, get to Cedar City on Saturday."

The millennials all attempted to speak at once. "But we'd have to take Friday off work. We can't get another day of vacation to do that!"

"Then, maybe you can fly to Salt Lake City after you get off work on Friday, and link-up with Ray and Charlene when they pass through on Saturday," I suggested.

Steven protested, "Woah, man. Like, that'll be expensive—if there are even any tickets available. Like, that's only a week away!"

I wanted to just put my foot down and say, "We will all be in Cedar City Saturday evening. You figure out how to make it happen."

But Ray got me off the hook. Looking at Joseph, he said, "Maybe you guys can find a way to get off work a little bit early on Friday. If we can get out of Portland ahead of the afternoon rush, we'll get to Boise before midnight. I'm sure we can find a motel that'll accommodate a late arrival. Then we can go with what Ken says, and meet him in Cedar City for shopping Saturday evening."

Thank you, Ray!

I looked around the room and saw that everyone was nodding in agreement. Just when I thought everything was settled, Ray raised his hand.

"We read that a lot of people stay at a motel up by the Navajo Bridges on the night before launch. We think that'll be easier than camping down at the launch site," he said.

"It's true. Some people do that. Is that what you want to do?" I asked in return.

"Well, we'll have real beds and showers," Charlene said.

I could see that Ray and Charlene had already made their plans and probably had included at least some of the others.

"That's fine, if that's what you want to do. You'll just need to be sure that you're back down at the launch site in time to get all of your gear loaded and the boats ready to go before the orientation lecture."

"What time do they do that?" Ray asked.

"Around 8:30 or 9:00."

"That should be easy enough," he said. "It looks like it's only about a ten-minute drive."

I knew it to be more like thirty, but there was nothing to be gained by pointing that out. They'd find it out when they got there, and I could only hope that they'd adjust their morning schedule accordingly.

"Okay then, who's staying at the motel?" I asked.

Ray, Charlene, Joseph, and Sophia raised their hands.

"And the rest of you will be camping?"

Krystal, Steven and Jeremy looked at each other and nodded.

The real lesson in all of this was that I probably shouldn't have done my Owyhee and John Day trips. I could have dealt with these issues as they came up, before people got entrenched in plans that deviated from what we'd discussed way back in the first few days of April. But it did seem like we'd worked it all out with minimal carnage, and we were back on track.

My first task on Sunday was to get my sister's raft off my trailer, and my own raft onto it. I rounded up a pair of four-wheel furniture dollies, and then pushed the *Miwok* off the trailer onto the dollies. Next, I backed the trailer into the garage and centered it beneath my big *Vanguard*, which was hanging from the ceiling on a pair of cable hoists.

I lowered the raft onto the trailer, pulled it out onto the driveway, and then I rolled the *Miwok* into the garage where *Vanguard* had been. I removed everything that I'd need for the Grand Canyon trip, including the gear I'd borrowed from *Vanguard* before the Owyhee trip.

At some point in the process, I turned my attention to something that had been on my mind ever since Ray had revealed that he was planning to takeout at Diamond Creek. His doing that meant that I'd be rafting by myself for three days, and there was no way I'd be able to lift the big SuperStove in and out of my raft.

Nor would I be able to lift the full-sized dry box that carried our big cast iron water stove, a Dutch oven, dish pans, a dish drying rack, a dull hatchet, a folding shovel, a cylinder pump, our water filtering system, and a variety of other useful things. Lettering on the end used to identify it as the "utility" box.

But because packing the utility box is like working one of those 3-D wooden puzzles, where each piece had to be put in a specific place at a specific point in the assembly process, that became the least-favored duty in camp every morning. That's why someone added an "F" to the lettering on the box, which has since been known at the Futility Box. And it is a very rare thing for anyone to attempt lifting the Futility Box without help.

This took me back to the thought process that had led me to build the half-sized kitchen setup that I'd taken down the Owyhee and John Day, and that, in turn, started me thinking about taking *both* kitchen sets along on the Grand Canyon trip.

On trips with my regular rafting group, we nearly always carried a small two-burner auxiliary cook stove, which we used mainly for making coffee in the morning, freeing up space on the SuperStove for the cooking. It also gives vegans a place to fry their cardboard bacon and tofu steaks.

Once I accepted the premise that the mini-kitchen would be a useful thing to have along, the only question was how I would carry it. I couldn't carry both kitchens on my raft. There simply wasn't room. But wait. Why did I have to carry *both* the SuperStove and the Futility Box?

Somewhere on the two big rental rafts, there *had to be* room for it. So, I moved the Futility Box into the back of my pickup and loaded the two half-size boxes in its place on my raft. I stashed my Scat-Packer bucket, which was carrying a twenty-pound bag of charcoal, in the very front of my raft.

It wouldn't be legal to use the Scat Packer while inside the national park boundaries, but once past Diamond Creek, it would be okay. And since the Eco-Safe toilets that we'd be using between Lee's Ferry and

Diamond Creek belonged to the rental company, I'd need the Scat Packer for the last few days of my trip.

At the very top of my priority list was ice. I should've checked it as soon as I got home. My big ice chest was in the freezer, where it'd been since my earliest planning for a group trip on the Owyhee. As was my standard practice, I'd spent a couple of weeks making a single massive block of solid ice, by adding a couple of gallons of water every-other day until the block was a foot thick. The ice and ice chest together were so heavy that I'd need to use a block and tackle to lift it out of the freezer when the time came. But my iceberg would last as much as a week longer than an equal volume of ice in regular ten or fifteen-pound blocks.

I had plenty of those, too, which would go into my smaller cooler in the front of the raft. This would be kept frozen for as long as dry ice would last, and would be available to replenish ice in other coolers as needed later in the trip. It would also carry most of the meat for the trip. The dry ice would keep it frozen solid for the first four or five days on the river. Nothing wrecks dinner like rotten chicken.

Better late than never, I checked the freezer and confirmed that it was still running and everything in it was still solidly frozen. I'm not sure what I'd have done if the freezer had thawed for some reason.

A related issue on a trip of this length is cooler space. On my past Grand Canyon trips, I'd gotten some extra space by deploying a pair of white-painted rocket boxes as evaporative coolers. It was a trick that old-time guides used. Covered with a couple of layers of burlap, which would be kept damp, the rocket boxes would keep certain durable produce adequately cool to survive until needed—things like eggs, bell peppers, cabbage, cucumbers and melons.

But I didn't have burlap, so I used old white towels that I got from a thrift store. That did keep the rocket boxes somewhat cooler, but the towel fabric was too dense to allow efficient evaporation. So, our evaporative coolers were marginal, at best. Next time out, I got hold of a stack of what were supposed to be burlap bags, but it turned out that they were made of a synthetic fiber, and did not absorb water. Those were even less effective than the white towels.

Real burlap seems to have become extinct. Fabric stores sell something that looks like burlap, but is actually made of a synthetic fiber. Art and craft stores sold the same stuff. I finally found some very old but unused burlap bags in a nut drying plant on property that a friend had bought in rural Marion County.

I had tested them out on my driveway and found that, even in direct sun on a hundred-degree day, the temperature inside the rocket boxes stayed below seventy. Nestled at the lowest part of my raft frame, floating on the fifty-four-degree water in Grand Canyon, they'd stay under sixty degrees.

Just one note about using this technique. It is essential that you air-out the rocket boxes first thing every morning, or else the humidity inside will build up and cause things to mold and rot. Yeah, I know. Who needs another thing to do in the morning?

By early Sunday afternoon, my raft and equipment were almost ready to go. I had to take time-out from my trip preparations, because Linda was throwing a farewell party for some neighbors who were moving away. It wasn't that I didn't have a good time, but all afternoon, all I could think about was what I might be forgetting to do.

On Wednesday, I changed the oil in my pickup and pumped grease into the wheel bearings on my trailer. I checked the condition and air pressure of all the tires. I refreshed my collection of audiobooks for the long drive and programmed key addresses into my GPS navigator. I'm an old person and need someone to remind me where I'm going.

With one day left before my departure, I was as ready as I could be, and that's when the idea of doing a "Whitewater Summer" floated to the surface of my imagination. One of the biggest obstacles standing in the way of actually doing such a thing was already gone—Charlene's Grand Canyon invitation had taken care of that.

There were plenty of other obstacles, for sure, but what if I could find *other* groups that would allow me to take advantage of their permits? Over the years, my groups had been approached at various launch sites by individuals wanting to piggy-back on our permits. It didn't happen often, but enough that we'd given them a name—Permit Parasites.

I'd never allowed a permit parasite to join my group, so my karma was in questionable condition for success, but wasn't it worth a try? At the same time, I knew that there were other ways of getting around the permit obstacle, so maybe it *was* worth trying.

Toward that end, I started contemplating the logistics. until I thought of one more thing I should do in order to prepare for any kind of solo trip after Grand Canyon. I went online in search of some kind of kitchen shelter that could be easily set up by one person. Repeated searches brought up numerous toy shelters for kids, pop-up canopies like those used at carnivals and outdoor events, which were very bulky when folded and, while they *could* be set up by one person, really required two. Eventually, though, I found a smaller version of the pop-up, sold as the Eagle Peak Day Tripper.

The ad had video of one person setting it up, and it folded to fit in a cylindrical bag about three feet long by nine inches in diameter. I read the reviews, and the main complaint was that it wasn't big enough for more than one person. Fine. That made it just right, so I ordered one. My Whitewater Summer required it.

On the night before departure, I packed the block-ice and meats into the 80-quart Gott cooler in the front of my raft. Next, I hoisted the big Icey-Tek 125 cooler out of the freezer and, with help from a neighbor, wrestled it into the raft. I packed dry ice in both, to postpone the start of the "burn time" on my regular ice.

I had a third ice chest for the food that we'd consume at Lee's Ferry. Most of that was pre-cooked and ready to eat cold, so that we wouldn't have to set up and take down our full kitchen. The ice that I put into that cooler would have to last only until launch day. The empty cooler would go into the back of my pickup before our departure from Lee's Ferry.

Before going to bed, I ran one final lap through all of my checklists.

On Friday (Permit Day minus three), I drove seven hours to my daughter's place outside Caldwell, Idaho. She was appropriately envious that I was heading to Grand Canyon and she wasn't, but I *had* invited her to go, back when we had an empty space to fill. I really wished that she'd been able to go, but her work schedule couldn't be changed. So, I got stuck with Jeremy, his kayak, and his soybean curd.

I told Tamara that she didn't need to get up early just to make breakfast for me, but of course, she did it anyway, and it didn't cost me any more time than an Egg McMuffin stop somewhere along the way. I took my second cup of coffee along, and freight-trained the 600-mile drive to Cedar City, Utah, arriving there at about 5:30.

I looked around the Motel 6 parking lot for Ray's Suburban, but didn't see it, so I called Charlene, who said that they'd be there in about an hour. I went ahead and checked-in, and then walked across the street to a restaurant, where I waited in the bar. With a beer.

When the others arrived, we ordered a couple of large pizzas, and while we waited for them, I went over our plan for doing the shopping.

"So, if we're waiting to do the shopping at the last minute, like, why don't we just do it in the morning," Steven asked.

"We'll do it after the sun goes down. If we wait until morning, we'll be loading our ice chests in full sun on hot asphalt. We'd lose more ice doing that than we will by doing it this evening."

"That makes sense. But does it really matter, since we'll be transferring everything into the rented coolers?"

I said, "That's true for you, but not for me. The ice that's in my coolers right now will have to last for the duration of the trip. Besides, if we do the shopping in the morning, we'll be that much later getting to Lee's Ferry. What time are your rafts being delivered?"

"They said that they'd be there to start rigging them at ten, and they'd like us to be there by noon."

"Good. We can do that. Then it'll probably take most of the afternoon to get everything inspected, loaded, and ready to go."

The grocery shopping went as smoothly as could be expected with a group of rookies. We were careful to keep everything sorted according to cook team and meal sequence. When we got out to the parking lot, we packed everything into numbered zip-lock bags.

Meanwhile, Ray opened his trailer and revealed that his ice chests were buried beneath all the rest of the gear, so everything had to be unloaded. I climbed up into my raft and opened the big cooler, where I found a few fragments of dry ice, which I transferred to the Gott cooler. You do not want to expose vegetables to dry ice! In fact, even the regular ice, once it's been pulled down to the temperature of dry ice, will destroy many fresh foods.

To prevent that, I covered the ice with an ensolite foam pad, and then layered the food on top of that, with the least vulnerable things on the bottom and the more delicate things on top. As always, it was a tight fit, and took some special care to keep anything from getting crushed. I laid another ensolite pad over the top and carefully put the lid down. With some more jostling of foods, I finally got it latched and strapped.

I had a number of things to add to the "leave-behind" cooler in the back of my pickup, including the things that would later be packed into the evaporative coolers, which would be like ovens until after the raft was in the water.

By the time I was done with my coolers, Ray had his uncovered and was ready to fill them. Charlene supervised, making sure that the food stayed properly sorted. The entire process, shopping and packing, took two and a half hours.

Chapter Ten

Setup Day Chaos

Since crossing into Idaho on Friday, we'd been on Mountain Daylight Time. Lee's Ferry, like the rest of Arizona, was on Mountain Standard, which is the same as Pacific Daylight Time. Arizona doesn't do Daylight Time. I didn't bother re-setting my watch or the clock in my pickup for the two days in the other time zone, and Ray hadn't changed his clocks either.

But everything we did while in Idaho and Utah was done by the local clocks, not ours. So, when I said we'd have breakfast at 7:00 at a pancake house down the street, I was talking about the time on the clocks in the motel rooms. Everyone else, it seems, thought I was talking about the time on our wristwatches.

When nobody had shown up in the parking lot by 7:15, I called Charlene and interrupted her shower. That's not the best way to start the day. Except for that little glitch, we'd have made it to Lee's Ferry by 10:30, when Canyon REO was expecting us. While Ray apologized to them for being late, I backed my trailer down the boat ramp into the river. Within a matter of minutes, my raft was afloat.

I pulled it over next to the blue Canyon REO rafts, and then went back to move my rig off the boat ramp, over to the setup beach next to the Canyon REO truck. I hovered around while the Canyon REO folks talked to Ray and his crew, explaining a hundred things, most of which would quickly be forgotten, about the rafts. The last thing they did was stress the importance of getting to Diamond Creek by 11 a.m. on takeout day.

We were approached by a park ranger carrying a clipboard and looking official. She introduced herself as Ranger Lucy and asked who was the permit holder. Ray raised his hand and introduced himself.

Each of us had to show photo ID as Ranger Lucy checked our names against those listed on the permit. All of that went well, and then she handed Ray a list of all the required equipment that she had to inspect.

Pointing to patch of beach near our rafts, she said, "Put all of these things right there, and when you're ready, I'll come over and inspect it."

We rounded up life jackets, first aid kits, oars, repair kits, toilets, dishwater strainer, fire pan, air pumps, satellite communication device, signal mirror, and an assortment of other things. The next time Ranger Lucy came by, she inspected everything and signed-off. From that point, we were free to load the rafts.

Photo by Jan Brandvold

Gear and supplies to be loaded at Lee's Ferry. This and all of the other photos in Grand Canyon were shot on my 2007 trip.

While Ray and I were dealing with that, the millennials set about unloading everything from the Suburban and trailer, piling it in heaps on the beach. I was astounded by the mountain of beer. I heard one of them say that there were sixty half-cases.

The only beer I'd brought along was the six-pack in the leave-behind cooler. Once on the river, the only way to chill beer would be in the river, and even though fifty-four degrees is cold water for swimming, it makes for what I consider to be warm beer. So, I'd brought wine in half-liter boxes, one for each evening in camp. Looking at Mount Heineken made me thirsty, so I went over to get a can of Deschutes IPA from the back of my pickup.

I sat down on the tailgate and snapped my beer open, ready to relax for a few minutes for the first time since getting off the John Day River. Apparently, someone saw me and decided that it must be break time. The millennials all stopped working, found beers of their own, and stood around talking as if they hadn't spent the last two days riding together in the Suburban. It seemed like half an hour before they got back to work.

I went over to Ray to talk about the Futility Box. Together, we walked down to find a place for it on one of the rented rafts. Each raft came with two full-size dry boxes with dimensions nearly identical to the Futility Box. We pulled one out from behind the oarsman's seat on Ray's raft, and called for Joseph and Steven to get the Futility Box out of my pickup and lower it into the raft.

"Where're we going to put the other box?" Steven asked.

Ray said, "Well, I think we're just going to leave it in the Suburban."

"But we have stuff to put in it," Steven protested.

"Let's figure that out later," I suggested. "First, let's identify which dry boxes we're going to use for food."

Ray's raft, where we'd stashed the Futility Box still had an empty full-size box, plus a half-size dry box on each side of the oarsman's footwell. The other raft had the Eco-Safe rocket boxes in that position, but still had two full-size dry boxes. One contained an assortment of loose equipment.

I said, "We have two full-size boxes and two half-size boxes for food. Let's save one full-size box for bread and other bulky fragile food. The other will go for Team Two—Ray and Charlene. The two smaller boxes will go for Teams Three and Four. Everyone okay with that?"

Photo by Jan Brandvold

Ranger Dave checking permits and required equipment before it can be loaded onto rafts.

Nobody offered an objection, so I called Sophia to bring the Team Three food. I demonstrated how to make best use of the space by squeezing air out of the zip-lock bags. I placed the bags in the box in order, so that the first to be used was on top. As expected, there were two loaves of bread that wouldn't fit, so they went into the designated bread box.

I then asked Steven and Krystal to load their box, and finally, Ray and Charlene packed theirs. They still had some space, so we stashed our toilet paper supply in there as well. Feeling pretty good about how things were going, I announced that I was going to move my raft down to the private boater's beach and claim a campsite.

Before making that short trip, I stacked my leave-behind cooler on my front seat, since it contained our dinner and breakfast. After tying my raft, I off-loaded the cooler, my mini-kitchen and folding table, and set them up in a little shaded area. I also put my dry bag on a good tent site, thus marking my territory in a manner more acceptable that that commonly used by wildlife.

With a fresh beer, I walked back to the setup area to see how things were going with the rest of the group. I found them in deep discussion about how to accommodate their mountain of beer. Since it was the heaviest thing to be loaded, they properly decided it should be as low as possible in the rafts.

Krystal and Sophia were busy wrapping all of the beer cases in duct tape. I've seen others do that, presumably on the belief that it will make the cardboard boxes less likely to fall apart when they get wet. It probably took about a mile of tape, and by the time they were finished, there were empty duct tape rolls scattered all around where they'd been working. I gave them points for coming prepared. And then I took them back for not have doing the job at home.

The rented rafts came equipped with a plywood gear deck in the rear compartment. In two layers, the beer was almost level with the tops of the raft tubes. As a general rule, square things use space more efficiently than round things. Round things leave gaps. Some of the significant round things that had to be accommodated were two propane tanks and the giant aluminum stock pot that we use for heating dishwater.

Photo by Jan Brandvold

We managed to get the propane tanks stuffed down in with the beer, and we found a gap in the very front of one raft for the water tub. Little by little the pile on the beach diminished, until all that remained were the ice chests and dry bags.

Someone told us that the temperature was over a hundred, so this was definitely not the best time to transfer the food from Ray's ice chests into the larger ones on the rafts, which contained fresh, solid ice. The plan was to do that first thing in the morning, before the sun hit the beach. As for the bags, they too would have to wait until morning. Some were going to the motel and some were going to our campsite.

It was around 4:30 when Ray and Joseph declared the loading finished and shuttled the rafts over to the campsite. I walked ahead to make sure they didn't go past the landing. Once the rafts were tied-up and the kayaks beached, I showed Jeremy and Steven where the tent spaces were.

I said, "I'm not going to use my tent. In fact, my goal is to do the whole trip without taking it out of my dry bag."

"Like, aren't you worried about rain?" Steven asked.

"No, not really. Rain here tends to fall in the afternoon, not at night. If I put up my tent, it'll probably be because of bugs."

Krystal said, "Bugs—ick! Steven, you need to put up the tent!"

It had been a long, busy afternoon, and because of our morning time zone faux pas, we'd skipped lunch. So, I went to my leave-behind cooler and pulled out eight chicken dinner boxes from the Fred Meyer deli and placed them in a row on the table. They came complete with plastic forks for the potato salad and coleslaw and napkins for the chicken.

"Dinner is served. Nothing to add but beer," I proclaimed.

Ray said, "Oh. That's okay. We're going to have dinner up at the motel after we take showers."

Well, shit. The no-cooking-needed dinner was something we'd talked about way back in the earliest part of our meal planning. But, of course, I couldn't force them to eat it just because we had it. So there sat eight boxes of dinner, while Ray and his family gathered their things and headed up the trail to their Suburban.

"Try to get back here by 7:00, so that we can be ready to go as soon as the ranger talk is over," I called after them.

What I meant by "try to" was "be damn sure to."

I said to Steven, Krystal and Jeremy, "Well, I guess we're going to have a lot to eat."

I carried a box to my chair, opened a beer and settled down to eat. Anticipating that we'd be extra hungry, I'd asked for larger than standard portions, so by the time I'd cleaned-up my "plate," I was finished. No way I could eat any more.

Steven and Krystal finished setting up their tent and then came back for dinner, but Jeremy wandered off without eating.

"He said he wasn't hungry," Steven said.

I simply shook my head.

"Who want's strawberry shortcake?" I asked.

I had individual angel food cakes, a zip-lock filled with sliced, sugared strawberries, and a can of Reddi-Whip. I got out three paper bowls and plastic spoons, and served up generous portions.

"Take seconds if you want," I said. "I hate to toss all this out."

"Can't we, like, just put it away for tomorrow or something?" Krystal asked.

I explained, "My experience with leftovers on river trips is that they almost never get eaten. They just take up space in the cooler until they go bad, and end up in the trash anyway. Besides, there just isn't room in the ice chests for all this."

"It's such a waste!" Krystal said.

"I think I can find someone who'll take care of it," I said.

Photo by Jan Brandvold

We carried the five untouched boxed dinners over to the boat ramp, where guides were busy setting up a pair of huge motor rafts. I've never met a guide who would turn down free food.

"Anybody here hungry? I have chicken dinners and strawberry shortcake," I announced to the guides.

"For real?" one of them asked.

"For real. Some of our party decided to get dinner up on the rim."

"Hey, that's great! Damn right we'll take it!"

Sundown comes earlier in the canyon than at home—partly because of the latitude, and partly because of the high canyon walls. By 8:30, we were well into twilight. I spread out my sand mat and air bed, which I inflated with the battery-powered pump.

I rolled-out my sleeping bag, but it was too warm to actually get into it. As on past Grand Canyon trips, I carried a queen-size bed sheet, which I used to cover myself until the temperature came down in the middle of the night. Sleep came very easily.

Chapter Eleven

Grand Canyon Launch Day

Long after dark, I woke up briefly when Jeremy returned from wherever he'd gone and started rustling around with his gear. I didn't know what to make of him. He didn't talk much—at least not with me. I hoped that he'd been able to find something to eat, though the only possibility for that would be the other private party, camped a hundred yards downstream, or the guides on the boat ramp.

My next awareness was at 5:30, as daylight crept into the early morning sky. There was no need to get up that early, but once awake, there was no hope of getting back to sleep. So, I pulled the plug on my air bed and sat up.

After a short stroll to the restroom over by the boat ramp, I rolled-up my things and packed my dry bag, which I then carried down to my raft. A thin, wispy layer of fog lay over the water, which was clear and smooth. From the leave-behind ice chest, I got the things that we were taking along, and loaded them into the evaporative coolers.

Photo by Jerry Baysinger

Permit day at the private boaters' camping area at Lee's Ferry

When I snapped them shut, the rocket box latches made a loud noise that echoed across the still water and should have served as a wake-up call to anyone still asleep. I arranged my burlap sacks atop the rocket boxes, strapped them in place, and wet them down with river water.

Seeing no sign of life from Steven, Krystal or Jeremy, I made no attempt to work quietly as I started the stove and put on a pot of water for coffee. I glanced at my watch, reading 6:05. I hoped that the motel group was awake. I'd have given a wake-up call, but there's no cell service anywhere in the canyon. Not even at Lee's Ferry.

I made some more noise topping-off the air pressure in my raft with a loud, high-speed electric pump. It's okay to use them at Lee's Ferry, but they are prohibited in the rest of the canyon. It's a rule that we've conveniently forgotten on our past trips and I probably wouldn't remember on this trip either, what with my advancing age.

It is generally considered bad form to tamper with someone else's raft, but I went ahead and topped off the two Canyon REO boats. By the time I finished, the water on the stove was boiling and I could hear voices from the tent, so I knew that Steven and Krystal were awake, and I could see Jeremy walking in the direction of the restroom.

By 7:00, there was still no sign of Ray and his part of the group, and the sunshine was creeping down toward our camp. I called for Steven to help carry Ray's ice chests down to the rafts. As soon as I opened the first one, I spotted something terrible: cartons upon cartons of store-brand margarine. I don't know how I didn't see that stuff when we did our shopping in Cedar City.

Like most Americans of my generation, I grew up on margarine, as the alternative to "the high-priced spread." (Makers of margarine were prohibited from mentioning "butter" in their advertising.) But at some point in my adult life, I learned that "hydrogenated vegetable oil" was the definition of margarine, and it was very detrimental to cardio-vascular health. And I already knew that it was flavorless crap.

I switched to butter in my personal life for the latter reason, long before the health issues surrounding marge-urine were known. And when I made that change, I went into the menu program for my raft trips and changed everything from marge-urine to butter. But I found that many shoppers considered the two to be synonymous and bought either what they habitually used, or what was cheapest.

So, to emphasize the point, I went back and edited the program again, to read "Butter (the real thing)." Until now, that had worked, and I hadn't been subjected to the indignity of having to ingest any marge-urine on a river trip for many years. I don't know how to be any clearer than that. Maybe I'll have to change "the real thing" to "yes, butter—the stuff that comes from cows, you pitiable moron."

An old Meg Ryan movie came to mind.

I quickly transferred the food into the larger ice chests on the rafts, careful to keep things sorted by cook team, as much as was possible. But there was still no sign of Ray and the others.

I'd already had two cups of coffee by the time Steven and Krystal finished taking down their tent and packing their dry bag. I made one last pot of coffee and turned off the stove, letting it cool down so that I could close it up. Jeremy returned and started rolling-up his sleeping bag.

Having waited long enough, I got out breakfast—fresh fruit and breakfast burritos made with made-at-home egg salad, cooked ham cut into small cubes, a couple of diced tomatoes, a can of vegetarian refried beans, and a package of large flour tortillas. I spread out all of this in a self-service buffet, along with hot sauce, sour cream, sliced olives, and a bowl of chopped onions. Demonstrating the proper use off all that, I made a couple of burritos for myself. The others took the cue and helped themselves, Jeremy avoiding the items that had mothers.

My mood was deteriorating fast by 8:00. The old "wrong time zone" excuse was no good this time. I moved the breakfast buffet from the table to the tops of the empty leave-behind coolers, folded the table and mini-kitchen, and carried them down to my raft. When Ray and the others finally arrived, my gear was all tied-down and my raft was completely ready to go—as theirs should have been.

Trying my best to conceal my annoyance, I cheerfully said, "Help yourselves to coffee and breakfast, and then we'll get packed up."

"Oh, thanks, but we had breakfast at the motel," Charlene said.

There were many things I could have said, none of which would have contributed to group unity. So, I simply said, "Then let's get to work."

I walked over to where two groups of river guides were camped and invited them over to finish-off our left-over breakfast. Several took me up on the offer, and before long everything was gone. I carried my empty ice chest up and locked it in my pickup, and by the time I got back to camp, Ranger Lucy was gathering everyone together for the mandatory lecture. There was a total of twenty-four private boaters in the two groups launching that day.

Ranger Lucy went over all of the rules and regulations that we already knew, reminded us how fragile the environment is and how any microscopic crumb left on the sand would cause the campsite to be overrun by voracious biting ants. She didn't fool me. I knew that the ants were already there. I'd seen them and had been bitten by them. I nodded and smiled a lot, and laughed at Lucy's tired jokes.

What I *didn't* do was ask questions or engage in conversation. But there was a lady in the other group who was hell-bent on showing everybody how much she knew by embellishing everything Lucy said and asking a barrage of inane questions. The twenty-minute talk ended up lasting over an hour.

It was 10:00, and time to be on the water. But no. Everywhere I looked, dry bags were open and people were cramming things in or digging things out. Joseph was fiddling with his oarlocks. Nobody showed any sense of urgency. Churning inside, I made helpful suggestions from time to time, hoping to get people motivated.

"When should we put all the food in the other ice chests?" Charlene asked.

"About three hours ago," I said. "I beat you to it."

My smile may have looked sincere.

"Seriously? It's already done?"

So innocent. So naïve. So clueless.

"But maybe you could get someone to help carry your empty coolers back up to your trailer," I suggested.

Charlene and Sophia took off up the trail with the first of the three ice chests.

"Maybe a couple of you could help with that," I said to Jeremy and Steven.

Steven said, "Yeah. Soon as I get my spray skirt adjusted."

At this point, I had to walk away. Doing any more of their work for them would just tell them that if they didn't do it, I would. And staying around supervising them might lead to someone saying, "Well, I don't see *you* doing anything," And that could lead to homicide.

Sorry. I've already done way more than my share.

I told Jeremy, "I have to go to the can. Might as well take one of these along. Grab the other end of this cooler."

We got to Ray's rig and put the ice chest into the open trailer, and I looked around for Charlene and Sophia. We should've passed them on the trail. But they were in the Suburban trying to get signals on their phones, or something. I walked up to the restroom. After allowing a few minutes for the others time to get started back to camp, I ventured out and walked down to talk with a group of oar-raft guides.

I asked a few questions about rapids or campsites that might have changed since the last time I went down the river, and we exchanged information about our float plans. I said I hoped to get to the camp called Hot Na Na that day, but we were getting further behind schedule with every passing minute.

When I returned to camp, I expected to see things ready to go. But dry bags were still on the beach, though most of them were closed. There were folding chairs, ammo boxes, a camera case, and kitty litter buckets scattered around. Only Joseph and Ray seemed to be doing anything. And the damned last ice chest still hadn't been carried up to the trailer.

"If we don't get going pretty soon, we'll have to start unloading for lunch," I joked.

Polite chuckles.

Completely out of patience, I grabbed the nearest dry bag and said, "Let's decide which stuff goes on which raft,"

Joseph looked up and said, "Over here."

When I pointed to the one next to it, he said, "That one too."

Charlene said, "I guess we should take that cooler up."

By then, Ray had finished whatever he'd been doing and was busy closing the last of the open dry bags. He separated the ones that he wanted on his raft, and I pitched-in carrying them down and positioning them on top of the beer pile.

Photo by Tamara Baysinger

Steven got the message and started carrying bags to Joseph's raft. Jeremy was too busy puttering around with his kayak to help.

I helped Ray spread the special-made cargo net over the pile of bags and secure it to the raft frame with about ten cam straps. It looked like it would be strong enough to support the weight of the beer if the raft got flipped. I strapped three of the folded chairs together, stacked them atop the rear load, and tied them down with more cam straps.

While Ray worked on the last odds and ends on his raft, I went over and gave Joseph the same help I'd given Ray. To be honest, I should have done all this earlier, instead of going up to the outhouse and taking the time to talk with the guides.

We might have been there all day if I hadn't finally jumped in. And it *still* took another thirty minutes before we finally pushed off, at 11:25.

I shouted, "Hoka hey, let's go rafting!" and pulled away from shore and into the current.

Photo by Jan Brandvold

In the Lakota language, hoka hey means, "This is a great day to die." It was the rallying cry used by Crazy Horse at the Battle of the Little Bighorn. He didn't mean it literally. He meant, "Let's get it done." So did I.

The water was sparkling clear and looked beautiful—exactly as it had on both of my prior Grand Canyon trips. On the first of those, we went only half a mile before passing the mouth of the Paria River, which was more mud than water. The Colorado was completely overwhelmed by Paria mud, and it stayed opaque with mud for the rest of the trip.

On our second trip, we managed to get three days of clear water before a monsoon over a side canyon filled the river with mud. I was hoping to have better luck this time, but the odds were against it.

It was past lunch time when the Navajo Bridges came into view and I spotted a sliver of shade along the left bank. I called out to the kayakers, who had paddled out ahead of the group, and motioned toward the little beach. With some effort, they paddled against the current and managed to get to shore.

Photo by Jerry Baysinger

I said, "Lunch is always a group activity. Everyone helps, and everything gets done. Pay attention to the process, because it'll be the same every day."

I gave an ongoing lecture as we went through the lunch preparation, hoping the people were paying attention. As much as possible, I expedited the lunch stop, because we were nearly two hours behind schedule, meaning that we wouldn't get to Hot Na Na camp until 5:30.

The first big rapid in Grand Canyon is at Badger Creek. It's rated Class 7, making it a fairly serious rapid. I should explain that there are two systems for rating rapids: the International Scale, which uses Roman numerals and rates rapids from Class I to Class VI, and the Colorado River Scale, which rates rapids from Class 1 to Class 10.

The ratings are always based on running the *softest* part of the rapid. Things can get much more challenging if you go into the rapid in the wrong place.

As we approached Badger Creek Rapid, despite my repeated warnings, the kayaks had once again pulled ahead of the group. I tried to get their attention to wave them to shore so we could scout the rapid, but they couldn't hear me and didn't look back.

Instead, they kept paddling obliviously downstream. Because of that, I had to scrap the plan to scout the rapid, and instead stood up and shouted back to Ray and Joseph.

"There's a straight-through chute just left of center. Stay close behind me and go exactly where I go. There's a huge hole to the right of our entry, and it can flip a raft with ease. Enter left of center. Everyone got it? Left of center."

I turned back around and looked downstream, and saw that the kayaks were too far to the right. There was nothing I could do but watch as first one, and then the other two, rode up the wave and dropped out of sight. At that point, I had to focus on making sure that I was in the right place, but I kept trying to spot the kayaks in the runout. I managed to catch a glimpse of Krystal's red kayak about two hundred yards ahead just as I was accelerating down the V-shaped chute into the rapid.

I ran straight down the wave train, getting a great roller-coaster ride. Still trying to see what became of the kayaks, I didn't look back to see how the rafts were doing. As the waves diminished, I finally spotted the kayaks. Steven and Krystal were still in theirs, but Jeremy was swimming alongside his. I turned my raft and started rowing toward him. And that's when I looked back upstream.

Ray was coming down right in my tracks, in full control and looking good. Joseph and Sophia were out of their raft, bobbing through back-curling waves that repeatedly buried them. The raft was caught in the hole beneath the big pour-over at the entry. Somehow, Joseph had gone far to the right of my line. The raft was being pummeled as the reversal kept pushing it back under the pour-over.

River Hazards: Reversals and Holes

A reversal, as the word implies, is the phenomenon where water flows in the direction opposite that of the main current. Most people understand what an "eddy" is—an upstream current along the banks of a river or downstream from an obstacle. It is a horizontal reversal.

Now envision an eddy standing on edge. That's a hole—a vertical reversal. These occur when water flows over a ledge or a rock lying beneath the surface. Over time, the downward plunging water creates a plunge pool beneath the pour-over.

When the falling water hits the surface of the pool, it pushes a portion of that water downward, creating a low spot—a hole. The surrounding water is pulled by gravity into that hole, creating an upstream surface current. Water rebounding off the riverbed creates a back wave, which as in this illustration breaks upstream.

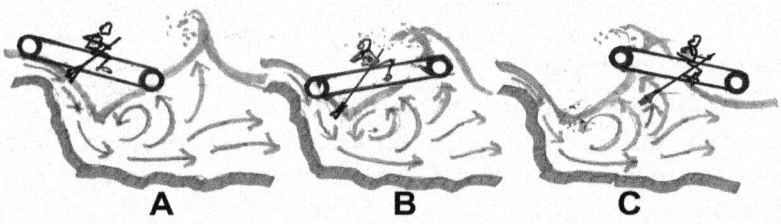

A raft can pass over a hole, providing it is long enough to span the hole and has enough momentum to punch through the back wave instead of being stopped by it.

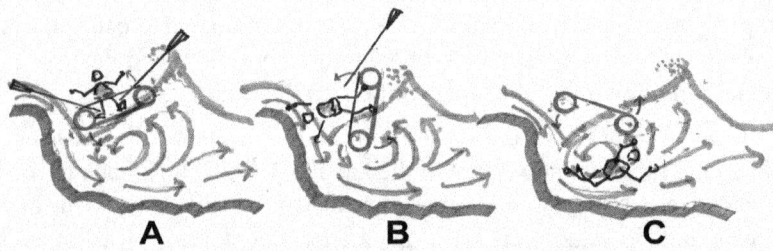

But if the raft hits the hole sideways, or if it is too short to span the hole, the result is that the pour-over pushes the upstream part of the raft downward, while the back-curling wave lifts the downstream part of the raft. Often that combination of forces will flip the raft.

Furthermore, whether the raft flips or not, the conflicting currents can hold it in place between the pour-over and the back wave. That can be an extremely violent event—enough to snap oars, rip gear off the raft, or tear the raft to pieces.

Sketches by Jerry Baysinger

I left the kayakers to their own resources and rowed hard to get in front of Joseph and Sophia, intercepting them just as the waves diminished. At about the same time I was helping Sophia onto my raft, their raft popped out of the hole and wallowed downstream toward us. I could see that the oars were still in the oarlocks, and it looked like all of the gear was still in place.

After getting Joseph aboard, I got back on my oars and chased-down the raft. When I nosed up against it, Joseph climbed over and crawled to the oarsman's seat. When he raised his oars, he found that the left one was broken. The lower third of the shaft dangled by the last few carbon fibers that hadn't been torn apart.

I stayed with him while he got one of his spare oars in place, and while he was doing that, Sophia climbed over. She took the pieces of the broken oar and stashed them out of the way. Ahead, Steven had paddled to Jeremy and his kayak, and Krystal had chased-down his runaway paddle. We all got to the right bank about half a mile below the rapid.

While the three swimmers caught their breath and tried to absorb some warmth from the rocks on shore, we inspected the raft and kayak for damage and lost gear. All had lost their hats, and the oar was destroyed. Only the blade and Oar-Right would be salvageable.

I asked Joseph, "How did you get so far off-line?"

He said, "I don't know what happened. I just followed Steven, and suddenly it was like I was looking over a waterfall."

"Did you not hear what I said when we were approaching the rapid?"

"Well, yeah, but it looked like Steven's route was more fun."

I then addressed the whole group. "We got a lucky break and learned a cheap lesson. You've seen the power of the river, and believe me, we'll see rapids a lot meaner than this one before we're done."

I paused to let that sink in.

"Nobody was injured, and all we lost was an oar. Now let me tell you how we're going to keep this from happening again. You brought me on this trip because I've been here before and I know how to keep us all out of trouble. But I can't do that if you don't follow my instructions."

Joseph said, "Yeah, well…"

"Here's the deal. Kayaks can go places the big boats can't. When you follow them, you are risking them leading you into just such a place. So, to prevent this from happening again, I want the kayaks to stay behind the rafts, and I want the rafts to follow *me*."

I did not miss Steven's eye roll.

Joseph and Ray inspected the raft and found that the left oarlock stand was bent inward, possibly from the same impact that had broken the oar. The rented rafts had come with spare oarlocks, but not spare stands, so we had to find a way to bend the damaged one back into shape. Joseph tired hammering on it with a rock, but that only broke the rock.

Photo by Jan Brandvold
Making repairs with the materials at hand.

Hammering on it with the back side of the hatchet made a lot of noise, but didn't accomplish much. But Ray understood how to bend metal, and he took over the job. He found a splintery ten-foot piece of lumber in a pile of driftwood and lashed one end of it to the raft frame on the inboard side of the bent oar stand. Then, with ten-feet of leverage, he and Joseph were able to bend the metal back close to its original shape. It wasn't perfect, but it would work.

While this was going on, Sophia dug her dry bag out of the big pile on the back of the raft. When she opened it in search of a hat to replace the one she'd lost, she discovered that the bag had leaked. Everything in the top of the bag was wet.

"Oh, damn! Water got into my bag. Like, everything's soaked," she complained.

I said, "The best thing to do is pull out the wet stuff and wring it out as much as you can. Then put it in a plastic bag, so that it doesn't spread the moisture to anything that's still dry."

She dug down to see how deep the water had seeped, and extracted a small pile of clothes. Krystal and Steven, whose bags were also on that raft, checked and found their things dry.

But all of this took time. It was 4:30 when we finally got back underway. When we got to Soap Creek Rapid, I waved everyone to the right bank, and we walked down to scout the rapid, which carries a rating of Class 5. I pointed out where I wanted to enter the rapid and explained :30 sounded argumentative, and I was in no mood to engage in any of that.

I suggested, "It's late, and we're still five miles from Hot Na Na. How about we set up camp here and run the rapid in the morning?"

It wasn't really a question.

Looking at Sophia, I added, "That'll give some time for you to spread-out your wet things to dry."

To everyone else, I said, "Pick your sleeping space and mark it with a piece of personal gear."

I pointed to where I'd hung my life jacket on a tamarisk bush. "That's my spot. The kitchen will go in the space close to the rafts. Let's all work together, get the gear off the rafts, and set up the kitchen."

I went to work pulling things from the front of my raft, starting with the two half-sized boxes and the folding table, all things that I could carry by myself to the kitchen area. As I was walking back to my raft after the first trip, I heard the snap of a pop-top. I gave it no thought, because there's no reason a person couldn't work on a beer while unloading the boats.

Photo by Jerry Baysinger
Soap Creek Rapid, Class 5.

My next move was to turn my raft around so that I could unload the gear from the back, starting with my beach chair and big red dry bag. I looked around and saw that Ray was unstrapping things and handing them to Charlene, who was stacking them on the beach. Joseph and Sophia had gotten the non-dry dry bag off their raft and were draping soggy things over the bushes.

But the kayakers were nowhere to be seen. I found them sitting on rocks down where we'd scouted the rapid, drinking beer and smoking something that I'm sure was not legal in Arizona. Of course. The rafts weren't theirs, so it wasn't their job to unload them.

Kayakers.

"Hey, we could use some help carrying things," I said.

"Yeah, like, we'll be there in a couple of minutes," Steven mumbled.

Should I set them straight, and risk alienating them for the rest of the trip? Or should I be congenial, let it slide, and risk letting them become entrenched in their privileged attitude?

I said, "We all work together on some things—loading and unloading the rafts, carrying things, setting up and tearing down the kitchen. Take your break when that's done. But *never* take a break while others are working.

"Yeah, yeah. I *said* we'll be there, man."

"Now would be a good time."

Jeremy said, "Who made *you* God?"

"Let's not make this an argument. Things need to be done, and everybody needs to help."

Steven flicked his roach into the sand and drained the last of his beer. "Sure. No problem."

They grudgingly followed me back to my raft, where I dispatched Krystal to help Joseph and Sophia. The two heaviest items that had to be carried to and from the rafts every day were the SuperStove and the Futility Box. I coached Jeremy and Steven in unstrapping and lifting the SuperStove out of its well behind the seat on my raft. I carried two propane tanks and they carried the SuperStove up to the kitchen.

With everyone helping, it took only about ten minutes to get all of the community gear into camp. I then conducted a short clinic on how to set up everything. I figured I'd have to repeat the clinic several times before everyone learned. I won't deny that it's a lot to absorb in one lesion.

Another round of beers appeared, and—now that the kitchen was set up—it was time to relax.

The cook team was Ray and Charlene, and they asked when they should start dinner. I checked my watch, even though I already knew what time it was.

"We're running kind of late," I said. "We should get things going right away. I'll walk you through the process. First step is to round up your food and supplies. There's a full set of meal sheets in the SuperStove. Grab an empty bucket."

We went first to my raft and found the things on the list that were marked KB, all of which were in my large food box. From there, we went to their dry box and found the bag marked "Camp 2 Dinner." And finally, we got the refrigerated items from their cooler.

I suggested that Ray ask a couple of the guys to carry buckets of river water up to camp to fill the big water tub, and another for the hand-washing station. I looked at the daily duty list and found that Team 3—Joseph and Sophia—had toilet duty in this camp.

"Are you familiar with the EcoSafe toilet system?" I asked.

Joseph said, "You mean the groover? What's to know?"

"I'll show you a few tricks to assembling it."

When I got back to the kitchen after that, I made a show of washing my hands and took the occasion to remind everyone to always wash hands before doing anything in the kitchen. Yes children, Ranger Lucy had already stressed the importance of that, but it was important enough to warrant repetition.

That's typical of how things always go in the first camp on a river trip with a new group. Lots of repetition, lots of questions, lots of standing around, lots of uncertainty as to what needed to be done. I'd done so many trips with my Clan of the Nose Hair group that I'd forgotten just how much they knew that these rookies didn't. I answered a hundred questions and explained a hundred "rules" that made our tasks go smoothly. It was exhausting.

Charlene did most of the cooking, and Ray did most of the "schlepping," and I stayed close by to show where needed items were stored in the SuperStove and Futility Box. The main course was creamed bay scallops served over avocado halves, with wild rice and fresh salad, one of the favorites in my menu system.

I cleared one of the tables and helped set up a buffet line, and finally gave the dinner call. Tradition holds that the cook team serve the first helpings, thus assuring that nobody would take too much and leave someone else short.

We once had a newbie on a Rogue River trip, and for some reason, he helped himself to a heaping plate-load of spaghetti, leaving only a child's portion for the cook—who happened to be me. I think everyone else saw what he did, but nobody could think of a tactful way to deal with it. Besides, it was too late. I made a mental note to never let it happen again. When everyone was finished eating, the offender's plate still had a substantial heap of spaghetti, which he generously offered to me. We buried his body in the forest.

The sun was down and it was rapidly getting dark by the time we finished eating. I was accustomed to hearing lavish praise to the cooks whenever this meal was served, and was surprised that nobody spoke up. Certainly, it was as good as it had ever been.

Millennials.

"My compliments to the cook team," I said loudly.

Sophia said, "Yeah, that was good."

When nobody else said anything, I said, "Well, Teams Three and Four, you're up for dishes."

"Yeah," Steven said without enthusiasm.

But who's *ever* enthusiastic about doing dishes?

I set up my folding dish rack on top of the SuperStove, and said, "I'll show you how we set up our dish line."

I stacked all of the dirty dishes at one end of the table and set out three dish pans, leaving room for the big water tub at the other end. The tub held about ten gallons of boiling water. I used a coffee pot to dip water into the first two pans. I added soap to those, and filled the third dish pan with cold river water, to which I added a tablespoon of liquid bleach. I asked the guys to lift the tub up onto the table.

"On one of my early guide training trips, I had half the people in my group get sick one night after dinner. After the trip, I asked a health expert what might've happened. She didn't hesitate.

"Food poisoning—either from contaminated food or poorly cleaned dishes."

I'd already guessed that, so I asked her to look at our meal preparation habits to identify a probable source of the problem. She took swabs from randomly chosen plates and silverware out of our kitchen set, and found bacteria living in a thin film of grease on nearly everything she tested.

She asked for a demonstration of how we washed dishes, and ultimately concluded that we weren't using enough hot water, and we were commonly using the old water long past its ability to clean anything. The thing that troubled me was that I already knew that the dishes felt greasy when they were returned to the warehouse.

I'd even installed a dishwasher in there to give everything a good cleaning between trips. When I told the guides what the expert had said, they told me that it was the way they'd always done it. That's when I went out and bought bigger water tubs and instituted new dishwashing protocols, which I still use in my private rafting.

I demonstrated as I said, "The first pan is the pre-wash. We use plenty of soap and the hottest water we can tolerate. The second pan is the main wash, and again, plenty of soap and hot water. We use long-handled dish scrubbers so that we can keep the water hotter that what you can put your hands in. And when the pre-wash water gets too dirty or cool, dump it and move the second pan into the pre-wash position. Get fresh hot water for the main wash.

"The third pan is the cold rinse. It is raw water, usually straight from the river, treated with a tablespoon of bleach. If suds start to form in the cold rinse, dump it and get fresh. The final rinse is in the big water tub—it is undiluted hot water. Use tongs. It's way too hot for fingers. The point is to get the dishes hot, so that they air-dry quickly. Dishes put away damp become petri dishes.

"One person does the first wash, and one does the second wash. The third person takes the dishes out of the cold rinse, dips them in the hot rinse, and puts them on the rack to drip dry. The last person dries off any remaining water with a dish towel, and then puts them away in the SuperStove."

Now, I *know* that's way too much detail for this story, but I want to make a point about how important it is. Besides, it's stuff everyone needs to know when you go on a raft trip with me. And nobody's gotten sick on my raft trips since I started doing it this way.

But this time, I felt that my group wasn't taking me seriously. I could almost hear them silently calling bullshit, and I knew I'd have to keep an eye on them.

I set up a pair of LED lanterns and said, "Let's wrap this up before the water gets cold."

After all the dishes had gone through the line, I demonstrated how to dump the used dishwater through a strainer to catch all of the chunks so as to keep the beach clean. The dish crew's final duty was to button-up the kitchen for the night and fill the water tub so that the morning crew needed only to light the stove.

It was my practice to give an evening briefing so that everyone would know what to expect the next day. We call it "Story Time."

"I'm going to keep this short, because it's late, and we'll need an early start in the morning. A lot of things happened today that leave us five or six miles behind where we wanted to be. That's not a big deal—we have plenty of time to make it up. But we need to always be conscious of where we are relative to our daily goal of sixteen miles.

"After we go through this rapid in the morning, we'll have some easy floating until we get to House Rock Rapid. It's rated Class 7, same as Badger Creek Rapid, so we'll stop and scout it. After that, we'll go into what's called 'the Roaring Twenties,' a series of rapids at half-mile intervals between float miles 21 and 27. Several of them will require scouting, so it'll be a busy day.

"Ideally, I'd like to get to Shinumo Wash, at Mile 29. It's a nice place to camp, and there's a great hike into the Silver Grotto. That's 18-miles from here. It won't entirely make up for what we lost today, but it'll be a good day's work.

"Let's plan on getting up at 6:00. While the breakfast team—Ray and Charlene—light the stoves and get started on breakfast, the rest of us will be rolling sleeping bags, taking down tents, and packing dry bags. Before breakfast, our personal gear needs to be all ready to load onto the rafts. After breakfast, while we do the dishes and break-down the kitchen, Ray and Charlene will take care of their personal gear. If we all do that, we'll get out of camp by 9:00."

The roar of Soap Creek Rapid made it easy for me to fall asleep. Later, I woke up and heard loud laughing coming from down where the rafts were tied. I sat up and looked in that direction, and saw light from a fire illuminating the canyon. There was another burst of laughter.

For some indeterminate period of time, I alternated between fragile sleep and unwanted wakefulness as the late-night party went on. When I finally woke up in the morning, I had no idea how much actual sleep I had gotten. I checked my watch. It was 5:45, and I had to pee.

I went down to piss in the river, as the regulations stipulate, and found the two rented rafts beached by the receding "tide" that results from the reduced overnight demand for electricity, which controls the outflow from Glen Canyon Dam, just upstream. My raft was still afloat, because I'd used a bungee anchor system to hold it off the beach.

During one of our pre-trip conversations, I'd talked about the tides and the need to be conscious of them when tying-up rafts. But I guess it was lost in the barrage of information. Among the rocks above the water line, I found the warm ashes and charcoal from the party fire. No firepan. We'd need to have a conversation about that.

Photo by Jan Brandvold

It wasn't yet 6:00, so I wasn't surprised that nobody was in the kitchen. I went ahead and lit the big "crab cooker" stove under the water tub, and then lit-up the small stove to heat water for coffee. Back at my nest, I packed up my gear and closed my dry bags.

After carrying my gear down to the beach, I took care of the morning ice chest maintenance. I started with the rented rafts, opening the drain valves on their ice chests to check for melt water. I hadn't expected to see any, and was both surprised and disappointed to see a brief drizzle, adding up to perhaps a pint of water, come from Joseph's cooler. On my own raft, I got no melt-water from either ice chest—and expected that I wouldn't for two or three more days. I closed the plugs, and then opened the evaporative cooler boxes to air-out in the morning coolness.

Knowing what was on the breakfast menu, I grabbed eggs and a melon from the "evaps" and carried them up to the kitchen. By then, the coffee water was boiling, so I made the first pot of coffee. Over the years, we've tried every known method of making coffee on river trips, and have settled on a single pass Melita cone filter system. As I waited for the filter funnel to drain, I checked the time. 6:10. I needed to stir things up.

Photo by JP Baysinger
Eight gallons of river water on the burner.

The lantern stand that we'd used while doing the dishes has the auxiliary function of a bugle. I gave a couple of blasts, and then shouted, "Coffee's done." I poured myself a cup and gave myself the luxury of a few moments of inactivity. Sitting comfortably in my chair, I watched the sunshine creeping down the canyon wall.

Charlene was first to reach the kitchen. She poured a cup of coffee and asked where to find the creamer. I showed her a jar of dry powder imitation cream in the SuperStove, and since I was there, I pulled out the meal sheet for breakfast and handed it to Charlene—my idea of subtlety.

Ray came along and noted, "Oh, you didn't have to make the coffee. We'd have done it."

I said, "I know, but I was up, so I took care of it."

"Thanks. When should we start making breakfast?"

"We always try to have it ready to serve at 7:00. So, it's not too early to start right now."

"The kids aren't awake yet," Charlene observed.

"You might want to give them a wake-up call," I suggested.

I turned to Ray and said, "Shall we go do the breakfast shopping?"

When we got back to the kitchen with a kitty litter bucket full of supplies, I poured my second cup of coffee and then stayed nearby to answer questions and give help where needed. It was troubling that none of the millennials seemed to be out of bed. How much should I push them?

It may have been the aroma of bacon on the stove that finally brought Sophia to the kitchen.

I asked, "Are the others getting up?"

"Not yet," she said. "I'm going to take Joseph a cup of coffee."

"Breakfast will be on the table at 7:00, so everyone needs to get moving."

I could see no way that they could have their gear packed before breakfast, as I'd explained during Story Time. I made a mental adjustment to my departure time. 9:00 was very unlikely. If it were only one or two people lagging behind schedule, the rest of the group could exert social pressure to get them moving. But with more than half of our group dawdling, my only options were to either become a dictator or let them experience the consequences of the late start.

A few minutes before 7:00, I gave another blast on the lantern-stand bugle, AKA "the Mogur Horn."

"Breakfast in five minutes," I shouted.

Sophia and Krystal showed up, so I said, "Serving line starts there. Grab a plate and go." I pointed to where the plates were stacked.

I followed the girls through the serving line, and since there was still no sign of the guys, Ray and Charlene helped themselves, and then put covers over the pans to keep the remaining food warm.

The guys still hadn't shown up by the time most of us were finished eating, so I asked the girls to go tell them that breakfast was getting cold—which it had already done.

Jeremy ambled in, grabbed a cup of coffee and plopped himself into his chair, looking barely alive. He was followed shortly by Steven and Joseph, looking equally corpse-like. Rather than watch them, I walked down to the beach.

After closing-up the evap boxes and wetting-down their burlap covers, I went up and took a look at the remains of the previous night's bonfire. I picked up the partially-burned pieces of wood and tossed them into the river. Then, I got a bucket and scooped up as much of the charcoal and ash as I could and dumped that into the downstream current. That was a violation of the rules, but the process of scooping it up had brought along so much sand and rock that it was too heavy and bulky to pack out. That's why fire pans are required. We had one along, but the guys apparently thought that the rule didn't apply to them.

I finished cleaning-up the fire pit by pouring buckets of water over it, to flush the remaining ash down into the river. I gathered two or three dozen empty beer cans and stomped them flat. I put them in pile to go into a recycle bag.

When I got back up to camp, I found that Ray and Charlene had gone up to pack their personal gear, and everyone else was drinking coffee and socializing. They'd eaten some of the bacon and melon slices, but most of the food was un-touched and destined for the garbage bag.

I rounded-up all of the K-box supplies in a bailing bucket, to take down and re-pack on my raft. "Un-shopping," as we call it, normally is the responsibility of the cook team, since they're the ones who would know where everything came from and ought to be able to return it all to its proper place. But I had to do something to keep from committing any of several major crimes that had come to mind.

When I started staging for the dish line, the girls finally got up to help. I don't know how it works in their home lives, but Joseph and Steven seemed completely at ease, letting their wives do dishes while they sat around. They didn't get up until after I had filled all of the dish pans, added Clorox and Dawn, and rounded up the dishwashing tools.

While they washed the dishes, I cleaned-up the stoves, disconnected the propane, and carried the tanks down to the staging areas in front of the rafts. Next, I collected all of the chairs from our lounge area, folded them up and took them down to the beach. That, at least, would discourage any more sitting-around.

This early in the trip, I understood that nobody would know where to pack everything in the SuperStove and Futility Box, so I set to work on that, attempting to teach in the process. It's a lot to learn, and I didn't expect anyone to pick it up in one session, but I do wish they'd at least pretended to pay attention.

Ray and Charlene passed through the kitchen on their way to the rafts with their bags.

When they returned, Ray asked, "When does the water come back up?"

"It won't come up until after noon," I said. "We'll just have to manhandle the rafts off the beach before we load-up."

I raised my voice for the benefit of the millennials, who I had concluded, must all be hearing-impaired, and suggested, "This is a good time to do that. We'll need everyone."

The eighteen-foot rafts were cumbersome because of their size, and were ungodly heavy, in part because of their beer load, which was still substantial even after the big party. With four on each side, we dragged the two rafts into the water. When Ray reached for the drain plug on his cooler, I told him that I'd already taken care of that.

"Oh, you didn't have to do that," he said.

"Well, I was down here, and it was the right time of day, so why not? We all have an equal interest in preserving our food."

At about that time, the sun line swept across the beach. Things would warm up quickly from then on. Ray and I walked back up and found the kitchen abandoned, except for Charlene, who was attempting to figure out the SuperStove puzzle. I helped with that, and then we undertook the more challenging Futility Box puzzle.

Because those two heavy boxes had to go on our rafts before we could load anything else, Ray and I lugged them down to the beach and lifted them onto the rafts. After that, I broke down the mini-stove and my table. Over the next twenty minutes, Ray, Charlene, and I took everything from the kitchen down to the beach.

My raft frame is engineered to make my raft very easy to load, so I was all ready to go at 9:00, despite the millennials' slow start. But Ray's raft carried gear that belonged to Jeremy. His gear was still up in camp, as was *everything* that belonged on Joseph's raft.

Charlene went up to see how they were doing, and reported back that they were just getting their bags packed—you know, the bags that were supposed to be packed before breakfast? Two hours later, they still weren't packed.

To suppress my annoyance, I had to remind myself that I wasn't the one who had to be in a certain place at a certain time. *They* were the ones who had to be at Diamond Creek to catch the bus to Peach Cove. But it still galled me that they seemed to hear nothing that I said about everyone helping with the group gear.

Chapter Twelve

River Time

We finally got out of camp at 10:00. As bad as I've made this sound, it was still only an hour too late, and even if you add the time it would take to make up the miles we failed to make the day before, it was only two and a half hours on a two-week trip. We had plenty of time to get back on schedule.

Relying on what we'd seen and talked about when we scouted the rapid upon arrival at Soap Creek, we avoided all of the rocks on the right side and pushed straight down the wave train with the main current. It was much less intimidating in its appearance at low tide than it had been when we scouted it.

The next five miles were easy, and we passed Hot Na Na Wash—which should have been our previous night's camp—at noon. I had to again caution the kayakers to stay behind the rafts, because we were coming to a rapid that we needed to scout.

I waved everyone to the left bank above House Rock Rapid, and we all walked together down to a point where we could clearly see the one-two punch—two massive holes up against the left shore. The main flow drives straight into the holes. At the top of

Photo by JP Baysinger
House Rock Rapid, Class 6

the rapid, the right half of the river was an ugly mess of boulders with no clear path through.

As we walked back upstream, I pointed out a course that involved threading our way through some of the boulders lying just to the right of the main current. We'd have to continue to pull toward the right bank, because the current pulled strongly to the left. Just at the bottom of the boulder field, there is a narrow gap between the last rock on the right and the huge hole on the left.

After making sure that everyone understood the plan, we went back to our boats and prepared to make the run. I instructed the kayakers to hang back until the rafts were through, in case one of us got tangled up in the boulder field. As I entered the rapid between a pair of "guard rocks" at the entry to the corridor that would keep us out of the main flow, I maintained an aggressive ferry angle to the right, to counter the strong leftward pull of the current.

With that angle, I could look to my right and see where I was going, or to my left, where I could keep an eye on those following. Ray turned his raft the same way I'd turned mine, but Joseph turned the wrong way. I shouted for him to pivot and pull, but I doubt that he could hear over the roar of the rapid. When I last glimpsed Joseph, he was pushing on his oars with increasing urgency, while the main flow reeled him in. As I neared the critical pull at the bottom of the boulder field, I focused all of my attention on that.

I kept pulling to the right as I washed past the towering piles of water a few feet from the bow of my raft, and I was swept into the tail waves without any trouble. I turned my raft around and looked back just in time to see Joseph's raft stand on edge and roll over. I pulled onto a sweeping eddy along the right bank, and hovered there until I spotted Joseph and Sophia. Ray was trying to row toward them, but he was still in the downstream current. I had a better angle, and was able to get to a place where they could grab the boarding ladder that is attached to my frame adjacent to my rowing seat.

Photo by Jerry Baysinger
Overturned raft but everyone okay.

Once they were onboard, I turned my attention to their overturned raft, which had stayed on the wave train and was already two-hundred yards out in front of us. Ray was chasing it, and seemed to be closing in, so I looked back upstream. My view of the kayaks wasn't clear, but from where I was, they appeared to be in the center of the main current, heading into the heart of the first hole. Then, I lost sight of them behind the big pile of water.

Steven's yellow kayak burst from the froth, right-side-up and still under control. A second later, Krystal's red kayak and Jeremy's green one flushed out, both upside-down. Krystal made a couple of unsuccessful attempts at executing a roll, and succeeded on her third try. Jeremy popped up, swimming alongside his kayak, so I set up to intercept him.

Joseph leaned out and plucked Jeremy's paddle out of the water, and a few seconds later I got to Jeremy. He grabbed the boarding ladder and held on, while I tried to go after his boat. Steven, after making sure that Krystal was okay, went after the green kayak. He caught up with it and grabbed a short piece of strap trailing from its bow eye.

As we all drifted into calmer water, Ray caught up with Joseph's raft and was trying to push it toward shore. When I caught up, Joseph stepped off my raft onto his, holding onto my bow line, so that I could tow him over to the left bank, a mile downstream from the rapid. Ray went over and helped get Jeremy's kayak to shore.

There followed a period of everyone un-winding, catching their breath, and recounting their own experiences. Our first task, once it was clear that everyone was okay, was to right the overturned raft. We started by un-clipping the oars, which were still attached by tether straps. They were undamaged, which was good, since one of his spares was already gone.

The raft was rigged with four flip lines, contained is small bags attached to each side of the frame. We uncoiled the flip lines on the side of the raft nearer to shore, and then Ray, Joseph, Steven, and I climbed onto the raft.

Each holding one of the flip lines, we backed toward the opposite side of the raft. As our weight pushed that side down, we leaned back and tugged on the flip lines to

Photo by Jerry Baysinger
Approaching Boulder Narrows, Mile 18.5

bring the other side of the raft up. Our first try failed, so we re-positioned ourselves and tried again. That time, the big raft stood on edge and crashed down right-side-up. The load appeared to be intact, but there was no telling what we'd find in the ice chest, where a hundred pounds of ice had crashed down on top of the food. But checking on that would have to wait until after sundown.

We went a short way downstream before finding a shady spot for lunch. It took longer than usual, because Joseph and Sophia took the time to check their dry bags, again finding that they had leaked. I suspected that either the bags were defective, or they were not closing them properly.

"How did you guys end up going into the big hole?" I asked Sophia when she came to get a Band-Aid for a little scrape on her shin.

She said, "Oh, Joseph went there on purpose. He says that he'd learned that the best way to go through any rapid is to aim at the biggest wave."

Of course. That was one of several stupid things that inexperienced boatmen told one another. Joseph was hardly alone in believing the myth. I'd heard the same line before, from boatmen with swamped or overturned rafts. I'd have to blow-up that myth at the first opportunity.

Photo by Jerry Baysinger
Approaching Indian Dick Rapid, Mile 23

At 3:00, we resumed our float downstream toward the "Roaring Twenties." Forty-five minutes later, we passed North Canyon, and soon arrived at 21-Mile Rapid. It's a straight-forward run down a clean, wide chute, with a nice, easy wave train.

Another fifteen minutes brought us to 23-Mile Rapid, also called Indian Dick Rapid. I'm not sure if that name refers to a person, or to the prominent stone spire on the bank adjacent to the rapid, which is rated as Class 4 and doesn't require scouting. But it was still capable of flipping any raft that ventured into the wrong line.

"Enter in mid-stream, and pull across the left-side laterals. Stay away from the big wave on the right," I shouted back to the group.

I approached the rapid with my raft sideways to the current, facing the right bank. With a few strong pulls on the oars, I rowed the raft up and over the lateral waves and past the flipper wave. This time, even the kayakers followed my line, and everyone came through dry.

A mile further, we stopped to scout 24-Mile Rapid, where the current likes to pull rafts against a boulder on the right side near the bottom of the drop. That could be avoided by pulling across the left-side laterals, out of the main current. Once again, everyone made a clean run.

We pulled over to the left bank to walk down and take a good look at 24.5-Mile Rapid. Here, the river makes a sharp right turn followed by a sharp left turn, at the brink of the rapid. There is a massive hole blocking the right half of the river, forcing boats to take a narrow chute near the left bank. We headed back toward our rafts after scouting, and passed through a decent campsite.

I said, "It's 4:30. If you're ready to stop for the day, we can run the rapid in the morning on low-tide. It is a lot less violent at lower water."

"I got no problem running it now," Steven said. "I mean, we came here for the *action*, man!"

Not to be outdone Jeremey said, "Yeah, like, I'm up for it."

Joseph said, "Dude, we need to dry out our stuff!"

"So, it'll only take like five minutes, man," Steven argued.

"It'll take longer than that," I said. "Once we leave here, the next campsite is two miles downstream, with this and two more rapids in between. Even if all goes well, it'll take over an hour. And if anybody gets in trouble…"

"I vote to stay here," Sophia said, and I saw Krystal nodding her head.

I guess that Ray and Charlene were willing to let the millennials make the decision, because neither spoke up. By my count, it was three "no" and two "go."

I said, "I think Joseph is right. If their sleeping bags got wet, they'll need the time."

Jeremy made a show of his distress at being denied the opportunity to demonstrate his masculinity, but everyone else was nodding.

Kitchen setup went more smoothly this time, and before long, Charlene, Ray and I were seated in the lounge area enjoying adult beverages. Joseph and Sophia joined us as soon as they had their things spread out to dry. Krystal and Steven discovered that their bags had leaked in the flip, so they too spread clothes and sleeping bags all over the beach, which soon assumed the appearance of a massive yard sale.

Joseph and Sophia had meal duty for this camp. Ray and Charlene had the day off, while the rest of us had all of the other duties. I set up the toilet at the end of a well-worn path, where thousands of others had set up their toilets over the years.

Charlene helped teach what she knew about using our kitchen setup, getting me off the hook, so I took advantage of the opportunity to set up a tripod using three oars, for my solar shower. There wasn't a suitable place for it that wasn't in full view, but that wasn't an uncommon situation. We always dealt with it by showering with our swimsuits on.

A hot shower is a true luxury on a raft trip. I had used only about half the warm water in my shower bag, so offered the rest to Charlene, but by then, she was busy helping Sophia cook dinner, while Joseph sat down on his raft, smoking a joint.

So, I extended my offer to Krystal, who happily took me up on it. I sat down with a glass of wine, and was talking with Ray about how things had gone that day. I didn't want to put myself between Ray and his son, so I avoided talking about Joseph's flip at House Rock.

While I was talking with Ray, Krystal called out, "Ken," somehow managing to make three syllables from the three-letter name.

"The water is, like, coming out too slow. Can you help?"

"Is the hose kinked?" I asked, as I turned to find Krystal stark naked, with the shower nozzle in one hand and a bar of soap in the other.

"Can you, like, fix it?" she repeated. "Pleeze?"

I awkwardly excused myself from talking with Ray and went to see what the problem was. I tried to keep my eyes on the ground, but Krystal caught me when I glanced up in a momentary indiscretion.

Giving me an ambiguous smile, she said, "So, we're all naked under our clothes, ya know, like, I don't *care* or anything if you want to look. I mean, I just want the shower fixed."

Focusing on that, I took care of the problem by cleverly turning the valve all the way to the ON position—which was impossible to do without observing that Krystal was remarkably well constructed. You'll have to take my word for that. There are no photos. Sorry.

Dinner was chicken enchiladas, and again I had to lead the way in complimenting the chefs. The dishwashing process and kitchen shutdown went fairly smoothly, although (as expected) I still had to show where to pack everything and remind the cook team to do their un-shopping.

Our after-dinner social hour was a relaxing time, and I told how I'd once been sitting at home and heard a knock on the door. When I opened the door, there was nobody there except for a big snail. I picked it up and tossed it across the street. Three and a half years later, there was another knock on the door. When I answered it, there was the same damned snail. He said, "What the hell was that all about?"

My Story Time glossed over the fact that instead of being five miles behind schedule, we were now nine miles behind schedule. The truth is, on my first Grand Canyon trip, we'd made our second river camp in this same place, and had still managed to get back on schedule and arrive at Diamond Creek in time for a couple members of our party to catch the bus out.

Photo by JP Baysinger
Closing-down the kitchen by lantern light.

"Once we get through the rest of the Roaring Twenties, we'll have easy going for the next thirty miles. If we can get out of camp early, we'll have time for a hike at Silver Grotto."

...where we had been planning to camp tonight.

"I'd like to do about sixteen miles tomorrow, and camp at Buck Farm Canyon. Along the way, we'll stop at Vasey's Paradise and Redwall Cavern. Time permitting, there are some other interesting places we might get to see."

...but only if you do your part to keep us moving downstream.

Finally, I raised the topic of bonfires.

"This morning, I cleaned up the beach where you had your fire last night..."

Jeremy interrupted, "Like, you didn't have to. We woulda done it, ya know."

I said, "That isn't the point. The point is that you need to use the firepan. The fine for the permit-holder, if you get caught not using it, is a thousand dollars."

I made up the number, but achieved the desired result.

Ray said, "No more bonfires without the firepan."

"And a quick reminder," I said, pointing toward the trail to the toilet, where my oar lay flat on the ground. We always use an oar to signal whether or not the toilet is in use, to prevent embarrassing encounters.

"Oar up means pants up. Oar down means pants down," I said, repeating what I'd said in the last camp. "Right now, there might be someone desperately trying to hold it in, tempting the kind of accident that none of us wants to see."

So many little rules...

There was no bonfire, and no late-night partying. One thing about being a trip leader, whether private or commercial, you are always on duty, all day and all night. Twice during the night, I woke up for no apparent reason, but as long as I was awake, I went down to the beach to pee in the river.

Both times, I noted the drop in river level, and pushed the rented rafts out before they became stranded. Despite the effort, when I got up in the morning, I found them beached, though not as badly as the day before. While down by the rafts, I performed the morning cooler maintenance, and once again, there was nothing to drain from my ice chests, and barely a drizzle from Ray's. But Joseph's drained for about half a minute—probably about half a gallon of water.

I opened the evap coolers to air out, and fetched the eggs and a bag of oranges, since they were on the breakfast menu. I was not surprised when I got to the kitchen and found that the cook team hadn't started the stoves. So, I took care of that, and then went up to my nest to roll my gear and pack my bags.

Now honestly, I didn't mind having to light the stoves. I'd be happy to do it every day, because I was always going to wake up at the same time anyway. Lighting the stoves was a half-minute job. But when the cook team still wasn't up by 6:30, I gave a good loud blast on the reveille horn. If they'd come straight to the kitchen, they still could have had breakfast ready by 7:00.

My obsession with the clock was rooted in leading many, many commercial river trips, where getting things done on time gave the guests the illusion of a relaxed pace throughout every day on the river. On a private trip, things like this relied entirely on consensus, and it was increasingly apparent that this group was more interested in late sleeping than in getting an early start.

So, breakfast was late and nobody else had their gear packed when it finally was ready. Once again, everyone abandoned the kitchen as soon as the last fork was washed, leaving Charlene, Ray, and me to break-down the kitchen and lug the "heavies" down to the beach and load them onto the rafts.

At 10:00, when the rafts were all ready to go, we went back and re-scouted the rapid. It had changed considerably from the previous afternoon, and it was much easier to see a clear path with a left-side entry, avoiding the gargantuan hole and rock garden on the right. The run went well, and half-a-mile downstream, we stopped to scout the next rapid, which was very similar to the first.

Photo by Jerry Baysinger
25 Mile Rapid, Class 6

At Mile 29, we scouted and ran one more rapid, and at 12:30 I pulled ashore for lunch at Shinumo Wash.

"Hey, isn't this the place with that grotto you talked about?" asked Joseph while we were all gathered around the table consuming our shrimp ring lunch.

I said, "It is, but we sort of burned our sightseeing time in camp this morning."

Ray said, "You know, we may never have another chance to see this place, so shouldn't we do it while we're here?"

"We can, but we'll still have to cover our miles," I said.

When we started up the narrow, vertical-walled wash, I had to confess that I'd never gone up to Silver Grotto. On my first trip, we were too far behind schedule to spend the time, and on my second trip, we could see clear evidence of a recent flash flood, and there

Photo by Tamara Baysinger
Filling water jugs at Vasey's Paradise

were rain clouds threatening to unleash another torrent down the wash. Getting caught in that could be deadly.

Scrambling, wading, swimming and climbing, we made our way up the creek, through three plunge pools and up four steep, slick stone chutes. A fifty-foot waterfall dropping into the fourth pool blocked any further exploration. Silver Grotto is a special place, and is well worth the effort and time it takes to climb up the stone chutes—providing you actually *have* the time.

It was after 2:00 when we got back to the rafts. Three miles downstream, we stopped at Vasey's Paradise, where huge springs burst from the canyon wall and plunge into a dense mass of greenery. Even though the greenery is mostly poison ivy, the water is pure and cold. We filled all of our water jugs and canteens.

Just downstream, we stopped at Redwall Cavern, one of the most spectacular places in the canyon, and a compulsory stop for all Grand Canyon trips. Joseph had read about Redwall Cavern, and brought along a ball and bat for a brief softball game in the cavern. It was good fun, but the afternoon heat kept the game short.

Photos by JP Baysinger
Spectacular Redwall Cavern

Still, it was 4:00 by the time we left. I had hoped that by this time of day we'd be eight miles further downstream. An upriver wind made it increasingly difficult to row, and we managed only two miles in the next hour. I pulled in for the night at Nautiloid Canyon camp, having made just ten miles that day.

The duty team for this camp was Steven and Krystal, and at times they seemed to be *willfully* dense. I had to explain so many things, so many times, that it would have been easier to do it all myself. At some point, Steven lost interest and busied himself with other tasks, which he deemed more urgent than his dinner duties. Sophia stepped up to help Krystal, and Steven assumed the role of OWB—Observer with Beer.

Our morning pattern was set, and nothing changed with a new day—our fourth on the river. I calculated the distance to Diamond Creek—190 miles—and divided by the number of full days remaining—eleven—before we had to get there. That was easy. We had to average just over 17 miles a day for the rest of the trip. So far, we were averaging 11.3. Something had to change.

Photo by Jerry Baysinger
Kayaks in Redwall Canyon

Every group finds its own pace, and it isn't my prerogative to dictate how other people choose to spend their vacation time. And yet, as trip leader, I remained responsible to the group to see to it that they were at Diamond Creek at the appointed date and time.

In order to *average* 17 miles a day, knowing that some days—those with time-consuming scouting to be done, not to mention the possibility of on-river difficulties—we were bound to come up short, our daily goal needed to be closer to 20 miles. We were in one of the easiest parts of the canyon, and if ever there was a place to make-up some miles, this was it. I set Nankoweap as our day's goal, near float mile 53.

From past experience, I knew that it was possible to average four miles per hour. If we could do that, we'd still need to spend a full five hours rowing. Getting out of camp by 10:00 and allowing an hour for lunch and potty breaks, meant that we had to be on the river until 4:00—easy enough, as long as we didn't encounter an upriver wind.

Nobody else in the group was doing the arithmetic, and it seemed that nobody was interested in hearing about it from me. They dawdled their way through breakfast, cleanup, pack-up, and load-up,

Photo by JP Baysinger

so we were twenty minutes behind my timeline before we pushed off from shore.

Photo by Jerry Baysinger
The Royal Arches

Photo by Jerry Baysinger
The Triple Alcoves

I encouraged everyone to enjoy the scenery, because we were in one of the most spectacular parts of the canyon, with deeply eroded, bright red rock, towering cliffs, and historical sites. For the most part, I avoided mentioning the latter, because I didn't want to raise the topic of sightseeing hikes, for which we had no time.

At 12:30, we hit the first of only two significant rapids for the day—President Harding Rapid. Scouting was not necessary, but I urged everyone to follow my route, because the huge eddy on the left at the foot of the rapid was notorious for grabbing rafts. After our successful run there, I kept us moving until after 1:00 when we arrived at a place called Duck and Quack, where an overhanging ledge provided a shady spot for lunch.

To that point, we'd done okay, and were on track to reach our mileage goal by 4:00. As much as possible, I expedited our lunch stop, but it was pushing 2:00 when we got going, and we immediately encountered an upstream breeze. It wasn't as bad as the wind that stopped us the previous afternoon, but it did slow us down.

Approaching the Nankoweap area at 4:15, I felt pretty good about having reached our goal. As we prepared to enter Nankoweap Rapid, I called back to the group, saying that it was long, but easy, carrying a Class 3 rating.

"Hey, isn't Nankoweap where the cliff dwellings are?" Ray asked.

"The Nankoweap granaries," I corrected.

We pulled ashore at the main Nankoweap beach, at the foot of the rapid. I gestured toward the cliffs to the west, where the stone structures were visible.

"Can we hike up there?" Ray asked.

"I think that's about a two-hour hike," I explained. "So yeah, we can do that. The quicker we set up camp, the more time there'll be for the hike."

I picked a kitchen site and marked it by setting up my table. I dropped my dry bag on my chosen patch of ground for sleeping, and proceeded with de-rigging my raft. I supervised the arrangement of the kitchen, since Jeremy and I were on duty for this camp.

"Okay," I said, when I was satisfied that the group work was done, "Who's going to hike up to the granaries?"

I think everyone raised a hand.

"I've been up there before," I lied, "so I'm going to stay here and work on dinner. I'll have it ready at 7:00, so make sure you're back by then."

They had two full hours, so that ought to have been plenty of time, but they dawdled around changing shoes, rounding up cameras and binoculars, beverages, and snacks for the hike. Without telling them, I adjusted dinnertime to 7:30.

After they left, I set up a tripod of oars and hung up my solar shower. The water turned out to be so hot that I had to drain some off and replace it with cold water from the river. I allowed myself a long, leisurely shower, and then dressed in fresh, clean clothes.

Preparation for dinner started with filling the dishwater tub and lighting the water stove. Next, I set up the fire pan for doing my legendary salmon bake over charcoal. This is a dinner that is always a group favorite, but one that nobody else wants to prepare, mostly because of the perception that the folding of aluminum foil into covered "trays" for the salmon is somehow a difficult thing to do.

The key to my salmon recipe is the sauce, which includes a secret combination of ketchup, butter, lemon juice, Worcestershire sauce, and horse radish cream. I was serving it with saffron rice with peas, and sliced tomatoes. And I didn't mind doing this without Jeremy's help. The nose ring, tattoos, and ear hoops were still things I couldn't stand to look at.

From time to time, I looked up at the cliffs, following the progress of the hikers. They got to the granaries at 6:40, so that's when I lit the wadded-up paper in the bottom of my "charcoal chimney." If you don't know what that is, you should. It's the easiest, fastest way to light charcoal, and it doesn't require the use of any chemicals.

Ten minutes later, the charcoal was ready, so I dumped it into the fire pan, spread it out, and put on the grill. Then I placed the aluminum-foil trays containing the salmon filets on the grill. While the salmon cooked, I heated the pre-cooked rice, added the peas, and sliced the tomatoes.

The dinner buffet was on the table, hot and ready to serve when the hikers arrived back in camp at 7:30. I dished-up the first helping, and as expected, everyone gave lavish praise—except Jeremy. Fish have mothers. And the saffron rice has butter and cheese, derived from products produced by cows, who might be offended and whose mothers certainly would be. He ate something that looked like grass clippings and putty.

Photo by Jan Brandvold
Breakfast on the SuperStove

Once dinner was served, I was officially off duty until morning. I afforded myself the luxury of a leisurely glass of wine, while relaxing in my chair watching the river and listening to the confusion in the dish line, and as darkness fell, a stunning full moon rose over the canyon.

Breakfast was ready at 7:00. I had kicked Jeremy awake at 6:30 and made him help, even though I'd already done most of the work. I assigned him to tend the coffee and slice the cantaloupe, while I cooked the sausage and French toast. He cooked something that looked like soggy cardboard for himself on the coffee stove. I hoped it was nutritious.

We managed our earliest start so far, getting out of camp at 9:30. Forty minutes later, we stopped to scout Kwagunt Rapid. There's a massive pour-over hole in the middle of the river, with an obvious chute on its left side.

"As soon as you're past that big hole, move to the right, because there's a powerful back-roller that you can't see until you're almost in it down near the left bank."

Our run went well, and half a mile below the rapid, I spotted a partially submerged mid-stream bolder, which I believe was where one of the big motor rigs flipped, and a passenger died, a month earlier.

We continued making good time, arriving at the mouth of the Little Colorado River at 11:15. On my two previous Grand Canyon trips, we'd found the LCR flowing pure mud, so it was a thrill to finally see the turquoise-colored water for which it is famous. We simply could not pass without stopping for a swim.

And our stop lasted 45 minutes, as we repeatedly hiked upstream and floated back down in our lifejackets. At 1:00, we stopped for lunch at Lava Canyon. It was a quick and simple lunch featuring crackers, cheese, and sardines, and we wrapped it up in half an hour. We were ready to leave when Steven spotted a mine shaft in the canyon wall above Lava Creek and insisted on exploring it.

Photo by Jerry Baysinger
Lunch in the only shade around

He and the other millennials scrambled twenty feet up the steep bank to the mine's entrance, and ventured inside. Since they hadn't thought to take along any kind of light, they didn't go very far in. And when one of the girls heard the buzz of a rattlesnake, they bolted out of the mine and back down to the rafts.

At 3:30, we pulled ashore on the right bank to scout Unkar Rapid, rated Class 6, with a 25-foot drop. The scouting path led through the ruins of a huge Indian encampment. Most of the artifacts have been illegally plundered, though pottery shards are scattered all throughout the area.

In the rapid, the main flow presses the left bank, where there is a powerful hole concealed behind the first big wave. I cautioned against the temptation to run that route, even though we watched a pair of big motor rigs go that way.

"Those rafts are 33-feet long. Yours are 18. They have stability that you don't."

Photo by Jerry Baysinger
Scouting Unkar Rapid, Class 6

I pointed out a run just to the right of the main channel, and a safer route to the right of that, which followed a narrow but clean channel through the rock garden on the right side of the river. That's how I had run it twice before, and was going to do it again.

Back where our rafts were parked, I pointed out the two boulders that flanked the entry to the right-hand chute, and when everyone was ready, I rowed into the current. When I was lined up and moving toward my entry gate, I looked back and was surprised to see that Steven was rowing Joseph's raft with Krystal onboard, and had replaced Ray in the second position, and was on a track toward something to the left of my chute.

For the next ten seconds, I had to focus all of my attention on picking my way through the rock garden, and couldn't let myself be distracted by what the other rafts were doing. When I got to smooth water, I looked back to see Steven, swamped and rowing hard to intercept Ray's overturned raft. Ray and Charlene were holding onto the lifeline. The kayaks were just plunging into the big hole, which swallowed them whole.

Sophia popped out right-side-up, followed by Joseph who was upside-down, attempting to execute a roll. Jeremy made two or three attempts to right himself, and then bailed out. Joseph was successful on his second try, and maintained control through the long wave train. I rowed hard toward the left side of the river below the rapid, where everyone else was heading.

As the water drained from Steven's raft, he was able to get better control, and he got to Ray's raft. Krystal leaned over and grabbed Ray's bow line, and Steven started pulling toward the right bank. I picked up Jeremy and his paddle, and Steven collected his kayak. We all got to shore in a cove half a mile below the rapid, where we righted Ray's raft and made sure everyone was okay.

At 4:30, we resumed our journey, and soon arrived at Upper Rattlesnake Camp, near Mile 74, bringing us to within six miles of our trip plan. We'd made 21 miles, despite the time spent after the flip. Two consecutive days without slipping further behind schedule was cause for optimism, even though it was tempered by the knowledge that the next thirty miles contained some of the most challenging rapids in the canyon.

Ray and Charlene had the duty, so it was a good thing that they found that their bags had kept everything dry while their raft was overturned. The same could not be said for the Futility Box, where we found several gallons of water sloshing around.

On my first trip here, the Futility Box had been aboard the raft that had flipped twice in our first two days, and both times it had taken in water—plus a whole lot of mud, requiring an extensive clean-up effort. After that trip, I'd replaced the gasket on the lid, but obviously, it still leaked. At least we didn't have to deal with mud this time.

Still, everything had to be taken out and dried, so I helped with that task. Charlene and Ray had dinner ready by 7:00, and the dishwashing crew managed to get the kitchen closed down before dark.

Since I did not have dishwashing duty, I set up my shower and washed off two days of Grand Canyon sweat. Charlene and Ray shared the rest of the hot water in my solar shower.

"Is there any hot water left in there?" Sophia asked.

I said, "No, but you can re-fill the bag with the rinse water left from washing dishes."

Uncharacteristically, Joseph and Steven pitched in and helped the girls transfer the still hot water from the tub into the shower bag. Next time I looked in that direction, the girls were under the shower, wearing nothing they weren't born with.

It had been a long day, so I retired early, not risking the possibility of catching a glimpse of the guys when it was their turn to shower. Later, they started a bonfire—in the firepan this time—and stretched their social hour into the night.

Chapter Thirteen

Thermodynamics

In the morning of our sixth float day, I followed my established routine, beginning with cooler maintenance. For the first time, I got a drizzle of melt water from my main cooler. The smaller cooler had exhausted its dry ice three days earlier, and showed its first melt water the day before.

This time, it drizzled out about half a gallon. It is an 80-quart Gott cooler from the 1980s, and is not especially well insulated, so the best thing to do with the ice was to move it to one of the big high-efficiency ice chests on the rental rafts.

Ray's ice chest still hadn't reached the point where a lot of ice was melting every day, but Joseph's was producing an alarming amount of melt water, so that was where the ice would be most needed. I opened it up to move things around and make room for the ice, and immediately saw the reason for the accelerated ice consumption. There was a large number of beverages in the cooler—beer, soft drinks, wine coolers and energy drinks.

And most of the ice was gone. I removed all of the beverages and stacked them on the floor in the oarsman's foot well and moved all of the ice from my old Gott cooler into Joseph's cooler. I noted that the cooler had holes for a padlock in the latch, and I had a padlock in an ammo box.

Charlene was in the kitchen making the first pot of coffee when I got back up there. I blew a loud reveille before helping Charlene with the breakfast shopping. This was the first time I'd seen inside Ray's cooler, and I was pleased to see his ice holding up pretty well.

I commented, "You know, most of the ice in Joseph's cooler has melted. I put all of our spare ice into it this morning."

"Really? The coolers look identical. Why would that one melt ice so fast?"

This was the opportunity I was hoping for. "It seems that they've been cooling their beer in it."

"I thought they were cooling it in the river," she said.

"So did I, but I pulled about twenty cans out of it this morning."

"Does it make all that much difference?"

"Putting cans of warm beer in the cooler melts ice faster than just about anything else you can do. And every time you open the cooler to get a drink out, you introduce hot air, so all of that energy has to be absorbed by the ice. Yeah, it makes a huge difference."

Charlene sighed. "I'll talk to Joseph."

When Ray and Charlene had breakfast nearly ready, I sounded another long, loud blast on the reveille horn, since none of the late-night partiers had shown themselves. They straggled into the kitchen about the time we were finished eating. It was a replay of our morning at Soap Creek, except this time I was not going to bail out the dishwashing crew by doing their jobs.

When Jeremy got up, he went down to the raft, spotted the pile of beverages in the footwell, and looked around, as if trying to spot the perpetrator. When he saw me watching, he quickly looked away and pretended that nothing was amiss.

But after Steven and Joseph came down to the kitchen, I saw Jeremy pull them aside and talk to them. The quiet urgency of that short conversation told me that he was reporting what he'd seen. They held several furtive discussions during the next half-hour, presumably deciding what to do.

Finally, Steven asked me, "So, did you, like, take our stuff out of the cooler?"

"Yes. It never should have been in there. We talked about that to great length before the trip," I answered.

"So, what's it to you if we want our drinks cold?"

"What's it to me?" I repeated. "What's it to all of us? If you melt the ice, we lose our food."

"Yeah? Well, *you're* the one who's wasting the ice, like, every time you drain the ice water out. Ya know, I've seen studies about that, and they say ice lasts a lot longer if you *don't* drain the water."

I sighed. This topic has been debated to death.

"The issue is preserving food, and that's not entirely about conserving ice. If you leave the melt water in the cooler, it becomes contaminated, fosters bacterial growth, and spreads the bacteria to the food, which quickly spoils. So, maybe the ice lasts longer, but what's the point if the food is contaminated?"

"Bullshit. All ya gotta do is package the food better, so that the water can't get to it."

"Did you do that?"

"Yeah. Like, we put everything in zip-lock bags, ya know."

"And how many of those bags ruptured when you flipped the raft?"

"You know everything, so you tell me."

"Okay, here's what I know. All of the ice in your cooler right now came out of *my* cooler. That makes it *my* ice, and if I see anyone opening that cooler for anything other than food, I'll slap a padlock on it. Is that clear enough?"

"Goddam Nazi!" he mumbled.

The others had listened to all of this without comment. I guess they'd appointed him spokesman, probably because he was so articulate.

Photo by Tamara Baysinger
Watching a 33-foot motor raft run Nevills Rapid, rated Class 6.

We finally got out of camp at 10:30. Nevills Rapid, a mile downstream, carries the same Class 6 rating as Unkar, but on my past trips, I'd found it to be pretty easy. Nevertheless, we stopped and scouted it. The entry tongue drives straight into a line of boulders, forcing all boaters to break the left-side lateral waves and run down the left side.

Photo by Jerry Baysinger
Lunch in the shade above Nevills Rapid

"This is a perfect place to practice your downstream ferry angle," I explained. "When you set up with your raft at 90-degrees to the lateral waves, you'll actually be rowing downstream as much as toward the left bank.

I always carry a little toy raft for demonstrating what I'm talking about when there's a difficult move to make. The move at Nevills was not difficult, but when we got to Crystal Rapid, the downstream ferry would be critical.

"If you attempt to make this move with your conventional upstream ferry angle, which works fine on smaller rivers, you'll find yourself sideways against the lateral wave, and it'll funnel you right back into the main flow. With the downstream angle, you'll be rowing directly *at* the wave, so your raft can climb over it. Timing is everything."

Photo by JP Baysinger
Scouting the left run at Hance Rapid

As expected, the run was pretty easy, and I was pleased with the way everyone executed the downstream ferry. Hance Rapid was just a mile ahead, and Hance has always been considered one of the most difficult in the canyon.

On my 2007 Grand Canyon trip, I found a left-side channel that avoided any confrontation with the submerged boulders in what is called "the Land of the Giants" in the main channel.

But in 2012, a blowout of Red Canyon Creek filled the left side of the river with rock and blocked the safer run. So, on our 2013 trip, we were left with no choice. We tried to enter the rapid close to the right of the midstream rock pile, intending to break into the "duck pond," an area of calmer water below the rock pile. No one in our group made it to the duck pond, and we had one raft flip and the boatman on another washed overboard, as we blasted through the Land of Giants.

During the past few months, I'd heard that a new left-side run had opened up, and I'd even managed to find a couple of YouTube videos. If that run was open, that would be my first choice. But to keep our options open, I pulled to the left bank well above the rapid to walk down and scout.

That way, we'd still have plenty of room to cross the river and scout from the other side if we didn't like what we found on the left.

I was, in fact, able to identify a left run, though different from the old one. There appeared to be some risk of getting hung-up on rocks around the entry, but from there on, the rock-dodging would be easy for a person with technical rowing skills.
When I explained how to run the left side, Jeremy asked, "Shouldn't we look at the other side before we make up our minds?"

Others were nodding their heads, so we rowed across the river and scouted the main channel run. I pointed out the entry markers and explained what it would take to get into the duck pond, and how to get from there to the left of the major hazards.

"On balance, I think we should take advantage of the left run, since it is open," I said.

"Why do we always have to take the 'chicken routes?' I mean, we came here to run the rapids," protested Steven.

"I'm not telling you what you have to do. I'm just telling you what I think is best for the situation we're in."

But once the left run was labeled a "chicken route," it seemed that all of the young guys felt the need to demonstrate their courage. In the end, the group split 4-4 on which way to go. Among the millennials, only Sophia broke ranks and favored going left. The others were adamant about the main channel run. Nothing, it seemed to me, was going to change anybody's mind.

"Okay, here's my suggestion. Ray, if you want to go left, I'll lead the way. Sophia, you can ride with one of us. When we're down, we'll eddy-out and watch the rest of you come through, and if anyone gets dumped, we'll be there to pick you up. Okay?"

Sophia elected to ride with Ray, since there wasn't any good place for her to sit on my raft. Leading the way, I rowed across to the entry point, just to the right of a prominent boulder at the top of the rapid. I made a conventional eddy turn to the left beneath the boulder, and continued to work to the left until I could have touched the bank with my left oar. Ray stayed close behind me, and in thirty seconds we were pulling into an eddy along the left bank.

Steven led the way in his kayak, with Krystal close behind, entering just to the left of a pour-over rock at the entry. Jeremy followed, but missed the entry and plunged into the hole beneath the pour-over. He made a good recovery, but didn't get out of the main flow. Joseph set up to follow Steven and Krystal.

Ferry Angles Explained

Maneuvering in whitewater is accomplished by rowing at an angle to the current. A ferry angle is the angle between the direction the raft is pointed and the direction of river flow. Keep in mind that the direction of the current is often not parallel with the river banks. So you always need to watch which direction the water is moving and set your ferry angle relative to that.

In simplest terms, a zero degree ferry angle means that your raft is pointed in the direction of flow, and the boatman is rowing directly against the current, as indicated by the white arrow.

A boatman might choose a zero angle if he wants to simply slow his raft's downstream speed.

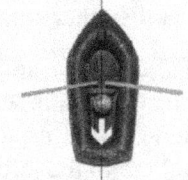

0° Ferry Angle

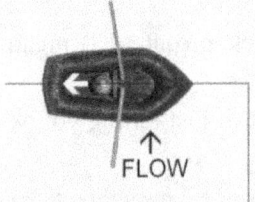

90° Ferry Angle

Now, suppose a raft is heading directly toward an obstacle that the boatman wants to avoid. He will turn his raft at an angle relative to the flow, enabling him to row to a point where the current will carry him past the obstacle.

In this illustration, with a 90° Left Angle, all of the boatman's rowing power will be applied to pulling the raft to the left, while its downstream speed remains unchanged.

In most circumstances, the boatman will also want to slow his downstream speed, in addition to repositioning the boat. The 45° angle will accomplish both. As he pulls on the oars, the raft will slow down relative to the current, and also move left. With the current pushing against the right-hand side of the raft at the 45° Left Angle, it acutally helps push the raft to the left. This is the most commonly used maneuver.

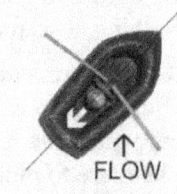

45° Ferry Angle

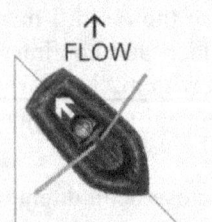

45° Downstream Ferry Angle

There are times where a downstream ferry angle is needed. In "big water" rapids, like those in Grand Canyon, lateral waves form at the edges of the main flow, and often, you will need to get out of the main flow to avoid an obstacle, meaning that you have to cross those laterals.

But when the lateral are high, a conventional ferry angle will not work. The lateral wave will surf the raft back into the main flow. You need to turn the raft so that it is at 90° to the lateral, and pull the raft over the waves. It is a bold, aggressive move.

Jeremy went straight into the biggest, meanest hole in the rapid and got mauled, losing both his paddle and his boat. Steven and Krystal took a tumultuous ride down the left side of the Land of Giants, hitting several large holes, but making it through in good form. Joseph hit the entry chute, but failed to get over to the duck pond. Still trying to pull left, he hit the monster hole sideways and the back wave turned him over like someone flipping a pancake (as illustrated on Page 102).

I went after Jeremy, and Ray went after Joseph. Steven and Krystal went after Jeremy's kayak and paddle. We got to the swimmers just before we arrived at Son of Hance Rapid a quarter-mile below Hance, and went through with swimmers hanging onto our rafts. The calm water below allowed us to get Jeremy and Joseph out of the water and round-up the gear.

Joseph caught the bow line on his raft, and Ray was able to drag it into a calm eddy along the left bank, where we turned it upright.

"That went well," I said with a straight face.

A mile after that, we entered Granite Gorge, where the walls close in, and landing points become scarce. A mile into the gorge, we arrived at Sockdolager Rapid, rated Class 7. It features boulder piles on both sides of the entry, forcing boaters to approach the rapid on a tongue that pours directly into a boat-eating hole. The only way to miss the hole is to pull across the left-side laterals using a very aggressive downstream ferry angle.

Photo by Jerry Baysinger
Scouting Sockdolager Rapid

Immediately below the rapid, we stopped at a little beach with a diminishing sliver of shade. After a quick lunch, Steven and Krystal swapped places with Joseph and Sophia. Half an hour later, we arrived at Grapevine Rapid, which is a mirror image of Sockdolager.

We scouted it quickly, and I led the way, easily punching the right-side laterals to avoid the hole on the left. Ray came through right behind me. When I looked back, Steven was struggling with his left oar, which seemed to be out of its oarlock. He was unable to use it, and the raft was out of control, getting pulled into the hole. With only his right oar, all he could do was try to turn the boat and hit the hole head-on.

The raft stalled on the reversal, hovered momentarily, and then flipped on the back wave. The three kayakers breezed past without difficulty. So, once again, we chased the raft and swimmers downstream After righting the raft, we found that the bronze oarlock had fractured at the base of the horseshoe, which still rattled around on the oar shaft. The oarlock shaft had fallen out the bottom of the oarlock stand and was gone.

Since the oarlock that broke was on the side where the oarlock stand had been damaged at Badger Creek. It seemed likely that the oarlock was cracked in that event and finally fractured through at Grapevine. Fortunately, there was a spare oarlock in the repair kit provided by Canyon REO.

Photo by Jan Brandvold
Above Zoroaster is a beautiful campsite, and its location is critical.

It was about 5:00 when we reached a campsite at Mile 84.5, and we'd made barely ten miles on the day. I might have insisted on going further, but there were only two campsites between here and Horn Creek Rapid. I knew from talking with a passing motor rig that the camp called Cremation was already taken. That left only the camp below Pipe Creek, a mile from Horn Creek.

Now, let's be clear about our situation. Horn Creek Rapid is formidable at any water level, bordering on impassable at low water. I had a group of exhausted boaters. If we were to arrive at Pipe Creek and find that camp occupied, we'd be forced to run Horn Creek Rapid, and by then it would be about 7:00. As much as I felt the need to get some more miles behind us, the prudent thing to do was stay where we were, at the camp called Above Zoroaster.

The two flips had saturated everything in at least three of the bags on Joseph's raft. Once again, he and Sophia wrung-out their sleeping bags and clothes, and borrowed towels to dry the insides of their river bags. I should point out how fortunate they were that the river was running clear. Had it not been, their bags would've been half-full of mud, and they'd have been completely unable to get their things clean.

While they hung clothes on bushes, spread sleeping bags over boulders, I set up my solar shower. I used only about half the warm water and offered the rest to Charlene. Dinner was late, because getting things dry was a higher priority, and we found ourselves washing dishes by lantern light. I woke up a few times during the night and noted the rotation of the Big Dipper around the North Star.

Joseph and Sophia had the duty, and as in the past, Joseph left Sophia to do everything by herself. Once again, Charlene covered for her lazy-ass son. And once again, my bags were the only ones packed before breakfast. I'd given up trying to enforce that rule.

Late getting out of camp, we passed beneath the Kaibab Bridge at 11:00 and pulled up at the Phantom Ranch boat beach to fill our water jugs. A visit to Phantom Ranch is almost compulsory on Grand Canyon trips. The hike up and back, plus the time it took to drink a cool beer and mail a post card from the bottom of the canyon, all added up to another hour gone.

Photo by Jan Brandvold
Fresh water from the well at Phantom Ranch

So, at 12:30, we were standing on the rocks studying Horn Creek Rapid. With the clean water on this run, it was easy to see exactly what causes this rapid to be so challenging. On my two previous Grand Canyon trips, we'd had thick, muddy water, so this was a new experience.

The rapid features two prominent mounds of water at its brink, often called the "horns." These create big pour-overs with keeper reversals below. Many people think that it is the horns that give the rapid its name. but that is incorrect. Horn Creek is named after the famous nineteenth century Pinkerton agent, Tom Horn, and the rapid is named after the creek. The "horns" were named after the rapid, but have nothing to do with Tom Horn. I don't know what good that piece of information is, but there it is.

The most common approach to this rapid begins on the right-hand side of the right-hand horn. But at most water levels, this leads into either a big, mean back-rolling wave in mid-current, or into a huge boulder against the right bank. Either way, a flip is a common result. To prevent that, the boatman should approach the rapid with a downstream ferry angle set and as much cross-current momentum as he can get, and with perfect timing, blast the laterals into the choppy, fast water that will brush to the left of the suicide back-roller.

Most people who attempt that move are unsuccessful and wind up taking on the back-roller. But if they hit it straight and power through, they have a reasonable chance of success, with the black side down. On the other hand, if they hit it sideways, they're likely to go swimming, and might get to see the bottom of their raft.

Photo by JP Baysinger

Horn Creek Rapid with muddy water. The "splitting the horns" run is the smaller tongue, in the upper-center part of this photo.

I'd often heard of a run called "splitting the horns," which is an option that is available at certain higher water levels, when there's enough water to soften the big drop in the steep slot between the pour-over rocks. As we studied the rapid, I started to see that chute, and the more I looked at it, the better it looked. A perfect entry would lead to a tumultuous, straight-through run. It all hinged on being able to identify the slot from above.

A characteristic of many of Grand Canyon's bigger rapids is that the initial drop is so steep that it can't be seen from above until you are already accelerating into it. This is certainly true at Horn Creek, no matter which entry you choose. In scouting, you need to study the surface of the water approaching the brink, and identify subtle cues in the swirls and waves, which show where the water is going.

I pointed out what to look for in order to be in position to thread the needle and make the necessary perfect entry. There'd be only a few seconds after the chute became visible for a boater to correct his position, so it was essential to be very close to the line.

There is always a sense of breathless uncertainty in the moments before the drop becomes visible. I put my raft close to where I expected to find the line, and stood up for a better view as the speed of the current picked up. I was off by maybe a foot or two to the left, so I pivoted and made the adjustment. I glanced back at Ray following close behind, and saw him also pulling to the right.

As my raft dropped into the chute, I pivoted the bow downstream and pushed it into the wave that crashed into my lap. I kept the boat pointed downstream and rode out the rest of the rapid in a chaotic but straight line. I heard Ray shout for Charlene to hold on. For a moment, I thought that meant they were making a good run. But then...

"Oh no!" Charlene screamed.

I looked back to see Ray's raft upside down, and Joseph dropping sideways, directly over the right-hand horn. In the blink of an eye, he too was upside down. If there's a redeeming quality to Horn Creek Rapid, it is that it runs out into calm water almost immediately.

I released my boarding ladder and moved toward Charlene, who was closest to me. While I was helping her up

Photo by Jan Brandvold
Flipped raft below Horn Creek Rapid

the ladder, Ray and his raft caught up. He handed me the bow line from his raft and worked his way around to my ladder. Once onboard, Charlene went to the back of my raft and Ray went to the front, where he pulled his raft in close and clipped our bow eyes together with a carabiner.

Joseph and his raft came alongside, and Ray took hold of a strap and pulled it tight against his raft. Sophia was out of sight on the other side of the raft, but I could hear her coughing, so I knew she was okay. I started tugging hard on my oars to drag the three-raft barge to the right bank. The three kayaks were all upright, and the paddlers were gathering flotsam including hats, water bottles, oars, and whatever else they could catch.

When I got to shallow water, Joseph put his feet down and pushed my raft to shore. We were still securing the boats when a pair of Grand Canyon Expeditions motor rigs came around the bend. They immediately came over and offered to help right the rafts.

With the help of one of their guides, we quickly got the rafts turned upright and began assessing the damage.

Photo by Jan Brandvold
Guide helping right the flipped raft

There were poorly-tied bags hanging over the sides of both rafts, and on Joseph's raft, two of the folding chairs were hanging by a single strap. The other two were gone. I had stopped inspecting their tie-downs after our second day on the river, believing that I'd given all the instruction they wanted to hear. I was relieved, however, to see that all of the major gear was still aboard.

While Joseph, Ray, Charlene and Sophia worked on getting their rafts back in order, Krystal and I set up my table and put together a deli sandwich spread for lunch, in a patch of shade cast by a huge boulder. Note that I didn't mention Jeremy or Steven. An occasional whiff of pot smoke was the only sign that they were there.

Maybe if there hadn't been so much re-rigging to do on the rafts, or maybe if everyone had pitched-in and helped, or maybe if I'd conveyed a greater sense of urgency... Maybe, maybe, maybe. Maybe we could have gotten back on the river sooner. But it was 3:30 when we finally got underway, fifteen miles short of our day's goal.

Two miles downstream, we stopped to scout Granite Rapid, where a big rock bar intrudes half-way across the river from the left bank, forcing the current into a long row of tall, back-curling waves. A lot of rafters, mainly those in eighteen-foot boats, push straight down the middle of the waves, and get a great rollercoaster ride. But with my smaller sixteen-foot raft, I preferred to duck across the left laterals and ride next to the wave train, rather than on it. I found the group uncharacteristically willing to listen to my suggestions.

Having walked the full length of the rapid, by the time we got back to the rafts, it was 4:30. And there was no question that there were wet sleeping bags and clothing to dry out.

I said, "Okay, here's the situation. We haven't even made ten miles today, and we really ought to keep going. If we run this and the next rapid now, and everything goes well, we'll get to a good campsite at about 6:00 or 6:30. That'll give us five more miles, but won't give much time for things to dry."

Photo by JP Baysinger
An OARS dory takes Granite Rapid straight down the waves.

Ray said, "Well, we *have to* get things dry! And my shoulder is *killing* me. Can't we just camp here and run the rapids in the morning?"

"That might be the right thing to do, but what's this about your shoulder?"

"I don't know, I must've wrenched it when the raft went over. It didn't hurt too much at the time, but ever since lunch, it's been getting worse."

My Boy Scout first aid training was kind of limited, and that was a very long time ago, but I took it upon myself to check Ray's shoulder. I figured I'd be able to see if it was dislocated, and it didn't look like it was. But Ray winced when I squeezed and felt for the possibility of a fractured humerus. Nothing felt loose, and since he'd managed to row two miles, I figured it probably wasn't broken. I suggested a double dose of ibuprofen.

Applying ice is always the recommended treatment for this kind of thing, but that had to be measured against the fact that we had a finite quantity and no way to replenish it. I got the little axe out of the Futility Box and went down to Joseph's raft with a zip-lock bag. I broke a chunk from one of the ice blocks I'd put in there in the morning, sealed it in the zip-lock and took it to Ray.

"Wrap that in a dishtowel, and maybe it won't melt so fast."

Because of his dad's injury, I prevailed upon Joseph to help carry the "heavies" up to camp. When we went to lift the Futility box, we found it substantially heavier than usual. We opened it to find that it was half full of water. Tipping it on end, we drained most of the water out before carrying it to the kitchen site.

Before starting dinner, the duty team—Krystal and Steven—had to wring-out their clothes and sleeping bags, a task that took them over half an hour. And then, they took time-out to sit on their raft (since their chairs were gone) and drink a river-temperature beer.

Only after I reminded them that it was their turn to cook dinner, did they go to the kitchen and read their menu sheet. After helping Krystal with the meal shopping, Steven set up the firepan and started charcoal to barbecue steaks.

Then he wandered off to burn more weed with Jeremy, while Sophia and Krystal made dinner. If I hadn't helped with the steaks, they'd probably have been cremated, because the girls had no clue how to cook on a grill. That task entitled me to the extra steak—the one that Jeremy wouldn't eat. I shared it with Ray.

Photo by Jan Brandvold

A platoon of ringtail cats visited us during dinner, begging for handouts and looking cute. But they are Procyonidae, not cats

Ringtail cats visited during dinner to beg for handouts, which were generously provided, in violation of good sense and the rules set down by Ranger Lucy on launch day. We did the dishes by lantern light, and then the millennials tossed firewood onto the charcoal and started a smoky bonfire.

Photo by Jerry Baysinger
Kitchen under the Parawing canopy, doing dishes by lantern light.

I insisted that they carry the firepan down to the beach, away from where the adults were sitting. That party went on until long after I checked-out for the night.

Once again, I started my morning by lighting the stoves and draining the ice chests. At 6:30, I blasted reveille. When Steven didn't show up, I went up and nudged him. He grumbled, to let me know that he was alive.

He and Krystal finally showed up to start breakfast at about the time they should have been serving it. When Ray came down, he was cradling his left arm against his chest, so I didn't need to ask how his shoulder felt. After Steven went off to drink his Monster Energy, I helped Krystal finish preparing breakfast.

I still hadn't seen the rest of the millennials, so I gave another loud blast on the lantern stand horn. This was rapidly turning into a really crappy start to what already promised to be a difficult day on the river, with Granite, Hermit, and Crystal Rapids in our first five miles.

"Can we do a layover day?" Charlene asked.

I could see that coming. Ray looked to be in no condition to row a raft. And, honestly, neither did the guys who stayed up partying half the night. But a layover would put a huge amount of pressure on our float plan, and I didn't want to give-in to that too easily.

I compromised, "Let's look at making a late start—see how things look around noon, and maybe do half a day on the river."

I took another look at Ray's shoulder, which was swollen and turning purple. I chopped more chunks of ice for his ice-pack, until I'd used half of a block. I suggested that he take a couple of Advil tablets.

At 11:00, Ray seemed to be doing all right, so I announced that we'd be leaving in an hour. I had packed up my personal gear before breakfast, but everyone else still had to take down tents and pack their dry bags. It took until 12:30 to get the kitchen packed-up and the rafts loaded.

Before leaving, we hiked back for a fresh look at Granite Rapid. During the morning, we'd watched several groups run the rapid, and it seemed that most pushed straight down the wave train.

"I'm still going to get across the laterals and stay on the left fringes of the waves," I said, knowing that the young guys thought that was pretty wimpy.

Joseph said, "I want to hit the waves," and the kayakers nodded in agreement.

Ray said, "I'm going left. I think my shoulder will be okay, but I don't want to aggravate it first thing in the day."

We all got through right side up, although Joseph got blown out of his seat by one of the big waves. A mile and a half later, we arrived at Hermit Rapid and stopped to scout it.

Hermit features a line of towering irregular waves right down the middle of the river. The larger ones pulsed with no obvious rhythm. Sometimes the bottom would drop out of the trough between the waves, and the downstream wave would collapse into the resulting hole. Other times, the crest of a wave would curl upstream and crash like ocean waves rolling toward shore.

Photo by JP Baysinger
Huge waves in Hermit Rapid

Riding the wave train was a lottery. You might get a fun rollercoaster ride, or you might get buried, turned sideways and dumped. And the chances of those things happening were inverse to the size of your boat.

I punched the laterals and ran left, and Ray followed. Everyone else went down the waves. Jeremy got hammered and had to bail out, but stayed with his boat until he could swim it to shallow water and get back in.

At 4:00, we pulled ashore to scout Crystal Rapid. As we were tying the rafts, I noticed that Ray was having difficulty. In obvious pain, he was trying to do everything one-handed. There was no way he could row Crystal.

"Okay," I said loudly. "We're going to camp here and run the rapid in the morning."

The cooking duties belonged to Jeremy and me, and spaghetti was on the menu. After we'd done our meal shopping, I spread-out the ingredients for the sauce.

"Normally, I'd start by browning the meat, and then add everything else. But this time, I'm going to make the sauce without meat and separate a portion for you. I'll cook the meat separately, and then add it after we take yours out."

"Hey, Dude, that's, like, really cool," Jeremy said.

His appreciation was unquestionably sincere. I just wished he didn't have to call me Dude. The Ringtails were back, scurrying around our feet and being adorable pests throughout cooking and consumption of my spaghetti orgy.

Before retiring for the night, I urged everyone to get up early and be ready for a challenging day on the river.

Chapter Fourteen

Crystal to Lava

Maybe the group finally took me seriously when I said we needed an early start the next morning, or maybe it was simply because I was on breakfast duty. Either way, we managed to be ready to go by 9:15. But first, we had to take a good look at Crystal Rapid.

Crystal is known to be the deadliest rapid in Grand Canyon. That fact all by itself ought to instill a sense of respect. The massive hole that lies dead-center in the river has flipped uncounted numbers of boats, including a 37-foot motor rig. And if that isn't enough, there's a rock festival just downstream that collects boats that are out of control, whether upside-down or right side up, after Crystal.

I explained, "Crystal Hole can be bypassed on either side at most water levels. I've always favored the right-side run. It requires entering the rapid with a downstream ferry angle, punching the right laterals and continuing to counter the pull of the current into the hole. It sounds complicated, but actually, it's a pretty easy move."

Steven said, "The left side looks pretty good."

Photo by Travis Mauk

Scouting Crystal Rapid—the deadliest rapid in the Grand Canyon

"The left-side run has its own list of hazards, not the least of which is the big boulder garden downstream. Passing to the left of Crystal Hole involves keeping control of the raft in violently tumultuous water and taking one or two good-sized holes head-on. And amidst all of that, the current will try to send you into the left-side wall."

Ray asked, "So, you want to stay right?"

"What I like about the right-side run is that you can see it up close before you run it. Right now, we're standing thirty feet from Crystal Hole, and we can see exactly where we need to be and what it takes to get there. Run left, and you don't really see what you're getting into until you're in it."

After I explained the plan, Ray said, "I'm not confident that I can row this one. My shoulder still aches, and I just don't have full strength."

Joseph volunteered, "I can row your raft, if Steven will row mine."

"Like, someone will have to carry my kayak," Steven said.

I said, "I can carry the kayak. Sophia, are you okay riding with Steven?"

"No problem," she said. "Or, I could paddle the kayak."

I looked at Steven, and he shrugged. "I'm down with that."

"Okay. Kayaks: Sophia, Krystal, and Jeremy. Ray and Charlene will ride with Joseph. Steven and I will row solo."

Everyone agreed to that, so we made a quick review of the plan before going back up to the boats, where we checked all of our tie-downs and cinched our lifejacket straps.

I led the way, staying as close to the right bank as the shallow rocks above the rapid would allow. Once clear of them, I used a downstream ferry to pull across the laterals and slip between Crystal Hole and the shore. A secondary hole below the big one was easy to avoid, by just holding my line along the right shore.

Joseph stayed close and mimicked every move I made, and in the span of fifteen seconds, we were both safely through. I was concentrating on getting around the right curve into the eddy in the shelter of the Crystal Creek rock bar when I heard Ray shout.

"He's over! Flip! Flip!"

I then spotted Steven's raft, black-side-up, far over on the other side of the river. After all that we'd discussed, he'd tried doing the left-side run. Within seconds, I saw Krystal and Jeremy paddling furiously into the final hole in the left run. Sophia showed up on our side of the river, right behind Joseph.

From where I was, I couldn't see whether or not Steven's raft was going to clear the rock garden. Until that was determined, I had to stay where I was, to keep rescue options open, in case the raft got hung-up in the rocks. Krystal and Jeremy were paddling hard to chase-down Steven and his raft.

They all appeared to be staying left, so I pulled out of the eddy and started rowing downstream. Joseph and Sophia were close behind. We caught up with the overturned raft about a quarter-mile downstream. Steven was hanging onto Krystal's kayak as she paddled toward the right side of the river. We all arrived at an eddy where we could tie-up and take a breather.

Steven flopped down in a flat area and lay on his back, still coughing-up river water.

Ray asked Jeremy, "What were you doing over there?"

He said, "After you guys pulled out, Steven goes, 'the left run looks like a good ride,' and I was like, 'yeah, it looks like a straight-through run,' and we, like, just decided to go that way, ya know?"

I bit my tongue.

"So, what happened?" Charlene asked.

Krystal said, "We got over to the left side, and it was like real gnarly 'n stuff, but we got past the big stuff, ya know, and like, we thought we had it made, but all of a sudden Steven turned like sideways and crashed into a boulder that stuck out from shore, and like, the raft just climbed up the rock and rolled over."

How many times in human history has mob mentality trumped good sense? Steven and Jeremy had to demonstrate their masculinity, and the plan went out the window. I'd lost track of how many flips we'd had on this trip.

Our first order of business was to turn the raft back over. When Steven was finally able to help, we made two unsuccessful attempts before finally getting the raft right-side-up. How many more times would this happen?

The right-hand oarlock was bent inward, and the oar was gone. Maybe we'd find it somewhere downstream. We replaced it with one of the spares from Ray's raft, leaving them each with one spare. We replaced the bent oarlock with the last remaining spare from the REO repair kit.

The flip and recovery had burned over an hour of time that we didn't have. We still had 23 miles to go, in order to reach our mileage objective for the day. Steven didn't want to row, so he rode with Joseph, and Ray resumed rowing his raft, now that Crystal Rapid was behind us. Sophia continued paddling Steven's Kayak.

The next four rapids were easy, and right around noon, I pulled ashore just above Emerald Rapid, not to scout it, but because Ray was struggling, and needed a rest. Joseph and Sophia took advantage of the stop to open their waterlogged dry bags and wring out their clothes and sleeping bags, while the rest of us made lunch.

Of course, there wasn't time for things to get dry, but at least the weight of the re-packed bags was reduced to that of a small dumpster. We easily ran Emerald Rapid, but had to scout Ruby and Serpentine. Everyone followed my line through them, and avoided any trouble.

Photo by Jerry Baysinger
The Ross Wheeler, a steel boat, was built in 1914 by legendary Grand Canyon boatman, Bert Loper.

But we still had to confront the fact that we didn't have time for off-river sightseeing. The subject came up when we arrived at the wreck of the Ross Wheeler, and Charlene insisted that we had to stop. We did, but I had to say something.

"It is 2:30, and we still have twelve miles to go today. The fact is, we just don't have time for this. We burned our sightseeing time with that flip at Crystal Rapid."

"So, like, I didn't do it on purpose, ya know," Steven protested.

"No, I'm sure you didn't," I agreed. "But it *was* your decision to ignore my advice and put your raft in a position to get flipped."

"Hey, like you don't know everything, man!" Steven argued.

I held up my hand. "Well, I know how to keep my raft right-side-up."

"Oh yeah, like you're so perfect!"

"I never claimed to be perfect. But I am the trip leader. Does someone else want to take over? Steven?"

When nobody spoke up, I softened my tone. "We can still enjoy this trip, but you're going to *have to* agree to run the rapids the way I suggest. It won't guarantee that you won't flip, but it'll greatly reduce the risk. You do that, and you'll get to Diamond Creek by 11:00 on Sunday."

A mile downstream, we came to Shinumo Creek, where we had to replenish our water supply.

Charlene was again reading her guidebook. "We need to go up to the waterfalls," she insisted.

I reminded her of our earlier conversation.

"But it's only a hundred yards to the falls. It's not like a long hike or anything," Charlene said. "It'll only take a few minutes."

Photo by Travis Mauk
Shinumo Creek Falls

Forty minutes, actually, by the time we got back on the river. It was 4:30 when we ran Walthenberg Rapid, and it was clear that Ray had reached his limit. We had a raft-load of wet gear to dry, so I decided to stop for the day at Upper Garnet camp.

I hated to do it, because we were still six miles short of our daily goal, which now increased to an average of 25. We got camp set up without much help from Ray or Steven, who were convalescing with beers. Joseph, Sophia, and Krystal got busy again spreading things out to dry. The tone was somber for Story Time that evening.

I said, "In the last four days, we've made a *total* of about forty miles. For the next four days, we're going to have to cover 25 miles *every single day*, in order to get you to Diamond Creek when you need to be there.

"That means long river days, so we'll *need* to get an early start. No more sleeping-in. We'll need to be out of camp by 9:00 every day, and that will require everyone's help.

"Most of the way will be easy rowing, with only a few tough rapids. But some of them are *really* tough ones. We can do this. But not if we keep

Photo by Travis Mauk

Photo by Travis Mauk
Elves Chasm is a charming oasis deep in the Grand Canyon

failing to make our daily mileage objective."

The morning went just about the same way as every other so far. We managed to get out of camp at 9:45, and only because a few of us did way more than an equal share of the work.

Around 10:30, Charlene asked, "Now, when are we going to get to Elves Chasm?"

I'd hoped to sneak past without stopping. We ended up spending an hour there, plus another thirty minutes for lunch. We had made only three of our twenty-five-mile goal.

"Oh, we have to see Blacktail Canyon! I've read so much about it!" begged Charlene.

I genuinely liked Charlene, but she was becoming a pain in the ass. I simply had to draw the line.

"With only four days left to go a hundred miles, we're simply going to have to skip some things we'd like to see."

Photo by JP Baysinger
Scouting Specter Rapid

We arrived at Specter Rapid at 1:30. After quickly scouting it, everyone had clean runs, and just a mile downstream, we arrived at Bedrock Rapid. Rated Class 7, this one can be challenging

We pulled over to the right bank to scout the rapid. A massive boulder stands in the center of the river. The safe route down the right-hand side is made difficult by a rock bar that extends two-thirds of the way out from the right bank, just where the current accelerates into the rapid. The main flow pushes strongly to the left of the boulder island.

From shore, it is impossible to see what happens if you go left, but it's nasty. To keep from going there, you have to start pulling very hard to the right, as soon as you clear the right-side rock bar, and keep pulling as the current drives you straight at the bedrock island. Most of the boats that successfully make it to the right channel get close enough to the bedrock to reach out and touch it.

Photo by JP Baysinger

Bedrock Rapid. It's a lot harder than it looks from shore!

Ray's rowing strength was still impaired, and he actually bumped the rock. Fortunately, he bounced off to the right. Many boats that kiss the rock end up broaching.

Making good time, we arrived Dubendorff Rapid at 3:30. Another Class 7 rapid, Dubendorff is very long and filled with rocks and holes to avoid. There's a big back-rolling wave that is hard to see and equally hard to avoid. at the bottom. I squeaked past it, but Joseph and Ray both drove headlong into it. Fortunately, they had enough momentum to carry them through with nothing more than a good wash-down.

We made eight more miles before Ray announced that he could go no further. I pulled-in to Keyhole Camp at Mile 140 a few minutes before 6:00. For only the second time on the trip, we'd reached our mileage objective.

Our dinner was a pretty easy one to prepare, which was good, because Joseph didn't even pretend to help his wife and cook team partner. He was back in the rocks somewhere, smoking pot with Steven and Jeremy. Charlene jumped in to help after she was finished making Ray comfortable.

By the time dinner and dishes were done, it was

Photo by JP Baysinger

Dubendorff Rapid

Photo by Jerry Baysinger
Matkatamiba Canyon

getting dark. There was no partying that night. It had been a successful day, but everyone was exhausted.

I sounded the wake-up call at 6:00, as soon as I was done with my morning ice chest ritual. Sophia and Charlene had breakfast ready by 7:00, and at 9:30, we pushed-off and started the day that should take us to within five miles of Lava Falls.

We covered eight miles in the next two hours, and at 11:30, I led the group into the eddy at the mouth of Matkatamiba Creek. "Matkat" is one of the compulsory stops on any Grand Canyon trip.

"Let's be ready to go in half an hour," I said as we started up the canyon. "Then, there's a big rapid that we'll have to scout before lunch."

Forty-five minutes later, we headed out toward Upset Rapid, two miles downstream. This one is notorious for flipping boats. Many people like the left side run for the very reason that I dislike it. It takes you perilously close to the gargantuan hole that flips boats.

Photo by JP Baysinger
Upset Rapid: Its name says it all.

Despite some grumbling from the millennials, I insisted on a right-side run, and everyone came out right-side-up. We stopped for lunch at the campsite known as Upset Hotel, a quarter-mile below Upset Rapid.

Back on the river at 1:30, with fifteen more miles to go, I pushed hard downstream—a task that was not made easier by a headwind that had come up.

We arrived at Havasu Creek, which is another mandatory stop. The canyon is spectacular, and people sometimes spend an entire day there. We spent an hour and a half there—about twice the time I suggested. At 3:45, we were again rowing downstream, needing to get to Tuckup Canyon camp, eight miles away.

Arriving there at 6:00 I was moderately surprised to find the camp open, because it is one of the more popular in this part of the river. We had dinner after dark.

When we had the kitchen all buttoned-up for the night, I poured myself a glass of Black Box Chardonnay, and offered to pour some for Ray and Charlene. Once we were comfortably settled-in, I broached the subject that had been on my mind all day.

Photo by Tamara Baysinger
Tying-up rafts in the mouth of Havasu Creek.

"Tomorrow, we're going to run Lava Falls. It's bigger and meaner than anything we've done so far. But it's the last really big rapid before Diamond Creek. You have only two days to get within five miles of Diamond, in order to get there Sunday morning. That means you have to go 28 miles tomorrow and the next day."

Ray said, "I guess that won't be so bad as long as the wind doesn't come up."

I continued for him, "and as long as we don't have to make a long rescue at Lava."

"Well, let's hope that won't be necessary."

"Right. But here's the thing. After Lava, you don't need me. I'm old, I'm tired, and I'm not having fun. I'm

Photo by Jerry Baysinger
We hiked about a mile up Havasu Creek

going to pull-up short tomorrow and let you and the others go the rest of the way to Diamond on your own."

"But…" Charlene stammered.

"There are only two rapids that you'll need to scout—205 and 209. Take them seriously, and you'll be fine. But no matter what, make sure you get your mileage in before you stop for the day. Just remember that you need to camp around Mile 220 Saturday night, in order to get to Diamond Creek by 11:00 Sunday"

Ray sighed. "Yeah, I guess I see your point. But if we split up, we won't have a stove."

I nodded. "I've been thinking about this for two days. Now that the beverage load is greatly reduced, you can make room for the SuperStove in the back of your raft. I'll take the coffee stove, and that'll be all I need."

"But what about the food?"

"I already have most of what I'll need, and I'll transfer everything that you'll need out of my cooler and dry box. I'll grab a few things, but nothing that'll change your meals for the rest of the way to Diamond."

I added, "I'll really miss your company, but I *have to* do this." That was half true.

"Well, we'll miss you too," Charlene said, "but I guess I understand."

What I did not say was how little I would miss the millennials. I felt like screaming every time I heard someone say the word "like."

In the morning, before anyone else was up, I sorted-out the supplies, so that we both would have what we needed. And I made room on Ray's raft for the SuperStove. Krystal and Steven had breakfast duty, but only Krystal managed to make it to the kitchen. I volunteered to help, in order to get breakfast before noon.

It was after 10:00 when we started the fifteen-mile run down to Lava Falls. A well-worn trail leads to a viewpoint above the rapid, on the right bank. I pointed out all of the major obstacles that had to be avoided, and then explained how we'd accomplish that. I

Photo by Jan Brandvold
The black basalt boulder called Vulcan's Anvil means Lava Falls is one mile ahead.

described what they'd see and experience as we approached the initial drop.

"The difference between a successful run and a flip is entering at exactly the right place."

I pointed at the submerged boulder called the Death Rock.

"Pass just to the right of that. Then push aggressively into the waves downstream. Hit them straight on and duck down, so you don't get blasted out of your seat. Now for the hard part. As you approach the entry, you will not be able to see it. And you'll be moving very fast—some people say close to thirty miles an hour. That's probably an exaggeration, but it's fast."

Photo by JP Baysinger
First look at Lava Falls is terrifying.

I pointed to a line of swirls in the otherwise smooth surface current in the last thirty yards before the initial drop."

"See how the line of swirls leads right down to the Death Rock? Treat it like the centerline on a highway. Stay within a few feet to the right of it. The current will be pulling you left, so you'll have to keep pulling to the right as you approach the first drop. If you pass within five feet of the Death Rock, you're golden."

At 2:00, I pushed off. The sense of anxiety was palpable. I silently repeated my plea to any god who would listen, *"Give me the skill, give me the strength, give me the focus—and if I need it, give me the luck."*

A good run at Lava Falls takes about twenty-five seconds. A bad run… Well, I still haven't had a bad run. I crashed through the last wave and looked back in time to see Ray hit the first drop in just the right spot. First the V-Wave and then the Kahuna Wave buried the raft, as they'd done to mine, and Ray got flushed out into calm water.

Photo by JP Baysinger
We watched a motor rig run Lava Falls just before it was our turn.

Joseph hit the drop a little too far to the right, and while that's a whole lot better than being too far to the left, it changed the angle of the V-Wave relative to his raft. The right side pitched upward, toppling Joseph overboard. But the raft stayed upright and careened down toward the Cheese Grater Rock at the foot of the rapid. Just when it looked like the raft was going to wash up onto the rock, it suddenly flushed off to the left and passed between the Kahuna Wave and the Cheese Grater, into the calm water.

Sophia had not seen Joseph go out of the raft, and started cheering loudly at the successful run. It was only when she turned to share the celebration with him that she realized that he wasn't there.

I picked up Joseph, while Ray corralled his raft in the big eddy on the right, just below the rapid. I rowed over and delivered Joseph to his raft. The kayaks came through in a close cluster, but the Kahuna Wave turned Jeremy sideways and pummeled him until he had to bail out.

Ray collected both the kayak and Jeremy. We all floated down through the next rapid, called Son of Lava, and pulled in at Tequila Beach, where we celebrated being "Alive after Lava" in the traditional fashion, with airline-sized bottles of tequila.

Photo by JP Baysinger
Looking back up at Lava Falls from Tequila Beach, enjoying the Alive After Lava feeling.

After some awkward good-byes, the group moved out, with another ten miles to go. I set up my chair and slowly nursed another little bottle of tequila. Eventually, I moved my raft to the upstream end of the beach, leaving the main camp open for a large group.

It dawned on me at this point, that I had become a whitewater criminal. I was willfully violating at least three laws. I had no fire pan, the only toilet I had was my contraband plastic ScatPacker, and I was not carrying a permit, because I'd separated from my group.

If anybody challenged me, I was prepared to say that I'd felt too sick to go on, and the others had to get to Diamond Creek. Come to think of it, that was pretty close to the truth. I actually *was* sick—I was sick of them.

I spent the rest of my day relaxing in the shade of a big golf umbrella, dozing off from time to time, and enjoying peaceful solitude. Eventually, I set up my mini-kitchen and made an easy dinner of canned chili. By then, a pair of motor rafts carrying two dozen people pulled in and occupied the lower part of the beach.

With a week's worth of food, I could get to Pearce Ferry without going hungry if I averaged fourteen miles a day—a very leisurely pace. I'd done this arithmetic before we split-up, and had asked Ray to call the shuttle service and tell them I'd be landing on June 12th. With all of the pressure off, I fell asleep early and slept late.

By sleeping late, I mean I woke up at 5:45, as usual, but stayed in bed for another half-hour. When I couldn't stand it anymore, I got up and went through my established morning routine. I was ready to go at 8:00.

Photo by JP Baysinger
The Lizard Lounge at 202 Mile Camp on our 2007 trip.

I stopped at Whitmore Wash and hiked up to see the pictographs on an overhanging ledge high above the river level. Oddly, right next to the red ochre Indian paintings, faded white capital letters spells out AUSTIN SURVEYORS. In the absence of specific information, I am guessing that this was painted in the 1950s, during the heyday of dam construction.

Ten miles further downstream, I hiked up Parashant Canyon, something that I hadn't done on my previous Grand Canyon trips. All of the guidebooks speak of a distinctive block of stone called "the Book of Worms," for the many worm burrows penetrating the soft, green shale.

In the middle of the afternoon, I stopped for the day at Upper 202 Camp, having floated about 22 miles. It was the first day on the trip without any rapids.

The next day was somewhat more eventful, with Kolb Rapid at mile 205 and

Photo by Jerry Baysinger
209 Mile Rapid and its huge back-curling wave.

Photo by Tamara Baysinger
Running *Vanguard* through Little Bastard Rapid in 2007.

Photo by JP Baysinger
Pumpkin Hot Spring is heavily polluted with arsenic and other minerals—it is not popular for soaking.

Photo by Jan Brandvold
The Diamond Creek takeout is a busy place every morning during the rafting season.

then 209 Mile Rapid, which I had warned Ray about before we split up. I scouted 209, because it has a fearsome-looking back-rolling wave in the main current.

Little Bastard Rapid, four miles downstream is a simple wave train—a fun mini-rollercoaster. Less than a mile later, I stopped and dipped my feet in Pumpkin Hot Spring, on the off-chance that its toxic waters might kill my toenail fungus. I'll let you know.

Having again traveled over 20 miles on the day, I picked the small campsite at Mile 223.4, two miles upstream from Diamond Creek. I would have gone on past Diamond Creek, but I wanted to be there in the morning to get some ice from one of the big motor rigs that would be taking out there. They nearly always have extra ice to give away.

Stopping to beg for ice can be tricky, because the Hualapai Nation owns the beach and may charge a predatory fee if they see your raft touch shore. It seems to be hit-and-miss, depending on the temperament of the lookout on duty. If someone walks toward you as you approach, just hang off-shore and explain your purpose in being there. That's what has worked for me. One final bit of advice: Do not try to bribe him with tequila. That will backfire every time.

Mornings at Diamond Creek are chaotic, so it felt good to get away, now carrying about fifty pounds of ice, an unknown number of Tecaté beers, and a variety of other leftovers from a motor trip that had left Lee's Ferry six days after us.

Over the next few days, I would have ample opportunity to think about all that went wrong in the prior two weeks. Since I'm writing this story, I get to affix all of the blame on the Millennials, but in reality, when a group slides into conflict, it is nearly always a failure of leadership.

It is clear in retrospect that the Millennials never accepted my role as trip leader. They had not been part of the decision made by Ray and Charlene, so they placed themselves under their own leadership, and dismissed my role as irrelevant.

Divided or ambiguous leadership can lead to disaster in outdoor adventures, and while it would be an exaggeration to say that what happened on our trip was a disaster, it certainly was unpleasant and uncomfortable for everyone involved.

The fact is, I'd never before found myself in a position where I needed to define my role on a river trip. On my commercial trips, the fact that the guides were the leaders was established at the time of booking. On my other private trips, my position as leader was inherent in the invitations I made to participants. In both of these cases, my role as trip leader did not have to be spelled-out. Everyone there already understood it.

But this trip was different. I was the outsider, and even though Ray and Charlene had specifically recruited me to lead the trip, the Millennials considered me to be just another participant, and an old grouchy one, at that.

So, I'll take the blame. I should have seen it at the outset and made my position clear in our very first meeting. But that doesn't mean they *weren't* self-absorbed, arrogant butts.

Chapter Fifteen

Diamond Down

Three miles downstream from Diamond Creek, I stopped at Travertine Canyon, where there is a waterfall in a cave. It's the best place in Grand Canyon to spend a hot day. But it's not Travertine Falls, which is another mile and a half downstream. I have no explanation for that.

I pulled-in at the scouting stop for Killer Fang Rapid at Mile 232, and had lunch before running the rapid. It's normally the last big rapid before the slack water of Lake Mead a few miles downstream.

But that's when Lake Mead is full. This time, I found two more good rapids, at Mile 237 and 239.5. These have emerged from the depths of Lake Mead because of the twenty-year drought in the Southwest. At Mile 242, the river begins a huge ninety-degree bend to the left.

Photo by Tamara Baysinger

The waterfall in a cave at Travertine Creek is one of the things you miss with a Diamond Creek takeout.

Photo by JP Baysinger
Killer Fang Rapid at Mile 232 is the last rapid in the canyon when Lake Mead is full.

Halfway through the bend, I found a nice campsite in a secluded cove on the right bank.

My plan for the rest of the trip was to get out of camp early each day, and row until the upstream wind started blowing, typically early in the afternoon. If I could make eight miles a day that way, I'd arrive at Pearce Ferry on September 12th, the day the shuttle service would have my pickup there.

In the morning, I got out of camp at 7:30, and covered three miles in my first hour, with the help of a strong current that continued past Spencer Canyon at Mile 246. Then, as the current slowed, I had to work harder to keep moving downstream.

The wind came up before noon, and I knew when I pulled ashore at Mile 249.6 that it was futile to try going any further that day. I'd run out of current, and the wind was relentless.

For the next thirty miles, I would be rowing on flat water. On my prior Grand Canyon trips, we'd brought along a little outboard motor for this part of the run. But my raft was not rigged in a way that allowed for a motor. Any sane person, which I do not claim to be, would wonder if the two wonderful days I'd spent getting to this point after passing Diamond Creek were worth the effort it was going to take to row the rest of the way to Pearce Ferry.

Photo by Jan Brandvold
Spencer Canyon at Mile 246 – Potentially nice campsite, but badly littered.

It depends entirely on your priorities. There's plenty to see and do in the first 20 miles below Diamond Creek. But the end of the current doesn't mean the end of scenery. And as long as the wind stays calm, it's a stress-free float

My second day on the flat water took me to Mile 257 before the wind started up. I find peace in the serenity of the canyon—except around Quartermaster Canyon, where the Hualapai Tribe runs helicopter tours from dawn to dark. There is no serenity there.

The next day, I ended up camping at Mile 265, in the heart of the helicopter zone, and flights went past at five-minute intervals all day. I guess that's how you respect the natural environment and protect Mother Earth. The National Park Service prohibits such flights within the park boundaries, but has no authority over tribal lands.

Photo by Jan Brandvold
Mile 249.6 Camp at low water

Throughout much of my last full day on the river, my 19th since leaving Lees Ferry, I rowed through a gulch in the freshly cut channel through the silt that had accumulated on the bottom of Lake Mead between 1935 and 2005. In places, the dry silt cliffs were thirty feet tall. From time to time, chunks would break loose and crash into the river in a cloud of dust.

The phenomenon was both fascinating and oppressing. I was a prisoner between the silt cliffs, and couldn't step ashore for any reason. But as the canyon widened out, so did the river corridor, and I entered an area with actual beaches. I picked one on the left at Mile 273.5 for my last river camp.

Longstanding tradition calls for a celebration of

Photo by JP Baysinger
Looking up at Sky Walk (center of photo) where people pay a lot of money to walk on a glass floor hanging out over the canyon rim.

Photo by Jan Brandvold

With low water in Lake Mead, the river is cutting through a 75-year accumulation of silt, at this point about 30 feet deep.

some kind in your last camp on a river trip. But how do you have a one-person party? I spent the afternoon and evening in quiet relaxation, and consumed a discreet quantity of Bushmill's Irish whiskey.

My 20th float day would take me six miles to Pearce Ferry and the end of my Grand Canyon journey. As I rowed those last miles, I had plenty of time to reflect on the adventure. I had made the right decision when I split away from Ray and the millennials.

The drama and trauma of leading such a fractious group had stolen much of the joy from that part of the trip. Early on, I'd thought that Ray and Charlene would be good candidates for future Clan trips. They're nice folks, always ready to pitch-in and do more than their share of the work, and Ray was a competent boatman. But when things started turning sour with the millennials, Charlene was far too willing to cover for them, and that led to some tension between us.

Maybe, after some of the bad feelings become blunted by time, I could consider inviting them on one of my trips, but there is no way I will *ever* do any kind of a trip with any of the millennials. Steven and Jeremy were just plain lazy, and Joseph was far too willing to follow their lead. And his mother simply enabled him.

As for the two girls, they were always willing to do their share of the work in the kitchen—plus their husbands' share as well. So, I felt no particular malice toward them. And their presence on the trip *did* provide some actual entertainment.

And I'm not talking about their singing. As tone-deaf as I am, I could still feel the abrasion of their inability to sing on key. Nor was it their conversation, samples of which I have already included, and which accurately represent their tenuous grasp on the principles of communication.

No, their greatest contribution was turning shower-time into a public spectacle. None of the millennials had a trace of modesty. That's an observation, not a criticism. While I successfully managed to avoid the permanent trauma of seeing any of the guys taking their showers, Krystal had caught me off guard in our second camp on the river, and that set the tone for the rest of the trip.

In most river camps, the shower tripod is set up in a location that is discretely out of sight of the main seating area. But for reasons only they knew, the millennials adopted a habit of setting up theirs between the Lizard Lounge and the river, in full view, even when not forced to by the terrain, as I had been back in our Roaring Twenties camp.

Photo by Jan Brandvold

The bathtub ring shows how much Lake Mead has dropped.

There is nothing new about nudity on raft trips. Back in the 1970s, when I was first getting into rafting, there was a fairly large constituency within the whitewater community who believed that getting naked was part of the sport. I suppose it was an extension of the whole "getting away" mentality. Anyway, it was a near-certainty that you'd come across bare-ass people at some point during every river trip. It appears that we've now come full circle.

To be clear, I did not make a habit of leering at Krystal and Sophia when they took their very public showers. On the other hand, I didn't work too hard at *not* seeing what they gleefully displayed.

So, it would be unfair to not acknowledge the morale-boosting contribution the girls made. But, as entertaining as these moments of social enlightenment were, they still were not, by themselves, reason for even thinking about inviting them on any future raft trip.

The fundamental problem, aside from the implied inclusion of their worthless husbands in any such invitation, was that, based on everything

they said during the Grand Canyon trip, Krystal and Sophia combined had the I.Q. of a rutabaga.

I reveled in my leisurely pace as I drifted downstream, and I arrived at the Pearce Ferry landing at 2:30 on June 12. my first order of business was to get my raft onto its trailer. The boat landing was in decent condition, and I was able to back the trailer partway into the water, so, with the help of the power winch, I managed the takeout quickly, without having to beg for help from bystanders.

Photos by Jan Brandvold
Fresh Cinnamon rolls for breakfast

Chapter Sixteen

Grand Canyon to Grande Ronde

Once away from Pearce Ferry, the temperature soared well into triple-digits, and it was too hot to even consider trying to camp-out in the back of my pickup. I got a motel room in Boulder and made good use of running water, air conditioning, and WiFi.

While catching up on emails and Facebook, I was saddened to learn that the Galice Store had burned to the ground a few days earlier. Galice Resort had taken care of my vehicle shuttle for my very first Rogue River trip, and over the years, they'd done over a hundred shuttles for me. I got to know the owners, Gil and Marilou Thomason and their daughter Debbie, who currently runs the business. Sadly, they will not be able to rebuild the structure.

Photo by Author

The sad fate of a landmark on the Rogue River. I can't count the number of times I sat at a table in front of that stone fireplace for a pre-trip breakfast.

During the rest of my three-day drive home, I had plenty of time to consider what to do next. My Whitewater Summer idea was alive, and if anything, was more appealing than ever. I'd been rafting almost continuously for seven weeks. And after relieving myself of the stress of leading Ray's group, I felt healthier and more energized than at any time in recent memory. And, by the way, Kevin had just reached the halfway point at milepost 1,321 on the Pacific Crest Trail.

The Grande Ronde River, in Northeast Oregon is one of the very few rivers where you can still go rafting whenever you want to, without the need to pay a tax or get the government's permission. Five years from now, none of that is likely to be true, but for now, the Grande Ronde is a river of last resort for permit lottery losers.

By the time I got home from Grand Canyon, my plan was pretty well set. I went out to Ray's place to retrieve my Futility Box and SuperStove, and he told me about the group's last three days on the river. They'd done fine on the day we split up below Lava Falls, and had made it to Whitmore Wash at Mile 188. They'd planned to get to Mile 220 the next day, but Steven, rowing Joseph's raft, flipped at 209 Mile Rapid.

Then, they were unable to flip the raft upright until a guided group stopped and helped. So, they managed to get only to Mile 213, leaving twelve miles to Diamond Creek. With a 9:00 start, they still could meet Canyon REO at 11:00, as they had promised to do.

But they didn't get out of camp until 10:00, so it was close to 1:00 when they finally got there, and the outfitter was not happy. And those in the group who had plane tickets out of Las Vegas could not get to the airport in time, and had to re-schedule their flights. I was very glad that I hadn't been involved.

In preparing for my Grande Ronde trip, the first thing I had to do was decide which raft to take. Either one would work, and I argued back and forth before finally deciding that *Miwok* was the better choice. I did the big shuffle and got *Vanguard* into the garage and *Miwok* onto the trailer.

I re-rigged *Miwok* the way it had been for the John Day, and added my new Eagle Peak Day Tripper pop-up canopy, which had been delivered while I was in Grand Canyon. I tried it out on the driveway and confirmed that it satisfied the two primary requirements: It was quick and fairly easy for one person to set-up; and its size was adequate for my solo kitchen. And it actually packed down to about the same size as the big Moss Parawing.

Photo by Sabrina Luboch
At Minam State Park, ready to start downstream.

Linda was very helpful throughout all of my trip preparations, offering various suggestions as to how much I could get for all of this equipment in a big garage sale. About this time, I laid out my plan to keep rafting one river after another in my endless summer of whitewater.

"When I first started rafting, I conjured a fantasy about spending an entire summer rafting one river after another. Of course, it was totally unrealistic, since I didn't have the gear or the skill to do such a thing, and there was no way I could be off work that long."

Linda said, "So, now you have the equipment and you don't have a job, and you want to live-out your youthful fantasy."

She somehow made that sound like a bad thing.

"This is the first time I've ever had the realistic opportunity to actually do it."

"Realistic? What's realistic about doing this at *your* age?"

"The thing that matters is my *condition*, not my age. I may be in better shape right now than I was twenty-five years ago."

"Have you looked in a mirror lately?"

"Yep. And I've stood on the bathroom scales, too. I've just finished eight weeks of almost continuous rafting, and I'm stronger now than when I started."

"That may be, but what if you get injured, or have a heart attack? How're you going to get help?"

"I'm not alone of the river. There'll always be other rafts coming down the river. And I have my GPS messenger. I can press the red button and summon help whenever and wherever I need it."

"And how long will it take for someone to get to where you are?"

"You didn't worry about that when we went to Machu Picchu or Galapagos. I think that real medical help was a lot further away there than it is where I'm rafting. But in any case, it's a risk that I've always been willing to take."

"You've never been seventy-five years old before."

Photo by Sabrina Luboch
The big red boulder at House Rock Rapid

The logic had gone full circle. In the end, we made a friendly wager on whether or not I could actually do the entire thing, and I resumed preparing for the adventure.

I emptied my library box of all nature guides, geology books, and rocket box reading materials, and re-packed it with guidebooks and maps for the Grande Ronde, Selway, Middle Fork, Main Salmon, Lower Salmon, Snake, and Deschutes. Running all of those rivers might take until the end of August.

One of the last things I did before leaving was check the internet for any permits for the lottery rivers available through cancellations. It was an extreme longshot, with the predictable outcome.

On the nineteenth of June, I got up early and hit the road with a box of donuts and a thermos of coffee, for the six-hour drive to Minam, Oregon. Arriving there in mid-afternoon, I launched my raft next to the bridge over the Wallowa River.

Those who make this run will find that the ten miles on the Wallowa are the most challenging part of the entire trip. It isn't difficult, but it is fairly busy, with fast current and lots of maneuvering to avoid the many obstacles. It's great fun, but is not without hazard. Two weeks earlier, a boater had flipped his raft just a mile downstream from Minam. His three passengers managed to get safely to shore, but he did not.

After making my shuttle arrangements at the Minam Store, I walked back to my raft and pushed off. I stopped at Minam State Park just downstream, to fill my water jugs, and then floated a couple of miles further downstream, where I found a small flat place to camp for the night.

The thing that makes this run unique is the paradox of the river's relatively steep gradient and the nearly total lack of big rapids. The Grande Ronde and Wallowa rivers lack the pool-and-drop character that most rivers have, and instead runs at a steady gradient for almost the entire length of the run—ten miles on the Wallowa River and eighty-two on the Grande Ronde, assuming that you float all the way to the confluence with the Snake.

Most people don't. The last twenty-five miles, after passing under the Highway 129 bridge, features a lot of No Trespassing signs and thus a

Photo by Sabrina Luboch
In the rapid below Blind Falls

shortage of attractive campsites, very little shade, unspectacular scenery, and only two significant rapids. But those two are fun, and in my mind, make the extended run worthwhile.

Like most of the rivers in Eastern Oregon, the Grande Ronde is very seasonal. Most years, it gets too low for desirable rafting by the middle of July. So, launching on June 19 in a year with above average snowpack, I was in the prime rafting season.

On all of my past trips, I've found it astoundingly easy to make twenty miles in a short day on the river. In fact, the challenge has been to slow down enough to enjoy the scenery. I've even toyed with the idea of taking up fishing.

But then I came to my senses and decided to spend my extensive leisure time on this trip writing about my adventures thus far on my Whitewater Summer. Right away, I discovered how much there was to remember. Good memory exercise.

I had my laptop along, and I had the ability to run it on an inverter connected to my garden tractor battery, which I kept charged with a solar panel. This gave me something constructive to do with my leisure time, and didn't require the physical effort of taking long hikes away from the river.

Photo by Sabrina Luboch
The forest thins out as you approach Troy.

My first full day on this trip started six miles upstream from the Wallowa River's confluence with the Grand Ronde. It took barely an hour to cover those six miles. At the confluence, it's often difficult to tell which river is larger.

I found a nice beach for a lunch stop at about 1:00. Since I'd already floated fifteen miles that day, I decided to set up camp and stay for the night. I put my chair in a shady spot with a

Photo by Jerry Baysinger
I know of two really nice campsites in the lower canyon. And I'm not telling where they are.

nice view of the river, and spent the afternoon writing the first two chapters of this story. I saw only two parties go by that afternoon, and both were groups I'd seen earlier in the day in the Sheep Creek area, where they'd spent the previous night.

Photo by Jerry Baysinger
The best place to be on a hot afternoon

In the evening, I took a few minutes to review my notes from prior Grande Ronde trips. There is a long stretch between River Miles 60 and 37, where there are no desirable campsites. So, in order to set up to run that stretch in one comfortable day, my next camp would have to be in the area around River Mile 58-60.

A comment: On some rivers—most notably, the Colorado—the river is measured in "trip miles," starting at the launch site and counting upward. On most rivers in the Northwest, the convention is to use "river miles," which count upward from the river's mouth. So, on the Grande Ronde, your position based on river miles is a declining number as you go downstream.

I ran Martin's Misery and Grey's Rapid, both rated Class III in the morning of my second float day, enjoying the scenery and sunshine. With only a thirteen-mile run that day, I easily reached my destination camp in time for lunch.

I again checked my river notes, and confirmed that my next chance to camp without a road next to the river would be over twenty miles downstream. At the speed I was going, that would take four hours. But I knew that the river slows considerably in that stretch, so five or six hours was a better estimate.

The obvious decision was to camp where I was, and start the 20-mile run in the morning. I again passed the afternoon on the keyboard, and while I was writing about my preparations for the big Grand Canyon trip, I noticed that clouds were forming over the canyon.

When I started hearing distant thunder, I decided that it was time to set up my tent and new pop-up kitchen shelter. Just about the time I was finished preparing for rain, the sky cleared-off and the threat was over, thus reinforcing my theory about the perversity of nature.

Two hours after leaving camp, I entered my least favorite part of this river. For the rest of the day, a road ran close alongside the river. The town of Troy is now mostly abandoned, and all businesses are closed and boarded-up. You can't even get a drink of water in Troy, because the town's water supply is contaminated.

In the last two miles of that day's float, I crossed the Oregon-Washington state line three times, as the river makes two sweeping horseshoe bends. Since the road crosses the neck of the second bend, there's a mile-long roadless stretch, and that's where I stopped at a pretty decent little campsite, having floated 22 miles.

Photo by Jerry Baysinger
The lower chute at The Narrows

By then, I was seeing the formation of another afternoon thunderstorm, so I again set-up my shelter and tent. But this time, the leading edge of the storm passed directly through my location, with gusty winds and heavy rain. I had the pop-up pretty well anchored before the wind came up, and it stood up to the gusts all right. But as small as the canopy is, the wind brought in quite a bit of rain, and I started to believe that the critics had been right that the canopy was too small.

I was able to mitigate the rain intrusion by lowering the height of the canopy to about five feet—too low to do anything except sit in my chair, but at least it kept me dry. The wind abated after ten or fifteen minutes, and from then on, the canopy did a good job of keeping my thirty-six square-foot patch of ground dry.

Photo by Sabrina Luboch
Bridge Rapid—the last big rapid on the river. On the Grande Ronde the biggest rapids are all in the first ten miles and the last ten miles.

Rain continued into the evening, while I finished the story of my Owyhee trip. Sometime during the night, I got up and found a full canopy of stars overhead. My tent was still damp when I got up, but it didn't matter, because I'd already decided to do a layover.

The river re-joins the road half a mile below my campsite, and stays close to the road all the way to Boggan's Oasis at River Mile 26.3, where Highway 129 crosses. At Boggan's, I stopped to fill my water jugs and enjoy a giant ice cream cone. Back on the river, I floated for an hour and a half to a nice campsite at an undisclosed location.

My last full day on the Grande Ronde was uninspiring for the first thirteen miles. But that all changes at River Mile 4.5, where I walked down and scouted The Narrows. Most maps call it Class IV, but it varies with water level. There are two drops. The first is a narrow, long chute with large standing waves. The second drop follows a hundred yards of calm water, and features a single heavy drop. A left of center approach funneled me smoothly through the rapid.

There's one last rapid, around River Mile 3. It is a long wave train down the right side and under a bridge. A mile and a half later, I came to a campsite on the right bank. It's actually a car camp, but I've never actually encountered car campers there. The main attraction to the camp is that it gives you an easy run to Heller Bar for an early takeout in the morning.

Photo by Sabrina Luboch
Heller Bar is always a busy place.

It was Saturday morning, and the boat ramp was already busy when I arrived there at 8:30. I had to wait in line behind three jet boats that were launching, but when my turn came, I trailered the raft and cleared the ramp in five minutes. On the way to Clarkston, I stopped in Asotin to clean-out my toilet bucket at the Scat Machine, which was designed and built by a former river guide who, along with his wife had worked for me when I had my whitewater business.

Arriving in Clarkston before noon, I located a laundromat, and while I washed a load of river clothes, I used their WiFi to find a shuttle service that served Selway River boaters. By the

Photo by Sabrina Luboch
The last stop on every river trip is the Scat Machine—an automatic dishwasher for portable toilets.

time my clothes were dry, it was late enough to get a room at a nearby Motel 6.

On Sunday, I went shopping for ice and groceries for the next segment of my Whitewater Summer. Driving toward Lolo Pass, I found a Forest Service campground along the Lochsa River, next to US-12.

Chapter Seventeen

Selway Outlaw

Before leaving Clarkston, I'd used the motel WiFi to make a perfunctory check for a Selway River float permit. That miniscule possibility produced a strikeout and left me with only two options: go home, or run the river without a permit. My decision was already made.

The Selway is the most tightly controlled river in the nation. Only seven parties are allowed to launch each week during the short rafting season, and three of them are reserved for outfitters. In the private permit lottery, there are at least a thousand entries for each permit.

So, the question of the day was could I get away with running the river without a permit. The only time I'd floated the Selway was in 1993. During that five-day trip, we never saw a Forest Service official on the river. And there had been no official at the launch site to confirm that we had a permit (which we did). If those two things held true, I'd have no trouble. And yes, that's a pretty big "if."

One final possibility was finding a group with a permit, and talking them into letting me tag along. Over the years, I've been approached several times by strangers at launch sites, asking if I'd let them join my group. Most of these

Photo submitted by Tamara Baysinger
Selway River—steep, fast, and challenging at all levels, rocky and tight at lower levels.

permit parasites have been kayakers. A few haven't even had boats. I've never yet met one I wanted to take along. But if I found anyone at the put-in who might be open to accommodating a parasite, I'd ask the question.

My drive over Lolo Pass and up the Bitterroot Valley to the town of Conner took until early-afternoon. I found the shuttle service and made arrangements to have my rig delivered to the takeout at Selway Falls on July 4. Then I drove up and over Nez Perce Pass and down into the Selway River Canyon.

I spent the night in the Forest Service campground at Indian Creek, a few miles away from the launch site at Whitecap Creek. There is a nice campground at Whitecap Creek, but I wanted to minimize the possibility of having an encounter with any official there—the criminal mind is always at work and always paranoid.

Photo submitted by Tamara Baysinger
A law-abiding group on the Selway

In the morning, I made a quick breakfast before driving to Whitecap Creek, where I found a private group rigging their rafts. They appeared to be nearly ready to depart, so I stopped to watch. When the opportunity arose, I asked if they'd let me attach myself to their group. But despite the laundry list of wonderful things I'd have added to their adventure, they declined. So much for the parasite theory.

After they left, I slid my raft down the steep log ramp to the gravel beach, and then moved my rig to the parking area, where the shuttle service would find it later in the day.

My total time at the launch site was about thirty minutes, during which I was as nervous as a short nun on a penguin hunt. I relaxed only after pushing off and floating around the first bend, out of sight of any official who might happen by the launch ramp.

My criminal enterprise began in fast-moving, crystal-clear water, and within twenty minutes, I was a mile and a half downstream. I pulled into an eddy, where I poured a cup of coffee from my small thermos and took care of a couple of donuts left over from my driving rations. I hung around long enough to let the group out front get far downstream, so that I wouldn't overrun them.

At 3,000 cubic feet per second, the river flow was less than half of what I'd experienced on my first Selway trip. That meant a lot more rock-dodging, but it also meant that the current was slower and I'd have more time to maneuver the raft through the narrow chutes.

Most of the first four miles was easy floating, with a steady current and occasional shallow, rocky riffles. Slalom Slide was vastly different from what I recalled from 1993, when it was a tumultuous quarter-mile ride through a boulder-studded flume. This time, all of the rocks were exposed, making for a very busy run.

Photo submitted by Tamara Baysinger
Washer Woman Rapid—Good, clean fun.

There were three short rapids in the next mile and a half, and after running them, I started looking for a camping beach, even though it was barely past noon. My purpose in pulling up short was to put myself out of sync with groups in front and behind me. I found a small campsite on the left bank, just above the rapid called Holy Smokes.

My second day as the Selway Outlaw took me under the Running Creek pack bridge, where I passed beneath a string of mules hauling loads of lumber. Shortly after that, I came to Goat Creek Rapid, a long, steep, boulder-choked rapid that demands a lot of maneuvering—and provides lots of action and fun.

By mid-afternoon, I had floated thirteen miles, and I knew that I was approaching Rattlesnake Bar, which is a large and very popular campsite. Thinking that I might encounter the group ahead of me there, I decided to stop at a beach called Dead Elk Camp, below Pettibone Creek.

I hadn't yet seen another party on the river, but I'd seen several light planes flying over. That's hardly a surprise,

Photo submitted by Tamara Baysinger
The photos in this chapter were taken on a 2016 trip. That's Tamara Baysinger in the IK.

since there are airstrips at lodges and guard stations all along the river. I'd passed at least four already.

What worried me was the possibility that there might be river police in one of those planes, looking for outlaws, in which case, they'd spot me and dispatch SEAL Team Six to hunt me down like they had Osama Bin Laden. Putting my criminal mind to work, I made a point of moving to a landing spot where my raft might be somewhat concealed by overhanging trees, and selected a well-sheltered place for my camp.

On the river early the next day, I'd gone only a couple of miles when I came around a sweeping left bend and spotted a group of rafts beached on the right bank. It probably was the group I'd seen at the launch ramp, but I wasn't sure. So much for my criminal mastermind theory. They waved as I floated past, so now there were witnesses.

But they were still eating breakfast and showed no signs of being in any kind of rush to get out of camp, so maybe they were doing a layover. Either way, I figured I'd seen the last of them. Two miles further downstream, I came to a series of rapids that starts with a Class II, followed by a Class III, climaxed by Class IV Ham Rapid.

Photo submitted by Tamara Baysinger
This place is called The Shallows.

On my previous trip, we'd spent over an hour scrambling downstream on the steep left side of the canyon scouting Ham Rapid and the two lesser rapids leading into it. It was a particularly treacherous hike, and along the way I sprained my ankle. I knew better than to do that again. And the situation was different. On that trip, the rapids all ran together, with only a momentary respite between them. This time, there were pools of calm water that afforded the opportunity to stop if the route ahead was unclear.

I made it easily through the first two rapids, but looking ahead at Ham Rapid, I decided I'd better take a look before going into it. On my 1993 trip, I'd hugged the left bank and gave wide berth to the truck-sized midstream boulder. This time, the far-left route was blocked, so I ran the chute close to the left side of the rock.

In the three miles between Ham Rapid and Moose Creek, there are eight rapids, all rated Class II. They are spaced nicely, and just challenging enough to keep things interesting. I passed beneath the Tony Point pack bridge, marking the entry to Moose Creek Canyon, which is the most challenging part of the Selway River.

I cannot overstate how different the river was from the way it had been on my 1993 trip, when the current raced through Moose Creek Canyon, barely slowing between the individual rapids. This time, shallow riffles alternated with flat pools for the first mile, leading to Double Drop—an abrupt Class IV plunge followed immediately by a Class III drop.

Photo submitted by Tamara Baysinger
Preparing to leave Rattlesnake Bar.

The passable route was well defined and clearly visible, but the two drops were narrow and very steep. I squeezed the *Miwok* through the chutes, concluding that my *Vanguard* would not have fit. Double Drop is followed by another quarter-mile of riffles and pools, ending at Wapoots Rapid.

I stopped and scouted Wapoots, because this is where a long afternoon of mishaps began during my first trip. This time, I found a long rock festival that could be navigated with a careful entry and few good eddy-turns.

In '93, it was river-wide chaos. In the lead, I made a clean run, but our boats had become spread out in the flume-like rush of current after Double Drop. By the time I was through Wapoots, some of the boatmen behind me were too far back to see exactly where I'd gone, and they were counting on following my lead.

200 yards ahead was Ladle Rapid, which had to be scouted. I pulled to the right bank and waved for the rafts behind me to come in. That's when I saw the boatman—a helicopter pilot nicknamed Chopper—get dump-trucked out of his raft. The current was so swift that he was going to be in Ladle Rapid before I could possibly get out there to help. His only chance was to get back aboard and somehow make a controlled run without scouting. He made a couple of attempts to boost himself back in, but then lost his grip on the raft's lifeline.

I scrambled up the bank to a vantage point, and watched as raft and swimmer were swept directly into the heart of the maelstrom, first brushing past a tall, menacing boulder shrouded in a heavy veil of white water, and then tumbling into a bottomless hole of smoking foam. The raft crested the next wave, still right-side-up, but the swimmer had vanished.

Tense moments passed before the raft cleared the end of the rapid. Seconds later, Chopper's bright orange lifejacket came back into view. He was swimming, but was far from safety. The water was paralyzingly cold, and hypothermia would rob him of strength within minutes.

I told the rest of the group to stay there, as I hopped into my raft and gave chase. I'd just watched the small raft go down the center of the rapid without benefit of an oarsman, so surely, I could take my fifteen-foot *Cheyenne* down the same way. It was a terrifying run, but I got through unscathed and caught up with the exhausted swimmer a quarter-mile beyond, at the foot of another Class IV rapid called Little Niagara.

In 2021, as I stood on the scouting beach alongside Ladle Rapid, all I could see was rock. An impenetrable wall of boulders blocked the route I'd taken on my earlier trip, leaving only a far-right-side run open. I ran the *Miwok* through the tight maze, again appreciating my decision to use the smaller raft.

Back in '93, after picking up Chopper, I rowed across the river, left him with my raft and hurried back up the mule trail to the rest of the group. A couple of them decided to walk around the two big rapids, so we shuffled oarsmen and I took over *Mariah* to lead everyone down the right-side run. Unfortunately, I swamped *Mariah*—which was not a self-bailer—so, when I arrived where *Cheyenne* was tied-up, I was unable to muscle the heavy slug to shore.

I shouted for everyone to wait there, and went another half-mile downstream before I managed to find calm water where I could get to shore. By then, I'd punctured half a dozen holes in *Mariah's* floor by scraping over rocks that I was unable to avoid with the swamped raft.

After tying-up, I hiked back up the mule trail to the rest of my group, who had worked out a plan to recover Chopper's raft, which was sitting on a rock bar in the middle of the river at the head of the next rapid. Another member of our group suggested that if I would row his raft out to the rock bar, he could recover the raft. After I let him out, he gave me a shove back into the current, and then waded over to Chopper's raft, which was undamaged, with its oars still in the oarlocks. He pushed it off the rocks, climbed in, and rowed down to where I'd tied-up next to *Mariah*.

Once again, I hurried up the mule trail, this time to get *Cheyenne*, and along the way, I passed Chopper and another member of the party, who were not interested in doing any more rafting that day. I led the rest of the group down to where the three rafts were tied up. By the time we all got back together, it was about 8:00, and we urgently needed to find the campsite that we knew was close downstream.

Chopper still didn't want to row, so we left his raft there, to retrieve the next day. With three people hiking and the rest of us rowing, we ventured into the twilight. We soon discovered that our map was wrong. It showed the campsite *before* the rapid called Miranda Jane, but actually, it was *after* it. We arrived at the rapid wondering how we'd missed the campsite. But there was nothing to do but run the rapid.

All of my hiking, jogging, and rock-scrambling had severely aggravated the ankle I'd sprained that morning, and even my uninjured ankle was aching badly. That's why I let the less experienced boaters scout the rapid. The result was that the medical doctor rowing a red *Pioneer* led the way directly into a wide hole, which easily flipped his raft.

I was close behind, but saw the hole in time to miss the worst of it, so I went after the two swimmers from the flipped raft. They were able to get hold of their raft, and my passenger was able to grab its bow line, so I pulled them to shore. We righted the raft, and in near darkness ventured downstream to find the hikers, and fortunately, a place to camp.

That was a difficult day. My current trip was a lot less traumatic. After squeezing down Ladle Rapid, I approached Little Niagara, recalling that the clean chute was on the right-hand side. That hadn't changed with the lower water, and I ran it without scouting.

More shallows and pools separated the next three rapids, Puzzle Creek, No Slouch, and Miranda Jane. I stopped at the sand beach where our group and done a layover day after all of the drama in Moose Creek Canyon. From there, we had hiked back up and retrieved Chopper's raft.

I was tempted to stay, and maybe reprise my hike back up the trail, but it was a large camp, and I felt it would be better to leave it open for a large group. Like most other criminals I wanted to keep a low profile. I went on down to Osprey Rapid, which I scouted carefully before running, and then stopped at a small camp at Meeker Creek, shortly below the rapid. It had been a busy and satisfying day.

The idea of doing a layover at this camp was very appealing, and my schedule anticipated doing a layover. But there was a problem. As long as I was on the river, everyone behind me would be moving at the same speed I was. But if I stopped for a layover, I'd almost certainly be overtaken by at least one or two groups, and it was possible that a Forest Service patrol boat might also come through. I couldn't risk a layover in plain sight.

It's easy to lose track of the calendar on a long raft trip, and I'd been rafting almost continuously for over two months. So, I had to double-check what day it was—July 2. I wish I'd thought this whole thing through before I made my shuttle arrangements, because without a layover, I was going to arrive at the takeout a day before my pickup. One way or another, I had a day to burn.

A plane flew up the river at a surprisingly low altitude while I was eating breakfast the next day. I didn't see any markings that might hint at it being an official aircraft, but then again, I had no idea what such markings would be. If it was the river police, they had me dead to rights.

With my habitual early start, I passed Tango Bar half a mile downstream from Meeker Creek at 8:45. A good-sized commercial group was camped there, and it looked like they were just finishing breakfast. I floated past with the front of my raft pointed the other way so that the absence of a permit tag would not be conspicuous. The cunning criminal mind is always working.

Another pack bridge crosses the river at Mink Creek, and I half expected to see the National Guard, or some other armed force, there to nab me, but I got by clean. Shortly after that, I ran Class III Three Lynx Rapid, and at 10:00 I arrived at the wide pool above Wolf Creek Rapid, which many people consider the toughest rapid on the entire run.

Photo submitted by Tamara Baysinger
Wolf Creek Rapid—Challenging at lower water, Intimidating at higher water.

Scouting Wolf Creek takes you up the pack trail to a viewpoint fifty feet above the rapid. There is no "sneak route" in Wolf Creek Rapid. The whole left side of the river is choked with boulders, leaving only the main chute along the base of the cliff. The approach to that chute is obstructed by boulders and holes, so you have to start well away from shore, and then pull quickly to the right once clear of the obstacles. From there, you ride through semi-violent waves, staying off the ragged wall on the right, and then avoid the massive hole on the left at the foot of the rapid.

It's a boater's dream if all goes well, but could be a nightmare if you screw it up. On my 1993 trip, my group was still gun-shy from our adventures in Moose Creek Canyon, but everyone performed well at Wolf Creek and came out right-side-up and dry. My run this time was also without trauma.

At 11:30, I stopped and scouted Tee Kem Falls, where the river makes an abrupt left turn and drops over a ledge in a narrow, steep chute. I stopped below the rapid for a quick lunch, and then proceeded through two easy Class II rapids in the next mile. Two miles of basically flat water took me past Otter Creek on the left, and then I found a huge gravel bar on the right, separated from shore by a narrow, shallow channel, technically making the bar an island.

At the foot of the "island," a deep cove offered a place to get out of view. I rowed thirty yards up the back side of the island, and then got out and pushed my raft another thirty yards to a spot where a row of brush would conceal it from anyone not in an airplane. And there I finished writing about my John Day trip and started the long story about my Grand Canyon float.

But my Selway adventure wasn't quite over. In the early evening, another low-flying airplane went overhead on its way upriver. Up until then, I'd planned on doing a layover in my little outlaw's cove. Now I had to consider the possibility that a river patrol boat coming downstream might have been tipped-off about my hideout.

Photo submitted by Tamara Baysinger
Finding the best chute at Wolf Creek Rapid

If I got caught there, I would be in clear violation of the permit law. But if I went on down to the takeout and pulled my raft out of the river, I was nearly certain to encounter the authorities, but it wouldn't matter, because once my raft was out of the water, I wouldn't be breaking any law.

Taking no chances, I got out of camp at 7:00 and rowed the three miles down to Race Creek, past the Forest Service campground, to a sandy beach within sight of the big parking lot and takeout area. I jogged down and checked to see if my rig had been shuttled early, but as expected, it wasn't there. So, I went back and started de-rigging my raft, stacking everything next to a row of large rocks that blocked anyone from driving off the road down onto the beach.

Once I had the raft stripped down to the bare frame, I was able to drag it out of the water and up next to my pile of gear. And that's where I spent the rest of the day.

In the middle of the afternoon, while I was sipping wine and typing my rafting memoir, I was approached by a man and woman in Forest Service uniforms.

After the customary "how's your day" small talk, the lady asked, "Did you just float the river?"

Instead of answering the question, I said, "I'm just enjoying the afternoon here on the beach."

Pointing at my raft and pile of equipment, she said, "That's a nice-looking setup. How was your trip?"

Again, I evaded the question. "Thanks."

"Do you have a permit for floating the river?"

"I didn't know I needed a permit to camp here."

"Are you saying that you *didn't* float the river?" she pressed.

"I'm saying that I'm just sitting here drinking wine and enjoying the view."

"You don't need a whitewater raft to do that."

"I thought I might row across and see if there are any fish over there in the shade," I explained.

The man spoke for the first time, "Sir. Do you expect us to believe that?"

As innocently as I could make it sound, I said, "Well, I don't know why you wouldn't. I mean, my raft is right there."

"You and I both know that's not why your raft is here."

I just looked at him.

"So, that's how you're going to play it," he said flatly.

"I'm just an old fart sitting by the river drinking a glass of wine. If that's a crime, I guess I'm guilty."

"We've had reports of a solo raft on the river without a permit," the lady ranger said.

"I guess I should be flattered that you think I'm capable of doing that."

She said, "You look like you're in pretty good shape."

I winked and said, "What time do you get off work? Maybe you can come down and share some wine and talk about that."

"I don't think so," she said.

But I detected a trace of a smile.

They finally they gave up on me and left, without ever asking where my truck was parked, or if I was planning to camp where I was. I had a pretty lame lie ready for the first question—my buddy had to hurry back to Lowell because one of his tires was going flat. On the latter point, I had no choice. Until my buddy got back, I couldn't go anywhere else. Fortunately, they hadn't asked either question.

But I was a long way from being in the clear. All they had to do was interview people coming off the river the next day, and ask if they'd seen me. The guided group that I'd seen at Tango Bar had taken-out several hours earlier, so they weren't a threat. But the group that I'd encountered at the put-in was still out there, and probably would arrive at Race Creek the next day. I resolved to be gone before they got there. But that depended on my rig getting there before the rafting party arrived.

Photo submitted by Tamara Baysinger

Tamara Baysinger paddling into Wolf Creek Rapid, July 2016. All of the photos in this chapter were taken by a member of her party.

Not wanting to look like I'd intended to camp there, I didn't set up my table or stove. I made a cold dinner out of sandwiches and canned peaches. I camped that night without a tent, and slept on the hard ground, to maintain the charade of this being an unplanned emergency.

I got up at 5:00 and walked down to the parking area, where I found my dusty pickup and trailer, with the hood still warm from the overnight shuttle drive. I drove over to the turnout above my little beach and backed the trailer down close to the row of boulders.

It took half an hour to wrestle the raft onto the trailer and pile all of my gear into it. I moved back over to the main parking lot to tie-down a tarp over my raft and check all of my straps. I was on the road before the rangers had time to finish breakfast, let alone gather incriminating evidence against me.

It's a beautiful scenic twenty-mile drive down to Lowell, where the Selway and Lochsa Rivers join to form the Clearwater. Three Rivers Resort is across the Lochsa river from Lowell. I stopped there, uncovered my raft and re-rigged it properly, correcting my hasty loading at Race

Creek. I found the RV dump station and cleaned-out my Scat-Packer and deposited my trash in the campground dumpster.

With the hard labor finished, I went inside for breakfast. Over a much-needed cup of coffee, I had a long phone conversation with Linda, who thought I was a couple of days overdue. I'm not sure which of us got the date wrong, but I assured her that I'd had a spectacular trip without any problems.

"So, nobody caught you without a permit?"

"Well, I had a conversation about permits with a couple of rangers at the takeout," I said.

"A conversation?"

"Yeah. They thought I needed a permit to have my raft sitting on the ground near the river. I explained the whole thing to them, and that was the end of it."

"You're glossing over a lot," she speculated.

"Not a lot. Maybe a little," I acknowledged.

"You know, if you get locked up for this nonsense, I'm not going to pay your bail."

I'm sure she was just kidding. *Pretty* sure, anyway.

She gave me an update on Kevin's Pacific Crest Trail hike. He had crossed the border from California, and had made it to the rim of Crater Lake, but was concerned about forest fires further north.

My next calls were to my cohorts in my regular rafting group. After they had all declined to join me on the Owyhee, they had resolved to work the system and try to score a permit out of the cancellation pool.

"Nope. We finally gave up on that and decided on a Lower Salmon trip," my daughter Tamara told me.

We'd previously talked about the probability of this situation, and had agreed on a date where I could meet them if that turned out to be the case. The date we all settled on was Saturday, July 24th, and Tamara assured me that the group's preparations were proceeding on schedule.

Chapter Eighteen

The Middle Fork Caper

Trusting that the Selway SWAT team wasn't hot on my trail, I lingered over breakfast and another cup of coffee, calculating my next move. I needed to pin down a schedule that would dovetail with my rendezvous with The Clan at Shorts Bar on July 24th.

I was at least two days—and maybe three—from launching on the Middle Fork. The drive time from Lowell to Boundary Creek on the Middle Fork of the Salmon was about eight hours. But somewhere during that drive, I'd have to stop to do laundry and shopping.

My shopping would be a tricky thing, because once I start downriver, it would be nearly three weeks before I could re-supply, upon my arrival in Riggins. Anyone who's ever planned a raft trip of that length knows the problems. Under the best of circumstances, my ice couldn't last more than seven to ten days, and I wasn't sure that my dry box had the capacity to carry three week's food.

It occurred to me that the shuttle service might be able to help, since they are headquartered in the town of Salmon, about fifty miles from the confluence of the Middle Fork and Main Salmon. And they run shuttles past there almost every day during the rafting season.

Before calling the shuttle service, I had to figure out how long I'd be on the Middle Fork. The Forest Service limits the number of nights people can spend on the river—six for large groups, and seven for small groups. This has always struck me as ass-backward, since just about everything takes longer as group size increases.

On summer trips, most groups choose to use the maximum time allowed. Anyone I would encounter on the river was a potential informant, so I wanted to minimize contact with other groups. That meant floating at the same pace as the other groups. But large groups had to travel at a slightly faster pace than the small groups, so I had to decide whose pace I'd follow.

My threat analysis suggested that guides would be more attuned to my kind of crimes, and guided trips are always large groups. So, if I let the guided parties leave ahead of me on my launch day, the commercial groups from the next day probably wouldn't overtake me until my last day on the river, if I adopted the small group seven-night schedule.

I counted it out on the calendar and determined that with a July 7th launch, I would get to the Cache Bar boat ramp at the end of my Middle Fork trip on July 14th. I put in my call to the shuttle service.

"I'm going to need a one-vehicle shuttle from Boundary Creek to Heller Bar," I began.

"Heller Bar? Where is that?"

"Heller Bar is on the Snake River near Asotin, Washington."

"Oh, right. I know where that is, but uh, I don't think we go there. I mean, are you planning to float all the way from Boundary Creek to Heller Bar?"

"That's right. Can you quote me a price?"

"Yeah. I guess I can work something up," she said hesitantly.

"I have another request," I said. "Would it be possible for you to have someone buy some supplies for me and deliver them to me at Cache Bar?"

"Uh, I don't know about that—I mean, I'd have to talk with our drivers and see if anyone wants to take that on. What kind of supplies are you talking about?"

"Meats, produce, bread—perishables. And ice, of course. I can leave cardboard boxes and an ice chest in the rig you'll be shuttling, along with a shopping list and cash to pay for it all."

"That sounds like a lot to ask someone to do."

"It's easier than it sounds. The list has only about thirty items. And of course, I'll leave a generous tip for the person who does that for me."

"Well, okay… I'll have to see if we can do it, and then get back to you with a price for that shuttle."

"Excellent. I'll be in and out of cell-phone range for the next couple of days, so leave a voice-mail, and I'll call you back as soon as I can."

It was almost noon when I finally hit the road. I drove down US-95 all afternoon, passing through Grangeville, Whitebird, and Riggins before arriving in the town of Cascade at around 4:00.

Cascade was the last town of any consequence before the four-hour drive to Boundary Creek. I found a private campground with laundry facilities, showers, and WiFi. I set up my canopy and mini-kitchen, and after a shower, I went into town and got a bison steak dinner.

When I checked my voice-mail, I found quotes for the long shuttle and for the grocery shopping and delivery. After dinner, I put-in a return call to the shuttle service to pin it down.

"Pick up my rig at Boundary Creek after my launch on July 7th, and have it at Heller Bar in the morning on August 2nd. As for the groceries, I believe your shuttle caravans typically go past Cache Bar early in the morning."

"That's right. They deliver vehicles to Cache Bar and pick up others at Corn Creek. They usually do that before sunrise."

"I'll be camping at Cache Bar the night of July 14th. If they honk the horn, I'll wake up. That'll be early morning on July 15th."

"Okay. That should work. What about the shopping list?"

"I'll attach it to the envelope with the cash. There'll be cash for the supplies and for shuttle fuel."

"Perfect. We'll wake you up on the fifteenth."

In the morning, I washed my clothes and towels in the campground's two-machine laundry room. While waiting for the machines, I entertained myself by continuing the Grand Canyon saga, with frequent reference to the notes I'd kept on a tiny digital audio recorder.

Before going to the grocery store, I scrubbed-out my ice chest and purged my dry box of leftovers that I'd never use. My shopping list was the same one I'd used for the Grand Ronde and again for the Selway. This time, I tripled all of the quantities, except for the perishables. I bought a ten-day supply of those, and wrote-up a duplicate list for the shuttle driver.

I was pleased to find that the store had good ice. In urban stores, what they sell as block ice is actually ice chips compressed to look like blocks. But they're very porous and melt a lot faster than blocks of solid ice.

Arriving at Boundary Creek a little before noon on July 6th, I went straight to the campground and grabbed a vacant site, where I off-loaded my dry bag and set up my canopy. My "car-camping kit" included a one-burner Coleman stove that was too heavy for backpacking and too small to be much good for anything else. But it was adequate for heating my canned chili dinner and making coffee in the morning.

I drove down to the rodeo grounds at the top of the raft slide, where everyone rigs their boats. All of that day's boats had already started downstream, and the next day's people were starting to arrive, so I found myself second in line behind a pickup with a raft frame lashed over a pile of gear in the bed. I suggested that if he'd let me slide my raft down the ramp first, he could assemble his on my trailer, so that he wouldn't have to lift it up from ground level to the ramp. He liked the idea, so my raft was in the water before any inquisitive rangers came around to ask questions.

Photo by Jan Brandvold
The launch ramp at Boundary Creek. All of the day's permit holders had already left.

It took him a while to get his raft rigged and loaded. I helped where I could, and we talked as he worked. But I had already decided not to ask about piggy-backing on his permit, because of the number of Forest Service people around. If my new friend started asking others in his party about accommodating me, it would be too easy for a ranger to hear that I was there without a permit.

A couple of other people in his group pitched-in to help, because they were in line behind us. They had a group of eight, from somewhere in Colorado. I evaded questions about my group by saying that they hadn't arrived yet. Of course, they could see from my license plates that I was from Oregon.

Photo by Tamara Baysinger
Sliding a raft down the launch ramp.

When we finally got his raft off of my trailer, I drove back up and parked in the campground. I hiked upriver a short distance to Dagger Falls and shot a few pictures. I've seen video of people taking rafts and kayaks down Dagger Falls, but that's not something I've ever been tempted to try.

Back at the rodeo grounds, the afternoon chaos was in full swing, with a dozen rafts in varying stages of preparation and people laboring to get them rigged. There were guides from two companies rigging boats, along with people from two or three private parties. It was very easy for my solo boat to be lost in the growing swarm of rafts tied along shore downstream from the ramp.

I made coffee in the morning to go with a cold breakfast, and quietly packed up before most people in the campground were awake. I drove down to the rodeo ground, and then schlepped my dry bag and canopy down the long path to the beach, where I loaded them onto my raft. Then I drove my rig up to the shuttle parking area half a mile away.

Photo by JP Baysinger
Morning at Boundary Creek

People were up and about by the time I walked back down the hill, and some were starting to assemble for the morning campsite assignment session. I avoided getting too close to that. I would avoid the campsites that can be reserved, and camp only at sites that were infrequently used.

At about 9:00, everyone else gathered for the compulsory orientation lecture, and I made myself disappear up toward the outhouse. When people started coming back up the trail, I knew the lecture was over, so I walked down to my raft. By then, the guided groups had already left, and I saw that two private groups were about ready to leave.

I pushed-off between the two groups, so that each might think I belonged to the other. Once around the bend after the first rapid, which is cleverly called First Bend Rapid, I pulled into an eddy and made a bit of a show, wading out waist-deep to pee, while the second group cruised on by.

My plan was to pull up short, as I'd done on the Selway, and get myself into the gap between that day's groups and the next day's groups. But from the standpoint of boat traffic, the Middle Fork is like a freeway compared with the Selway.

Photo by Jan Brandvold
In the first rapid after safely sneaking away from Boundary Creek.

After the other parties were out of sight, I pulled back into the current and enjoyed the fantastic whitewater.

I stopped at Sulphur Slide Rapid, both to scout it and because I was catching up with the group out front. Then, when I was still in the busy water at the foot of Sulphur Slide, I spotted a patch of bright yellow where it shouldn't be. I rowed over to it and found an old Tahiti inflatable kayak mostly deflated and wrapped around a boulder.

Oddly, it was in fairly calm water. It seemed strange that it had made it through the tricky part of the rapid only to broach in easy water below. I grabbed the line that was trailing from the Tahiti, swinging my raft into the eddy below the rock. After working my way to the front of my raft, I put a foot against the rock and tugged on the line, and the Tahiti came free.

Photo by Author

I dragged it aboard and was wadding it into a ball, when I noticed the permit tag hanging from a loop on the Tahiti's bow. All of the tags I'd seen before launching were pale blue. This one was bright red. And it was numbered differently, too. Standard tags showed the month and a sequential number, like 07-032. This one said 83/28.

It dawned on me that this was a Special Use tag—the kind reserved for Native Americans, scientists, journalists and politicians. I could see that the Tahiti hadn't been in the water very long. And it wouldn't stay long either. Most outfitters would pick it up, just as I had, to keep the river free of litter. I doubted that it could have been there for as long as twenty-four hours, meaning that it probably had launched only the day before.

That meant the red tag was an active permit. And I know an opportunity when I see one. I inspected the Tahiti and found it to be complete trash. It probably was trash when it was launched. The vinyl was stiff and brittle, and I could feel it crack while I rolled it up. I guessed that it had split open the first time it was put to any stress.

I rolled it tightly and crammed it down into the front of my raft, next to my bow line. But I left the nose of the Tahiti hanging out over the bow of my raft, with its permit tag hanging in such a way that it might appear to be attached to my raft. This would keep almost everyone from being curious about a raft with no tag.

As I approached Velvet Falls, I saw the last boats in the group ahead of me disappear around the bend. I did a perfunctory scout in case something had changed since I was last there, and then ran it on the standard chute. Half a mile later, I pulled into Boy Scout camp for lunch. My quick breakfast had left me short on calories.

Photo by JP Baysinger
Scouting Velvet Falls

In no hurry, I beached my raft stern-first, so that my permit tag would be visible to anyone passing by. I set up my table and pulled out the makings for a tall deli sandwich. A private party went by and one of the boatmen gave a friendly wave. Even if he knew what my red tag meant, my tan was dark enough that I might be mistaken for an Indian, which was much better than having him think I was a politician.

It was a nice place, so I decided to stay. As the afternoon went by, two more private groups floated past—including the group from Colorado. After that, I enjoyed glorious solitude. Late in the afternoon, dark clouds started forming, and when rain looked eminent, I put up my tent and pop-up shelter.

That was the first rain I'd had since my fourth day on the Grande Ronde. I heard some thunder in the distance, but there were no lightning strikes anywhere near me. The rain came in hard, but quickly diminished to a light drizzle that continued into the night.

I didn't get up right away the next morning, even though I awoke at my regular time. The rain had stopped, but a

Photo by Jan Brandvold
Rams Horn Rapid circa 2006

thin fog prevented me from seeing what the weather was like. At 6:30, I couldn't stay in bed any longer, so I got up and made breakfast. By the time I'd finished washing the dishes, the fog had dissipated to reveal blue sky. I broke camp, loaded my raft, and was ready to go by 9:00. I floated a mile and a half to Trail Hot Springs.

One of the great features of the Middle Fork is the abundance of hot springs. I stopped and enjoyed a brief soak, giving the parties in front of me time to get out of camp, in hopes of not overrunning them. For the time being, I could float in the gap between yesterday's launches and today's.

After lunch at Sheepeater Hot Spring, I took a bucket of hot water and a scoop up to where I could bathe without risk of my shampoo or soap reaching the hot spring or the river. I was back at my raft when a mixed group of inflatable kayaks and rafts pulled in. We talked for a few minutes, and they said that they were going to camp at Dolly Lake, which was half a mile further than I was planning to go.

My afternoon took me through Artillery Rapids, a series of four read-and-run drops in a one-mile stretch of river. Not long after that, I came to Rapid River. The campsite there is not popular because it can be a difficult landing. But it's a nice place, and is not on the list of reservable campsites.

Photo by Jerry Baysinger
Explaining Powerhouse Rapid to my group on an earlier Middle Fork trip.

While I was typing away on my whitewater saga, with a glass of Chardonay at my side, I looked up to see a drift boat go by. It was occupied by two men wearing Forest Service shirts and hats. I held my breath, but they showed no interest in me, and I'm not sure they even noticed me before going into the rapid just below.

River patrols like that are fairly common on the Middle Fork and Main Salmon. They stop and inspect campsites for anything left by the previous night's campers. I once had a ranger stop and tell me that she'd found a fork in the sand where we'd camped the night before. I pointed out that it wasn't our pattern, but added it to the silverware tray.

I felt good about having the river patrol out front, because it probably would be two or three days before the next one came down. So, unless they had some kind of project that would hold them up, I might have clear sailing.

Still, chronic worrier that I am, I couldn't help thinking about what I'd have said if the river patrol had stopped to talk with me. I figured I had two options. I could simply tell the truth and let the chips fall, or I could fabricate a story that I could tell without lying too much. But I couldn't choose between these options without first concocting the story.

The dead Tahiti and its special use permit seemed like a good nucleus for the big lie. Under any circumstances, the river patrol's first demand would be for me to show my actual paperwork. I'd have to say that the trip leader had the permit, and he was somewhere out ahead of me. All true.

But since the river patrol launched sometime after the special use party, they'd probably be carrying information about the party. At the very least, they'd know the number of people in the party and the number and descriptions of the party's boats. If one of the boats happened to be a Riken *Miwok*, then I was set. If not—and that was by far the greater probability—then I'd need an explanation.

I could point at the dead Tahiti and say, "after this happened, there was nothing to do but hike back to Boundary Creek, get a different boat, and then set out to catch up with the group." That probably was a true statement, since I wouldn't claim to have been involved—even though my intention would be that they would infer exactly that.

The problems would come up if the river patrol also had a list of names in the special use party. First off, my name wouldn't be on it, and secondly, I would not know any of the names that *were* on it. I could think of no way out of that. Such is the criminal life.

At 9:30 the next morning, I passed the group camped at Dolly Lake, and soon arrived at Lake Creek, where a series of blowouts in the last twenty years have created a pool leading into a long, rock-filled rapid that is constantly changing. I took a quick look before running it, and then pulled ashore to scout Pistol Creek Rapid.

Photo by Jan Brandvold

Stopped at the debris fan from the Lake Creek blowout.

Over the past fifteen years, Pistol Creek Rapid has changed a lot. The preferred route used to start in the right channel, but as rock and gravel continues to wash downstream from the Lake Creek blowouts, the right channel has become too shallow to run, except during high-water. That leaves the difficult left channel as the only option. The main flow plunges over a shelf in a very steep, violent drop where all kinds of bad things can—and often do—happen.

The lower part of the rapid, where the river makes a sharp S turn, first to the left and then to the right, is pretty easy at the present water level, as long as your boat is right-side-up and you're in it. But the left channel leaves that situation something less than a sure thing.

Photo by Jerry Baysinger
Boat ramp at Indian Creek

Good fortune favored me, however, and I got through without doing anything that might lend my name to a river feature. The last thing I wanted was for future guide books to warn boaters about the perils of "Ken's Rock." Or worse yet, "Ken's Hole."

The character of the river mellows considerably after Pistol Creek. I made a brief lunch stop, and then drifted down to Indian Creek, where there is an airstrip and guard station. The possibility that I might encounter the previous day's river patrol at Indian Creek had been on my mind, but there were no boats there. I could once again put my criminal paranoia to rest.

Five miles downstream, I ran Marble Creek Rapid, and then immediately pulled into the eddy on the right, to the campsite called Marble Right. Most rafts carry so much momentum after going through the rapid that they blow past Marble Right without even noticing it. It's also a campsite that outfitters rarely use. I didn't want to have an outfitter find a solo raft occupying a campsite that they wanted.

My Saturday morning started with a stop at Sunflower Hot Spring, where warm water pours over a ledge ten feet above the river, making a delightful riverbank shower.

It was there, in 2012, that I first learned about the Special Use tags like that on the dead Tahiti. We were camped at Sunflower, when another group arrived and set-up camp on the opposite side of the

Photo submitted by Tamara Baysinger
Tamara Baysinger rowing into the big wave at Marble Creek Rapid

river. That evening, they paddled over to use the hot springs and proved themselves to be inconsiderate slobs. They left a dozen empty cans and bottles scattered all around the upper part of the springs, and they used their soap directly in the soaking pools and waterfall.

When we got up in the morning, we found our rafts, which were tied a few yards downstream, enveloped in suds floating a foot thick on the surface of the river. As we left our camp, we rowed across the river to return the trash they'd left behind. As we tossed the cans and bottles into their rafts, we noticed that they had the distinctive red tags. Rangers later told us what the tags were.

About 3:00, I passed Whitie Cox Campsite and pulled-in to a small campsite on the opposite side of the river. Lounging on the beach with a cold beer, I gradually became aware that nothing hurt—no backache, no muscle fatigue, no weariness. That was actually a startling realization.

Only a month earlier, as I approached the end of the Grand Canyon, I was worn out, mentally and physically. Throughout my three-day drive back to Oregon, I fought both sides of an internal battle over whether or not to continue my Whitewater Summer. In the end, my decision to go forward with the Grande Ronde run was mostly to rid myself of the residual bad feelings from having to babysit the petulant millennials for two weeks.

I don't know that I'll ever have fond memories of that trip, but had I not done the Grande Ronde trip, it is possible that I'd have never gone rafting again. I don't know how much of my physical pain had been induced by mental stress, but as I watched the Middle Fork of the Salmon River flow past that afternoon, I was free of both.

The next morning, about ninety minutes after leaving camp, I arrived at Hospital Bar, where the best hot springs on the Middle Fork are located. The campsite just downstream from the springs, and another directly across the river, were both occupied, as is to be expected, but there was nobody actually using the hot springs. So, I stopped for a relaxing soak before heading toward my first challenge of the day.

Photo by JP Baysinger
Done right, Tappan Falls is a big splash.

That would be Tappan Falls, which features a single abrupt plunge over a river-wide ledge in a four or five-foot drop. A narrow slot near the right bank is the only clean way to run the falls, and the penalty

Photo by Tamara Baysinger

Missed the chute at Tappan Falls. This boatman was launched over the head of his passenger, into the river.

for missing the slot ranges from ejection to flipping, with lots of other undesirable possibilities in between.

I made a smooth run through Tappan Falls, and half a mile later stopped to scout the rapid formerly known as Tappan III. In August of 2008, a flash flood in Cove Creek blew thousands of tons of rock into the Middle Fork, creating a new and more challenging version of Tappen III, now called Cove Creek Rapid.

While it has softened quite a bit over the years, it still provides a wildly chaotic ride down the boulder-choked chute. With a left-side entry, there is a nearly straight-through run, although one boulder on the left is pretty close. I made a clean run, so maybe it's easier than it looks. It is still evolving with every high-water season, so safety demand scouting.

Once again, I reached my daily quota of miles before 3:00, and had a long, leisurely afternoon at Broken Oar campsite. I walked downstream a half-mile in search of pictographs. I have a hand-written note saying that they are at a "shark fin" rock, but I failed to find either the pictographs or the rock.

The next day was pretty easy, with only four rapids of any significance. The first was Aparejo Point Rapid, which I unnecessarily scouted. Later, after a visit to Flying B Ranch, where I bought a t-shirt and an ice cream bar, I arrived at Haystack Rapid.

Photo by Jerry Baysinger

The lower part of Haystack Rapid was flooded by blowouts from Bernard Creek.

For years, Haystack had been considered one of the more challenging rapids on the river, but in 2003, a massive blowout from Bernard Creek just downstream created a pool in what had been the most difficult part of the rapid. I entered in the right-side channel and rode it all the way to the pool. Easy stuff.

Bernard Creek Rapid, created by the blowouts, is still a "young" rapid, subject to change in every high-water season. Long and rocky, it remains a read-and-run rapid. Just be ready for some quick maneuvering—some of those rocks come up on you pretty fast.

A couple of miles after that, I came to Jack Creek Rapid, which I scouted by standing atop my cooler, before taking the obvious route on the left and dodging a submerged rock at the bottom. Five more miles brought me to Grassy Flats.

Photo by Jan Brandvold
Waterfall Creek is half a mile before Big Creek.

Nearly everybody wants to camp between here and Big Creek, just over five miles downstream, because once you pass Big Creek, you are allowed to spend only one more night on the Middle Fork. But since I was already a criminal, I wasn't especially worried about that particular rule.

Still, I recalled that there is a tiny camping spot right at the mouth of Big Creek. And because it's so small, it is not a campsite that anybody ever plans in advance to use. When I arrived there at 4:30, I was pleased, but not surprised, to find it open, so I claimed it.

Big Creek marks the entry into the Lower Canyon, which is sometimes called the "Impassible Canyon." But since over a hundred people a day pass through it, that name seems more than a little bit pretentious. Still, it represents a stark change in the character of the river. After fifty miles of moderately easy floating since passing Indian Creek, the river gets walled-in and once again picks up speed.

Looking ahead to my last full day on the Middle Fork, I knew that I would face about seven or eight rapids where most guidebooks recommend scouting. In my experience, at least three of them are read-and-run rapids at the water levels I've seen. But don't take *my* word for it.

Photo by Jan Brandvold
Approaching Tombstone Rock Rapid

I left Big Creek at 9:00 the next morning, and half an hour later, I stopped and scouted Redside Rapid, which can be a tough one at some water levels. But with the proper entry and a couple of well-timed oar strokes, it is easy to make the cut around the dreaded "Airplane Rock," and cruise downstream.

I also scouted Weber Rapid, half a mile downstream. It is a complex rock garden, and the route through it is flanked by deep holes and powerful eddies. At high water, this one can be (and has been) deadly.

By early afternoon, three private groups had gone past, on their way to campsites further downstream, in order to set themselves up for an early takeout at Cache Bar. I had the mistaken impression that everyone who would be taking-out the next day was already in front of me, so I allowed myself a stop at Mist Falls for a leisurely hike and some photography.

Photo by Jan Brandvold
Mist Falls.

As I came back down toward my raft, I stopped short when I saw someone inspecting my red tag. I felt pretty stupid for having stopped at a place where *everyone* stops, because that was just asking for trouble. And now I had it.

"What kind of permit is that?" asked the stranger.

He wouldn't have to ask that question if he was an official, so that was a good sign.

"It's a Special Use permit," I said.

"What's it for?"

"I'm doing a documentary."

You could call this story a documentary, couldn't you?

"Did you get it through the lottery, or what?"

"More like 'or what.' They are issued without a lottery," I said.

"Okay, so what did you have to do to get it?"

"They don't hand them out to just anybody. I had to work pretty hard to get it."

Evasive, but true. And it seemed to satisfy his curiosity, because he wished me a good day and took off up the trail. My pulse rate was still elevated, and I felt like a sleazy politician for the ambiguity of my comments.

Opposite the mouth of Parrott Creek, I stopped to explore the remains of Earl Parrott's cabin. Parrott was a well-known hermit who lived in the canyon from about 1915 until his death in 1944. The popular story that he would shoot at interlopers in "his" canyon is utterly unfounded, but it defines his legend.

Photo by Jan Brandvold
Lower Cliffside Rapid

I cruised easily through Upper and Lower Cliffside Rapids, and floated past Otter Bar, a large, beautiful campsite that is occupied nearly every night throughout the boating season.

Rubber Rapid has never given me any trouble, but I didn't want this run to be a first, so I scouted it, just to refresh my memory of the locations of two submerged boulders near the bottom of the rapid. No problems.

Successfully running Hancock Rapid depends entirely on identifying the "shark's fin" boulder in midstream, and passing ten feet to the right of it. Once past the shark's fin, move left and ride the wave train. At my moderate water level, it is a read-and-run rapid for any competent boater.

A quarter-mile below Hancock Rapid, I spotted a sandbar along the left bank, which is the low-water campsite called Solitude. At this point, I was just three miles from the confluence with the Main Salmon, and six miles from Cache Bar. I pulled ashore and set up camp for my last night on the Middle Fork.

Photo by Jerry Baysinger
Devil's Tooth Rapid

I was in no hurry the next morning, but still found myself on the river before 9:00. A mile downstream, I came to Devil's Tooth Rapid. There are two theories about running Devil's Tooth—left of the tooth or right of it. I've always run left, and I've always scouted it first, looking for the reason that others go right. I still haven't found it.

The last two significant rapids on the Middle Fork are House of Rocks and Jump-off Joe, both rated Class III. After cruising through them, I floated the last mile of the Middle Fork, to its confluence with the Main Salmon, making me, for the moment, a law-abiding citizen.

Two miles on the Main Salmon brought me to Cramer Creek Rapid, which was formed by a massive slide in 2002. It seems to be getting easier as time goes by, but I still scout it

Photo by Jerry Baysinger
Scouting Cramer Creek Rapid

on every run.

Upon reaching Cache Bar, I went past the boat ramp and pulled ashore at the sand beach just downstream. I found a shady spot and sat down with one of my last cold beers to contemplate my next move. And the first question was whether I wanted to continue.

I had a one-time opportunity to call it quits. When the shuttle drivers came through to deliver my groceries, I could simply ask them to bring my pickup down the next night. I could pack up and go home. And a part of me wanted to do just that. I was increasingly bothered by the self-induced pressure associated with my life of crime.

I had nothing more to prove—I had already proven to myself that I could actually do it. And I wasn't trying to impress anyone else. And yet, the idea of quitting left me with the feeling that I was leaving a job unfinished. But was continuing worth the stress?

Or was there a way to reduce or eliminate the stress? Could I do that any way other than actually getting a permit for the next segment of my adventure? How about a stolen tag, or counterfeit tag?

Honestly, my Special Use tag was as close as I wanted to get to having an illegal tag. As long as it was attached to the dead Tahiti, I had plausible deniability, and it might ward-off river rangers. It seemed to have worked on the Middle Fork. But was it any good at all after I passed Corn Creek?

Photo by Jan Brandvold
Cache Bar boat ramps

It was a very warm evening, and my attempt to go to sleep early was a failure. And I was only sort-of sleeping when the rattle of trailers on the washboarded gravel road announced the arrival of the shuttle caravan. While drivers parked half a dozen rigs in every available nook along the road, the van driver pulled into the parking lot and tapped her horn.

I unloaded my ice chest and two boxes of supplies, while the shuttle drivers made their way to the van. They headed on down to Corn Creek to pick up a caravan of vehicles going the other way, while I transferred everything into the food box and ice chest on my raft. When the van came back, I had my last chance to quit. Instead, I loaded my empty cooler into the van and sent it on its way.

Photo by Jan Brandvold
Robert Baysinger 1942 – 2020
My brother on the Middle Fork in 2006

Chapter Nineteen

The River of No Return

The five-mile float from Cache Bar down to Corn Creek includes one pretty good rapid, at Kitchen Creek. I ran it without scouting, and arrived at Corn Creek at 9:30, right after the rangers concluded their daily orientation lecture. All around, people were making their final preparations and starting downstream.

I tied-up at a little sand bar at the upstream end of the Corn Creek campground. and walked down to the boat ramp, where two commercial parties and a private group were getting ready to leave. While the guides were busy giving their pre-trip lecture to their guests, I approached the apparent leader of the private group.

We socialized briefly, and during the conversation, I revealed that I was without a permit. As soon as I mentioned that, his demeanor changed from friendly to suspicious. He thought I was a permit parasite hoping to tag along on his permit. He was exactly right.

He preemptively said, "Well, good luck on that."

And then he added, "You might check with the rangers. A group that was supposed to launch today didn't show up for the orientation talk. I don't know how long they'll hold

Photo by JP Baysinger
Between Cache Bar Corn Creek.

their permit, but at some point, it ought to be up for grabs."

I hurried straight up to the little office between the boat ramp and the campground and asked about the no-show.

"Yes, there is still a party that hasn't checked-in," the ranger confirmed.

"If they don't show up, will the permit be available for someone else?"

"It will, but it's not too uncommon for groups to arrive here late—noon, or sometimes even later."

"Is there a cut-off time?"

"If they're not here by 4:00, we'll release the permit."

"Can I claim first dibs on it?"

She slid a clip board across the counter. "Put your name there, and be back her at 4:00."

I walked through the campsite looking for anyone who might be the missing group. Eventually, I ended up back at my raft. The good news was that I might actually get a permit. The bad news was that if I didn't, the rangers already had my name.

Back at my raft, I tried working on my story of the great adventure, but I was unable to focus my thoughts. With or without that permit, I was committed to starting downstream that day. For the rest of the morning and all afternoon, I kept my ears tuned for the sound of vehicles coming down to Corn Creek. Whenever I heard one, I'd rush up and see if they went to the boat ramp or the campground. Two groups went to the boat ramp and started unloading rafts and equipment. Both were outfitters.

A private group arrived and went straight to the campground. I watched them begin unloading camping gear, so I knew that they weren't the people with the permit I wanted. Another private group arrived, and my heart sank when I watched them go straight to the boat ramp. I moseyed over and struck up a conversation.

"You guys going out today?"

"No, our permit is for tomorrow."

I refrained from kissing him. It was 2:00, and I heard more vehicles approaching. Holding my breath, I watched them turn toward the campground. By 3:00, I allowed myself to feel some optimism. Another group arrived, and after a stop at the office, they went down to the launch ramp and started unloading gear.

Shit!

"Are you launching today?" I asked, as casually as I could.

He looked at me as though wondering if I was blind.

"Yeah. We have a lot to do," he said with finality.

"So, did you pick up your permit?" I gestured toward the office.

"No," he said impatiently. "They won't issue them until tomorrow."

"Oh. So, you're *not* launching today?"

"Yeah. We're launching right now, so that we can get going as soon as we get through the lecture tomorrow."

Why didn't you say that in the first place?

Forty-five minutes later, I went back to the office.

"Did that group ever show up?" I asked, wondering if they could have slipped past without my seeing them.

"Nope. If you want the permit, it's yours." She gave me some paperwork to fill out and took my credit card to pay the user fee."

"So, you're by yourself?" she asked.

"That's right."

"You look like you've already been on the river."

"Huh?"

"Your tan."

"Oh. Yeah. I did a Grand Canyon trip last month."

She finally handed me a numbered tag and a copy of my permit, but I had a strong feeling that she knew more than she was saying. I went straight to my raft, attached the tag, and pushed off.

I floated only a few minutes before finding a good beach for camping, just out of sight and earshot of the launch ramp. It was a wonderful evening, and it felt like I had the canyon all to myself. The Ranier Beer that the shuttle driver bought for me was perfect.

On the river at 8:00, the clear sky promised a glorious hot day. As I approached Lantz Bar, I spotted a Forest Service drift boat at one of the campsites above Lantz Rapid. Free of paranoia, I waved as I drifted past.

Photo by JP Baysinger
A nice beach half a mile below Corn Creek.

Photo by Steve Kernek

Class III rapids that day: Ranier, Alder Creek, Lantz, and Devil's Teeth, shown here.

By mid-afternoon, I'd floated almost fifteen miles, when I came upon a nice little campsite that wasn't on the long list of camps that I couldn't use. I claimed it and unloaded my gear. I was on my second beer when the Forest Service boat appeared around the bend just above my camp.

"How's your day going?" the first ranger asked.

"Couldn't be better," I said.

"Can you show us your permit, please?" the second ranger asked.

No surprise there. That's what they do. But the lack of warmth in his question was obvious.

He looked over my permit and wrote something on a note pad. The first ranger gestured toward my raft.

"That a fourteen-foot *Miwok*?"

I nodded. "Thirteen and a half, actually, but they call it fourteen."

He gave me a hard look. "We received a bulletin about someone in a raft like that, running rivers without permits. During the last two or three weeks, he was seen on the Selway and the Middle Fork."

I pretended indifference.

Photo by JP Baysinger

Overhang Camp—Room enough for a party of one, but not much more.

He smiled. "There were photos. You know, the guy wore a hat just like yours."

Oops.

I shrugged. "I'm sure I'm not the only person with a Filson hat."

"This permit seems to be in order," the other ranger said. "Looks like you got lucky and scored a no-show."

"We Irish are known for our luck," I said.

I am actually only 1/8 Irish, except on St. Patrick's Day, when I'm full-blood.

The first ranger said, "We're not stupid. We know it was you."

He was trying to stare me down. I just smiled vacuously.

"We heard that you were displaying a Special Use Permit." He pointed to the rolled-up Tahiti, where a corner of the red permit was showing. "Is that it?"

Damn! I thought I'd stuffed it out of site. I'd wanted to *get rid* of the Tahiti, tag and all, but I found that there are no trash dump facilities at Cache Bar or Corn Creek.

"That's just some trash that I fished out of the river," I said.

"Sir, I must tell you that displaying an invalid permit in a federally-protected wilderness area is a punishable offense."

"That isn't exactly on display," I pointed out.

"No. It isn't," he agreed. "If it was, I'd be writing a citation."

Luck of the Irish, indeed. I would have been displaying it if I hadn't picked up the no-show.

"May I explain something here?" I asked, and without waiting for an answer, I continued, "I'm 75 years old. I've been entering permit lotteries every year since the lottery systems were put into place. You know how many permits I've won by lottery?"

I held up four fingers. "Four permits in forty years."

"And you think that entitles you to break the law?"

"No, but if I *had* broken the law, I think I could make the case that it's a mitigating circumstance."

"So, you've run the Selway, the Middle Fork, and now the Salmon. That's quite an odyssey."

"I never said anything about the Selway or Middle Fork, but if you think you have to bust me, have at it."

"We're not going to cite you. As far as I can see, you're not breaking any laws in our jurisdiction. I'm just curious," he said with a smile.

Was that smile genuine?

"I'm not admitting anything here," I said, "but for years, I've fantasized about floating all of the Western rivers, one after another."

I looked at the rangers and said, "I've never heard of anybody ever having done that. But if I ever do it, I'll write a book, and you can read all about it."

"You can't just go around ignoring laws, simply because they are inconvenient."

"Get serious. At my age, there is virtually *no chance* that I'd even be *capable* of doing it."

...again.

"You know, it would be an expensive ticket, if you were to get caught."

"Would it be more than what I've spent on about 200 unsuccessful permit lottery applications?"

"That's not the point."

"It is *precisely* the point. I've spent a thousand dollars entering permit lotteries that I didn't win. You think a thousand dollars would be too much to pay for doing the thing we've been talking about?"

"In a way, I can understand what you're saying. So, where do you go from here?"

"I'll stay on the river all the way to Heller Bar on the Snake."

"Well, listen. I admire your adventure and wish you the best. Just try not to break any laws along the way."

Fine. So, who ratted me out? On the Selway, it probably was the ranger at the takeout. But on the Middle Fork, it must have been another boater—probably an outfitter, since they're the ones most likely to have satellite communication.

Photo by JP Baysinger
Mountain goat, sighted a mile downstream from Overhang Camp

But I didn't have to worry about that, now that I had a permit for the next hundred miles. And I wouldn't need a permit for the hundred miles after that. I was able to kick back and enjoy the trip for what it was, at my own pace.

I had sixteen days to float 200 miles to Heller Bar. It would be easy to average fifteen miles a day, and at that pace, I could afford a couple of layover days. This seemed like a good time to take one.

It was my first day of total rest since my layover at Horseshoe Bend on the Grande Ronde over five weeks earlier. Alternating between writing, swimming, and napping, I spent a very pleasant Sunday at Overhang Camp, where the cave provided cool refuge from the afternoon heat.

By 9:30 the next morning, I had gone six miles, and was floating over the boulders that used to be Salmon Falls. In April, 2011, a flash flood in Black Creek washed hundreds of tons of rock and debris into the river, forming a pool that permanently covered the falls. At the same time, the debris formed a new rapid that is arguably more formidable than Salmon Falls had ever been.

Photo by JP Baysinger

Salmon Falls is now gone, flooded out by a major blowout at Black Creek in 2011.

Scouting Black Creek Rapid requires patience and care, as you climb over boulders to a viewpoint on the left bank. From there, I watched half a dozen boats pass through, most using a chute on the right-hand side, and a couple of larger rafts taking the left-side run.

Photo by Jerry Baysinger

Black Creek Rapid, formed by the 2011 blowout—Class IV with lots of violence.

A mile and a half downstream, I spotted the trail that leads up the left bank to Bathtub Hot Spring, where a stone and mortar soaking tub can comfortably accommodate ten people. Since this is the only usable hot spring in the River of No Return section of the Salmon, I couldn't pass it without stopping.

I stopped for lunch at Hancock Bar, where I had camped on a trip a few years earlier, while forest fires were burning nearby. Our camp was all set up, and we were in the middle of dinner when the flames came into view half a mile downstream, on the opposite side of the river. Mostly, the fire stayed on the ground, and there was no wind to spread spot fires, so we felt fairly safe staying there.

Photo by JP Baysinger
Bathtub Hot Spring. There is another hot spring just downstream, at river level, but it is much too hot for soaking.

Photo by Steve Kernek
Forest fire burning opposite Hancock Bar.

It would have taken until after dark to break camp and load the rafts, and then, we'd have been floating toward the heart of the fire. Staying there and trusting the fire to stay on the other side was our best option. Throughout the night, the fire crept down the steep canyon slope, until morning, when it reached the river's edge almost directly across from our camp. But in the coolness of the night, the fire had lost a lot of its punch, and never was an immediate threat.

On this trip, I couldn't stay at Hancock, because now it is a reserved camp, and my late launch didn't allow me to make any campsite reservations. I knew that I was in a part of the river where there are few campsites, and it was seven miles before I'd find one I could use.

I stopped at Dillinger Creek to fill my water jug and found a small flat spot to sleep on. It wasn't a documented campsite, but I could see that I wasn't the first to use it. And that's where I had an encounter with a black bear. Now, I've always considered black bears to be fairly easy to get along with, but they can be pretty destructive in their determination to get to your food supply.

I always carry a "bear-proofing" kit, consisting of a cow bell hanging from an old fishing rod, a few small tin bowls, and a bottle of ammonia. I wedge the fishing rod between my cooler and frame so that any bear attempting to get to my food will rattle the cow bell. And to further discourage them, I pour a few ounces of ammonia into bowls that I put atop coolers and food boxes, on the theory that bears, with their extremely sensitive sense of smell will avoid the ammonia.

I can't say for certain that my "bear-proofing" is the reason, but I've never been raided when I've used this system. That night, I was jarred from sleep by a thumping sound I turned my Tac Light toward my raft and saw that a large bear was trying to climb aboard. The Tac Light has a strobe feature that they claim will blind attackers, but I've always been advised that shining a light in a bear's eyes will just piss him off.

It's one thing to have a bear in camp, but quite another to have a pissed-off bear in camp. So, I've always used the "make noise and act big" approach, and it has usually worked—the lone exception being a particularly bold Rogue River bear who was not intimidated in the least by a noisy river guide. She grudgingly backed off, but returned multiple times in broad daylight to try again.

Photo by Author
That was just a medium-sized bear.

The Salmon River bear seemed surprised by my noise, and abandoned the raft. She was starting to retreat upstream, when I was startled by the sudden appearance of two cubs from the other direction, in a panic-induced charge to catch up with Mom. I belatedly set-out my bear-proofing kit, but I slept very lightly—if at all—for the rest of the night. But the bears didn't come back.

A beautiful, warm morning greeted me, and I cruised five miles down to Big Mallard Rapid, which I stopped to scout. The most popular run is to squeeze between a monster pour-over rock and the left bank, but I've also used a mid-river run that is favored by jetboat operators. This time, I took the far-left channel, and succeeded in getting through without bumping into the rocks on shore, which can bounce you out toward the big pour-over hole.

Three more miles brought me to the start of a half-mile stretch of fast water, starting with Elkhorn Rapid. I've never felt the need to scout anything in this series, but the guidebooks recommend it. The last rapid in the series is Growler, but just above it, Little Trout Creek comes in on the

Photo by JP Baysinger
The second drop in Elkhorn Rapid, Class III-IV

left. There is a small, but pretty campsite hidden behind some boulders, and I'd gone nearly 15 miles, my longest one-day run since I got off the Grande Ronde.

In the morning, right after passing under the suspension bridge at Campbells Ferry, I pulled in to Jim Moore Camp. From there, I hiked up to explore Jim Moore's abandoned ranch and the Campbell's Ferry townsite.

At River Mile 145.5 (Float Mile 44 on the official map), I came to Whiplash Rapid, which can be a formidable Class V+ drop when the river is high. At Summer flows, it's an easy riffle. I stopped for lunch at a large flat-faced boulder on the right bank, just above water level. The pictographs on the rock have faded significantly since the first time I came down the Salmon. Unless someone figures out a way to restore them, they'll be completely gone in a very few years.

After Lunch, I stopped at the Sylvan Hart homestead. Nicknamed Buckskin Bill, he lived there from the 1930s until his death in 1980. A small museum displays many of his creations, and the descendants of his cats roam the grounds. There's a gift and snack shop, where you can get a Black Butte Porter ice cream float. Which I did.

Photo by JP Baysinger
"Buckskin Bill's" fort

Don't skip this stop, and while you're there, crawl up into the fort, for a commanding view.

Bluebird Hole is a large camp on the right at River Mile 135.8. It is not reservable, so I pulled-in. I found a nook at one end of the beach, and when a large party came in later, there was plenty of room for them. They invited me over for their evening campfire, where I told a greatly shortened version of the story of my great adventure.

I passed McKay Bar the next morning, and then pulled into the cove where the South Fork of the Salmon comes in. At the upstream end of the cove, I could look up the South Fork and see one of the best river camps anywhere.

But I couldn't get there. When the river is higher, there's a small chute that flows down from the shallow water above the gravel island that separates the South Fork from the Main Salmon. If you can drag your raft up that chute, some hard rowing will get you across the river and a hundred yards upstream, to South Fork Beach. By the time you get there, you'll need a layover, and there's no better place for one.

Photo by JP Baysinger

To get to this great campsite, you have to drag your raft 200 yards up the South Fork, in a narrow chute on the east side of the island at the confluence with the Main Salmon.

Following an afternoon stop at the Polly Bemis Ranch, I went another three miles to the small campsite at Whiskey Bob Creek, where I spent my last night in the controlled access section of the Salmon.

The next day took me through half a dozen good rapids before I arrived at the Vinegar Creek boat ramp, the first public road access to the river since Corn Creek. Just past the boat ramp, I stopped to scout the Class IV Vinegar Creek Rapid. It's a straight-through run, but your entry point is critical. Miss it by a couple of feet, and things will get violent.

When the Wind River pack bridge came into view, I pulled-in to a sand beach on the right, at the mouth of Wind River. Now outside the controlled section of river, I could camp anywhere.

From the time I left Corn Creek, I had made a point of stopping at all of the mayor off-river attractions along the way, and reveled in the comfort of not having to endure permit anxiety. During

Photo by JP Baysinger
Vinegar Creek Rapid, Class IV

the six days since I left Corn Creek, I had floated 80 miles through one of the most beautiful forested canyons in the world. For the next 57 miles, the river would be paralleled by a road or highway. But even with the sense of wilderness compromised, the scenery remains superb.

Chapter Twenty

The Lower Salmon

The boat landing at Carey Creek just below the Wind River Pack Bridge is generally considered to be the end of the River of No Return section of the Main Salmon and the beginning of the Lower Salmon, where float permits are not required.

For that reason, the Lower Salmon has been one of my go-to rivers for rafting after striking-out in the permit lotteries. When the government instigates a lottery for the Lower Salmon, I'll probably quit rafting altogether.

After leaving my Wind River camp, I encountered a long stretch with no significant whitewater. Four miles downstream, I stopped at a big beach opposite French Creek. There used to be a cable car across the river here, and there was a trail to a great little hot spring high above the north riverbank.

From the beach, I laboriously trekked up the steep hillside and intersected the trail, which appeared unused and unmaintained. I hiked it for a quarter-mile eastward, at times having to beat my way through brush that had overgrown the trail.

Photo by Friends of Cable Car Hot Springs
The cabin at the hot spring has fallen into disrepair since this photo was taken.

I finally found what appears to be an old mine tunnel with a low dam of stone and mortar creating a shallow pool just inside. I tested the water and found it comfortably warm, but the bottom of the pool was loose silt that immediately turned the water brown with mud.

A few yards further I came to the broken-down, overgrown remains of the hut that used to house a carved wooden bathing tub. The hot spring used to be maintained by a group of volunteers, but it looks like the organization is no longer active. I'd love to see someone save Cable Car Hot Spring, but I don't know who that would be.

Disappointed, I returned to my raft and resumed my float downstream. After a quick stop for lunch, I cruised through a pair of Class II rapids at Kelly Creek and Van Creek, and then, two miles past the boat ramp at Spring Bar, I stopped for the day at a huge beach on the left.

First thing the next morning, I ran Ruby Rapid, followed a mile later by Lake Creek Rapid. Both are Class III at summer water levels, and great fun. In mid-day, when I arrived at Shorts Bar, just upstream from Riggins, I was pleased to see my yellow *Vanguard* tied-up next to my brother's blue *Aire* and Tamara's *Cheyenne* on the little beach next to the boat ramp. The fleet appearing to be all rigged and ready to go.

I moved my personal gear from *Miwok* to *Vanguard*, and the new guy in the group—Other Ken, or "OK", as we called him—loaded his gear onto *Miwok*. OK was an experienced drift boater, but had never rowed a raft before. He would turn out to be a great boatman, and he adjusted easily to the comparatively sluggish handling of the raft.

While OK packed his share of the group food and supplies, I took advantage of the fact that I had cell phone coverage for the first time since leaving Cascade, Idaho sixteen days earlier, and called Linda.

"Well, I didn't see anything about you on the news, so I figured you'd be calling," Linda said.

"I've covered over 200 miles of river since the last time we talked, and by the time I put the raft back on the trailer, I'll have floated 315 continuous river miles."

"Better you than me."

We talked for half an hour, and among other things, she told me that Kevin was taking a break from his Pacific Crest Trail hike. He left the trail north of Crater Lake, because he had a wedding to perform and a funeral to attend, and then he decided, because of the fires, to put the rest of the hike on hold—probably until the next year. But my adventure continued.

By the time I got off the phone call, everything was ready to go, except for drinking water. I had thought—incorrectly—that there was water at

Short's Bar, and told everyone that there was no need to fill their water jugs before getting there.

We rowed down to the boat ramp at city park and filled our water jugs. Just downstream, we ran the rapid at 911 Hole, and by then it was 3:00. So, when we saw a large gravel bar opposite the northern tip of Riggins, we stopped and inspected its potential for camping.

None of us who'd made this run in the past could recall seeing any decent camping spots between there and Lightning Creek, five miles downstream, so despite the urban nature of the beach, we decided to stay.

The sound of traffic on busy Highway 95 was mostly covered by river noise from 911 hole just upstream and Race Creek Rapid just downstream. I enjoyed my first can of beer in a week before setting up camp.

First thing in the morning on July 25th, we ran Race Creek Rapid, followed by Time Zone Rapid, where the

Photo by Delrena Ogg
Entering Time Zone Rapid, Class IV

safe run is down the left side. Half a mile later, we took the right-hand chute past Tight Squeeze Wave. This stretch is very popular for day-trips, because of the lively rapids.

Five more good rapids in the next six miles led us to the tiny town of Lucile., where most of the day-trips end. We stopped for lunch at China Creek Beach, and then then continued down to Long Gulch and Box Canyon Beach, where we camped for the night.

Half an hour after leaving camp the next morning, we ran down the left side of Blackhawk Rapid, carefully avoiding the massive hole on the left at the foot of the rapid. Then we stopped at the Slate Creek boat ramp, where I emptied my Scat-Packer at the RV dump station, and put all of my trash, including the dead Tahiti, into a dumpster in the campground there. It was a

Photo by Delrena Ogg
Camping on Box Canyon Beach at RM 70

leisurely float for the rest of the day, and we made only 10.5 miles before stopping at what we call Goose Shit Beach, opposite Campbell Flat.

It was mid-afternoon the next day when we arrived at Hammer Creek, where most Lower Salmon trips begin. I was surprised that nobody was on the boat ramp. Normally, even this late in the day, there'd be at least a group or two rigging rafts. We stopped to get water and fill-out a self-issued permit for the last 57 miles of the Salmon River.

A guy approached me while we were filling water jugs and asked, "You know about the fires downstream?"

I said, "We've been smelling smoke all day, so I figured there was fire someplace."

"Yeah, it's been burning for a couple of weeks. Hardly anyone's been launching because of it. I heard a guide say that the river is closed."

"I don't see anything about that on the bulletin board," I said. "It seems like they'd post something if the river was closed."

The guy shrugged. "The smoke's not so bad today. Maybe they're getting the fire under control."

I related this conversation to the group, and we all agreed that there'd have been some kind of notice if the river actually was closed, so when we had our freshly topped-off water jugs strapped down, we pushed off.

Right after leaving Hammer Creek, a shift in the wind caused a marked deterioration in air quality. Whenever the wind blew upriver, it brought smoke that blotted-out the sun and burned my eyes.

We camped that night at Christmas Tree Beach about five miles past Hammer Creek. Fortunately, when the wind died down in the evening, the air cleared-out a bit and made breathing easier.

Photo by Delrena Ogg
Entering Green Canyon

For two weeks, I'd been riding a declining river flow, and at this point it was at about 6,000 cfs, which is considered optimum on this stretch of river. Still the intervals between rapids were flatter and slower, forcing us to put a lot more effort into pushing downstream.

In planning this trip, I had anticipated slow water and had given us five and a half days to get from here to Heller Bar. The first time I floated this stretch of river, I did it easily in four days. So, this wasn't a particularly aggressive schedule, and I anticipated a generally easy float.

On my guided trips, we always stopped in the eddy just above the entry to Green Canyon to see an array of pictographs. Some members of our current group had never been there, so we stopped, and I tried to recite what my niece Katy, who grew up on the Spokane Indian Reservation, had said about the meaning of the pictographs.

We went through Green Canyon, easily managing the Class II and III rapids, and after we passed Pine Creek, the smoke again descended on the river and turned the sun orange. Between Pine Creek and Rice Creek, there is a road along the river, and desirable campsites are scarce.

Photo by Delrena Ogg
Snowhole Rapid, Class IV

At River Mile 34.5, we stopped at Wickiup Creek, the first in a series of six or seven good campsites after the end of the road. The next day, we floated Snowhole Canyon, including the Class IV Snowhole Rapid. It's always kind of spooky to look at, but the run is easy, as long as you enter at the right spot—which everyone did.

Shortly below Snowhole, the river starts a broad bend to the north. On the right, at River Mile 22, where the river straightens out, we found a great camp that the BLM map calls Otter Poop Beach, or OPB. Delightful. We spent the afternoon going in and out of the water, because swimming was the only relief from the heat, until the sun went down.

After OPB, the river begins a huge horseshoe bend to the left. Near the end of this bend the next day, we ran China Rapid. The river hooks sharply left as you get into the rapid, so you can't see the boulder garden below. Stay left and watch out for a big pour-over hole thirty feet from the left bank.

Photo by Delrena Ogg
Rounding the bend in China Rapid. The sneaky hole is not visible at this point, but this is where you need to start moving left.

A couple of miles further, we first saw the burned-over hills extending from the right-hand riverbank as far as we could see. There were smoldering piles of ash, but the fire was mostly out. we camped on the left bank, opposite China Creek, and after dark, we could see glowing embers all over the hillside.

Here, the river is mostly flat, and it was slow going for most of the next six miles, until the start of Blue Canyon, where sheer vertical walls tower overhead. At River Mile 3.5 we floated over the site of notorious Slide Rapid. At high water, it becomes a Class VI monster. But at low water, it is barely a riffle. Five Class II-III rapids finish-out Blue Canyon.

Photo by JP Baysinger

The entrance to the upper mine shaft was partially blocked, and getting in involved crawling over jagged gravel. Once inside, it opened-up, and extended a quarter-mile deep.

Within sight of the Snake River Confluence, we stopped to walk up to see the Pullman Mine relics. The mine shafts used to be a great place to go on a hot afternoon, until the government put bars over the entrances, to protect bats from human intrusion.

I had known about the bars on the lower shaft, but I hadn't gone up to the upper one to see if it was also blocked. So, we scrambled up the steep scree slope and located the hole. It was more obstructed that it had been the last time I actually ventured down, so we didn't try going in. Who knows, maybe bars were not installed.

Feeling defeated, we went back down to our rafts and consoled ourselves with lunch and cold beer. We rowed the last hundred yards of the Salmon, into the Snake. About three miles down the Snake, we came to Cherry Creek, where a waterfall at river level features a bathtub-sized plunge pool, deep enough to sit in and get pummeled by the falling water. In times past, I had climbed up Cherry Creek Canyon to a whole series of additional waterfalls.

But the climb can be pretty treacherous, and now being a somewhat fragile old fart, I decided not to take the risk. So, after a brief cold shower, we returned to our rafts.

Half a mile of easy rowing brought us to Geneva Bar, and since we were in a relatively smoke-free area, we called it a day.

This part of the Snake River is often called "The Great Snake Lake" by people rowing against the ubiquitous headwind. Fortunately, the wind the next day was pretty mild, and we were able to make headway without busting a gut. Whenever the hillsides above the eastern canyon wall came into view, we could see the blackened ground from the huge Snake River Complex Fire, which by then had been burning for nearly a month.

After eleven miles of rowing, we stopped in a cove on the left bank just above Wild Goose Rapid. There's a great little shady grotto at the head of a big sandbar, and it has for years been my preferred place for a last-night camp above Heller Bar.

Photo by Joni Scott
Cherry Creek Falls

There was still a lot of smoke in the air, and we figured that was the reason there were no jet boats on the river. Normally, we'd see two or three jet boats an hour, so their absence was striking.

The run down to Heller Bar the next morning was uneventful. As we approached the boat ramp, instead of the customary chaos, we found an eerie silence. There was nobody else around. I walked up to the huge parking lot with Tamara and my brother Jim, and we quickly found their rigs, but not mine. The last time that had happened, it was because my alternator had crapped-out during the shuttle, and the driver had to stop and have it replaced.

Figuring something like that had happened, I walked around until I found a spot where my phone got a signal, and called the shuttle service in North Fork. They acknowledged that my shuttle was running a little bit late, but they assured me that my rig would be at Heller Bar before noon.

We all set to work de-rigging rafts and loading them onto trailers. We worked first on Tamara's raft, since she and her husband Travis had a much longer drive ahead of them than either Jim or I had.

After sending them on their way, the rest of us completely unloaded *Miwok*. I swapped the SuperStove for the Mini, and rigged *Vanguard* for solo rafting. We loaded Jim's raft, *Big Blue* onto his trailer and stacked *Miwok* on top of that.

About then, my phone rang, and Tamara told me that they'd just seen my rig in Asotin, twenty miles north of Heller Bar, heading our way. Since I could easily load *Vanguard* onto my trailer by myself, I sent the others on their way.

I walked up to the parking lot and met the shuttle drivers when they arrived a few minutes later, and saw for myself the reason for the delay. The front of their van was caved-in from hitting a deer, and they'd had to wait for daylight to continue, because their headlights were gone. The van still had to go all the way to Carey Creek to pick up a load of drivers who'd shuttled rigs for floaters coming down from Corn Creek. It was going to be a long day for them

I backed my trailer down the ramp and winched *Vanguard* out of the water. In twenty minutes, I was on my way, without having seen a single other party coming in or going out. But when I stopped to change clothes in the outhouse, I saw a notice on the bulletin board saying that the boat ramp was closed due to the fires.

But despite the fires, the twenty days I had just spent on the Main and Lower Salmon River were some of the most enjoyable I've experienced on the hundreds of river trips I've taken over the years. There was little drama, lots of excitement, and no stress.

In thinking about the next leg of my make-it-up-as-I-go-along expedition, I couldn't help wondering if I should quit while I was winning. What if my next float turned out to be such a letdown that it tarnished the glow I was feeling after my Salmon River float?

Chapter Twenty-One

Hells Canyon Then

The logical next place to go was the Snake River—the same river I'd just pulled my raft out of, and, in fact, duplicating the last twenty miles of my Salmon River trip. But upstream from that twenty-mile stretch lies fifty miles of wild river in Hells Canyon.

The Snake River in Hells Canyon holds a special place in my whitewater portfolio. It was where I had my very first whitewater adventure, in November of 1964, right around the time of my nineteenth birthday. I was a complete novice. Not even that. Novice implies some small and insignificant level of experience, inadequate for the task at hand. I had no experience whatsoever.

But it didn't matter, because I was just a passenger on a hunting trip organized by some guys in a fiberglass shop where I worked. I was invited to join the group to fill a vacancy left by the untimely firing of a co-worker. I'd worked in the shop for barely over a month, and hardly even knew the men I was going with. But heck. I had a chance to be one of the guys.

That's the best explanation I can give for why I joined a hunting expedition, when I wasn't a hunter and didn't even own a hunting rifle. But the fiberglass shop was going to be shut down for a week to replace windows blown out in an explosion that was caused by the guy who lost his job. So, why *wouldn't* I go?

Now, I had some vague idea that there were big rapids in Hells Canyon, but nobody in the group talked much about that. However, I did know from lunchroom chit-chat that some of the guys had rowed their boats in the famous McKenzie River Whitewater Parade, so I felt that I was in good hands.

The leader of the party, an affable guy named Bill, had actually been there once. He'd gone on a hunting trip a few years earlier, and was thus our "guide." Eight of us in four drift boats launched from a gravel beach at the tiny town of Homestead, after driving half the night and spending the other half trying to sleep in two pickup trucks and a 1951 Chevy Suburban that had been a "crummy" in a logging camp during its early life, and still had a faded Weyerhaeuser logo on the door.

Photo by Jerry Baysinger
A wooden drift boat on the Middle Fork

It is said that after you row a boat in whitewater, you'll never see a river the same way again. I would expand that and say that you don't know what whitewater *is* until you row it. As a passenger in a boat, you never understand the full power of the river, unless it dumps you. But as long as the boat stays upright and you stay in it, it is easy for a beginner to get the idea that rapids are just wet, noisy entertainment.

I later learned that Bill had been a first-timer and a passenger on his one and only visit to Hells Canyon, at least five years before. It turned out that his memory of the rapids was severely tainted by this rookie phenomenon. His hired professional boatman had handled the boat well, and had taken them through the rapids with hardly a splash. The fact that some of these were genuine Class V rapids meant nothing to Bill. From his perspective, they'd been easy.

Our plan was simple. Bill's recollection was that it would take a day to float to where we would set-up our "basecamp," on a huge sandbar on the Oregon side of the river. Hunting there would be great, and there'd be deer for everyone—just like on his first trip.

Things went pretty well for our first half day on the river, although I was getting a lot wetter than I'd expected. Wearing rubberized nylon rain gear over old camping clothes, I kind of wished I'd brought the wetsuit that I owned for scuba diving, but the subject hadn't come up during our preparations.

In the middle of the day, we passed a temporary city comprised of trailers and portable buildings on a big flat terrace above the right bank. Someone on shore honked a horn as we went by, so we happily waved and commented how surprised those guys must be to see us out there in boats.

The whole thing surprised me, because I thought we were going into a wilderness area. Bill said that he didn't remember there having been a road, and speculated that maybe it was some kind of mining operation.

Late in the afternoon, when Bill was assuring us that our destination should be around the next bend, we found ourselves approaching a rapid that was clearly bigger than what we'd been running all day. With no maps or guidebooks, we didn't know the names of the rapids, but years later I figured out that this was Kinney Creek Rapid—the first in a series of Class IV and V rapids that made Hells Canyon famous.

Photo by Jan Brandvold

The fiberglass dories used in Grand Canyon are a special class of drift boats. There are no photos of the 1964 hunting trip.

Today, I'm astounded by our casual attitude about these rapids. We gave them no respect whatsoever, and plowed into them as though we were on a thrill ride in an amusement park. To me, Kinney Creek looked fearsome, but my boatman, Carl, followed Bill straight down the mid-river tongue, and we had a smooth ride.

Squaw Creek Rapid, not far downstream, was a beast on a whole different level. Bill later confessed that we probably should've scouted that one, but the guide on his first trip hadn't scouted anything, so he figured we didn't need to either. I didn't learn the term "read-and-run" until twenty years later.

I've seen old films of these rapids. I have no idea why we didn't all die that day and become Democrat voters in perpetuity. Carl got us through, but hardly dry. I got busy bailing as we regrouped, laughing with forced bravado. Squaw Creek was a monster.

Buck Creek Rapid was even bigger and meaner. When the rapid came into view, I looked over the brink where the current funneled into a steep "V" that ended in a mammoth back-rolling wave flanked by massive, churning eddies. Out in front, Bill aimed his boat at the towering wave and pushed on the oars. In front of the wave, his boat dropped from sight into a deep trough, and when it came back into view it seemed to be standing on end, just before the wave broke over it. And then it was our turn.

I experienced a moment of sheer terror when I looked into the depth of the trough in front of the wave that swallowed Bill, but just as we started into it, the wave collapsed and filled the trough. We bounced over it, and then were lifted high as the wave re-formed. I was furiously bailing as we rolled through the wave train and caught up with Bill.

We made it to shore as the November twilight closed-in on us. All four boats were swamped, but upright. We were wet, cold, and had no idea what lay ahead or how far it was to that "hunter's paradise" that Bill had promised us. After a very brief discussion, we decided to set up camp, rather than risk encountering another monster rapid in near-darkness, a decision that quite possibly saved our lives.

Our gear for the basecamp consisted of three large, white canvas wall tents, wood-framed folding chairs and cots, plus tables and Coleman stoves. It was intended to be a comfortable basecamp that we'd set up once and occupy for the week, or until we had all bagged our deer. But it was way too big a project to do for a one-night stay. So, we set up just one of the tents, spread a tarp on the ground inside, and rolled out our sleeping bags on that.

Some of the guys rounded up a pile of driftwood and started a huge campfire, which we gathered around to dry-out and get warm. We ate beef stew from cans heated in a washtub of boiling water propped up on rocks over the fire. The jokes about our day's adventures had a hollow, insincere ring to them.

Throughout the uncomfortable night on the hard, lumpy beach, we heard the sound of heavy trucks on a road cut into the side of the canyon, high above the river on the opposite side. We all accepted Bill's opinion that all of the traffic must be associated with that mining operation.

After a light breakfast in the morning, we reloaded the boats and got underway. Within a few minutes we arrived at a boulder-choked drop that must have been Sawpit Rapid. We entered it hugging the Oregon shoreline, trying to stay dry by avoiding the big waves.

Fifteen minutes later, we arrived at the construction site for Hells Canyon Dam. There was no big mining operation. Most of the excavation at that point was on the Idaho side, and the diversion tunnel loomed huge, right at water level, an ominous, gaping hole in the canyon wall. There was a massive rock pile extending along the right bank and intruding into the river where the diversion dam was being constructed, using rock blasted from the tunnel.

Someone on shore saw us and waved frantically for us to get to shore. After we landed, they told us that the river ahead was impassable, and we shouldn't even be on the river. A manager of some kind showed up and got some of his men to help us pile our boats and gear onto a lowboy trailer and portage us around the construction site, which was right on top of Copper

Ledge Rapid, once considered to be the toughest rapid on the river. Except for that portage, we almost certainly were the last people ever to float the true Hells Canyon.

By the time we were back in the water, it was starting to snow. Bill had assured us that Hells Canyon was a "banana belt," and the temperature probably wouldn't go below forty. Yeah. And it was snowing. We pressed on, confident that we'd find our destination at any moment. The sounds of construction, muffled by the snow, quickly faded away.

A new sense of isolation accompanied the light snowfall, and after about an hour, we arrived at what I now know was Wild Sheep Rapid. As I remember it, Bill led us down the Idaho side, close to the shore, though on subsequent trips, I've failed to recognize any runnable course there. We went another half-mile, and pulled up on the right bank to wait for the other two boats, which were lagging behind.

The guys got out cigarettes and were lighting up, when someone spotted something orange out in the river. It looked like a life jacket, and whatever it was, it had to have come from one of our boats, so Bill sent Carl and me out to pick up anything we could salvage. He waited there to watch for swimmers. We were able to pick up a few items, and saw ample evidence that a wooden boat had been reduced to splinters.

I had just grabbed a floating oar when Carl muttered, "Holy shit!"

Ahead of us, the river was squeezed against the left side of the canyon by a massive boulder bar. As we rode the tongue down the center of the steep drop, a towering green wave suddenly rose up in front of us. For a brief moment, it felt like the boat was going to fall over backward as we went up the face of the wave. I gripped the oar I had recovered as though it was the safety bar in a roller coaster. For a fraction of a second, we were actually *inside* the curl of the wave before it crashed down on top of us. The icy water was stunningly cold and felt like a hundred knives being shoved through my skin. Panic momentarily swept over me with the realization that my life vest hadn't kept me afloat.

Underwater and disoriented, I thought that I had been swept out of the boat, but when I finally broke the surface, the boat came up beneath me. It was completely full of water, and Carl had lost his oars. One of them popped up alongside the boat, and he managed to grab it. I quickly handed him the oar that I was still holding onto, and Carl was able to get more or less back in control. I bailed frantically with a small plastic bucket, while Carl looked for a place to pull ashore.

By the time he finally found a beach where he could wrestle the boat to shore, we had floated another mile downstream. While I kept bailing, Carl started hurriedly unloading gear from the front of the boat, hoping to get our bags out before too much water leaked into them. When I finished bailing the boat, I was shivering, and my fingers were numb, as I fumbled to untie the parachute cord that held my gear bags shut.

I was overjoyed to find that my things were dry. Carl and I laughed hysterically at the scene, as we stood on the beach in the snow and stripped off our wet clothes. I felt giddy as I put on dry clothes and felt a hint of warmth. My only jacket was waterlogged, so I put on two sweatshirts and covered them with an army surplus rubberized poncho.

It was getting dark when the remaining two boats finally arrived. Nobody had drowned, and that was a miracle. As we unloaded the boats and stacked up the things we had managed to salvage, the two guys from the wrecked boat mournfully took inventory. One of the tents was gone, along with a couple of rifles, some chairs, and a pair of cots. Fortunately, they'd managed to recover their waterlogged sleeping bags and clothes, which had been in canvas sea bags that had floated out of the boat.

Snow continued falling and was beginning to stick, turning the beach around us into a smooth carpet of white. Bill looked around and suddenly broke into a broad grin. He happily proclaimed that by pure chance, we had landed at the beach we'd been looking for. This was "Bill's Paradise."

As the snow came down harder, we set up our two remaining tents, end to end, on the huge beach. We'd use the larger one for a bunkhouse, and the smaller one for a cookhouse. We had to use oars and scavenge some driftwood to replace the tent poles that had been lost, but eventually, we got everything under cover inside the tents. Darkness was complete when we dragged the boats out of the river into a shallow pool at the head of the sand bar.

Once we got the tables set up and the lanterns and stoves going, it warmed right up inside the tents. We spent the next half-hour wringing out clothes and sleeping bags, which we hung up in the cookhouse tent. Now, these tents were huge. The smaller one was probably about 12 by 16 feet, the other maybe 16 by 20. That night, Ted and Hugh, who had lost their boat, slept in folding chairs in the kitchen, because their sleeping bags were still too wet to use. They kept a stove going all night to keep warm.

And it snowed all night. By morning, there was a foot of snow on the ground. The weight of the snow on the bunkhouse tent had cause it to sag-in against us, and it was in imminent danger of collapsing entirely. The cookhouse tent had stayed warm enough to melt-off the snow as it hit, so we determined that from then on, as long as it kept snowing, we'd have to keep both tents heated, using Coleman lanterns. The clothes and sleeping bags eventually got dry, and we got things organized better, so that it was actually pretty cozy. The canvas tents retained heat pretty well, and just burning the lanterns kept it fairly comfortable.

And it still kept snowing. At times, we could barely see the river fifty feet away, but that first morning, we took it all in good spirits. We went out and had an epic snowball fight, and even played a sort of football game in the snow, using a rolled-up life vest for a ball. Sometime during the afternoon, Carl came in and excitedly announced that there were deer at the edge of the river, on the downstream end of our sandbar.

There was a mad scramble for rifles, and everyone bolted from the tent. We saw a doe with a pair of fawns, but no bucks. Nevertheless, everyone was suddenly optimistic that the deer would come to us, and we'd get our hunting done in spite of the weather.

By our second morning in Bill's Paradise, however, the reality of our situation had become apparent. The snow was close to two feet deep on the ground, and it was still falling, although in smaller flakes. That was because it was getting colder. For the most part, we stayed in the tents, where it was warm. Bathroom functions were about the only thing that took any of us outside. And we didn't see another deer.

We passed the time bullshitting and playing a rowdy card game they called "Oh Hell," which involved a lot of good-natured bickering and congenial insults. Occasionally, someone would look outside, hoping for a change in the weather, but the icy draft that blew in whenever someone untied the door flap told us all we needed to know.

Four or five days into our forced confinement, we discovered that we were nearly out of fuel. Over dinner that evening, we decided that we had to leave in the morning, regardless of the weather. We slept without heat that night, and it was so cold that even fully clothed in my sleeping bag, I had a hard time getting any sleep.

We started packing up at five in the morning. Once everything inside the tents was packed up, we divided into two teams. Four guys went to work digging out the boats, while the rest of us took down the tents.

We quickly discovered that the snow melting off the tents had run down the sides and formed a dam of solid ice around the bottom. The lower six inches of the canvas was encased in ice. We tried chipping it away with a hatchet, but it was slow going. Meanwhile, the boat crew found that the puddle the boats had been sitting in had turned to ice. The boats were solidly frozen in place.

They struggled with the boats, and we struggled with the tents. Everyone was getting wet and cold. When we saw that two of the boats had been freed from the ice, we felt that it was almost time to go, so we decided to cut-away the part of the tents that was encased in ice. It isn't easy to deliberately destroy your equipment, but in the end, there was no choice.

Carl's was the last boat stuck in the ice, and the guys resorted to violence in the effort to break it free. Two big guys in unison threw their weight onto the high end of the boat. There was a loud crack, and the boat came loose. Sort of. A large chunk of plywood had remained stuck in the ice, and there was a grapefruit-sized hole in the center of the floor. And upon turning the boat over, we found additional damage, where about four feet of the floor seam had separated up one side of the boat.

It seemed clear that the boat was a lost cause. But putting all four of us in the two remaining boats would mean that we'd have to leave most of our gear behind. The guys who owned the cots, stoves, kitchen boxes, tents, and lanterns objected strenuously to the idea of abandoning their gear, and Carl wasn't ready to give up on his boat.

During our first evening on this beach, while setting up camp, we'd built a bonfire. While gathering firewood, I'd walked up from the sandbar to some pine trees to break off dead branches. I'd seen big gobs of pitch where the trees had been damaged by a fire, and now it seemed like we could put it to good use. I suggested that we might be able to melt the pitch and use it to laminate a patch over the hole in the boat.

We were fiberglass guys, and we knew about laminating. So, we took knives, hatchets and empty cans up to the pine trees and collected all the pitch we could scrape off the trees. We fired-up one of the stoves, and carefully melted the pitch. Someone cut pieces of canvas from one of the tents, and we laminated three layers over the hole, and felt that we'd made a pretty secure patch. We drizzled melted pitch into the seam, to seal that up, and then turned the boat over and put another three-layer patch on the inside.

It was afternoon by then, and after slogging through waist-deep snow all day, we were soaked and frozen. Having no idea how far it was to our takeout at Pittsburgh Landing, we decided that we'd have to stay another night. We put up one of the tents, packing snow around the cut-off bottom in a marginally effective effort to close it off from the weather.

With everything in one tent, there wasn't room to move. We mixed up can after can of Campbell soup, and gulped it from tin cups to warm ourselves. We made pancakes until we ran out of fuel, and then hunkered down to wait-out the night. I hardly slept. It was just too damned cold.

At four, someone asked quietly if anyone else was awake. Everyone was. Using the two flashlights that hadn't yet gone dead, we packed-up again. It was still dark when we started downriver, but at least it had stopped snowing. We arrived at three or four good-sized rapids just about the time it was getting light.

One of them, as I determined years later, was Waterspout Rapid, and that's where Carl lost his grip on one of his oars. Out of control, we slipped sideways into a hole and got battered for several excruciatingly long seconds, while Carl and I scrambled to climb to the high side. With a hard thump, the boat crashed down right-side-up.

But the thrashing had opened-up the floor seam, and there was a steady seepage of water into the boat. About every five minutes for the rest of the trip, I had to bail a couple of gallons of water out of the boat. Waves of ice water sloshed around and over our feet the whole time.

There was no sunrise, but it gradually became light as we floated between the snow-covered slopes that stretched endlessly above the river. From time to time, we would see trenches in the snow where animals had plowed through, but we never actually saw any wildlife. We didn't stop all day. We had some cans of V-8 Vegetable Juice to drink, some crackers to eat. We saw a few ranches with smoke rising from the chimneys, but as much as we were tempted to stop, we all knew that if we did, we'd have had a very hard time going back to the boats.

By mid-afternoon, we were frozen, exhausted, and hungry. I don't know what anyone else was thinking, but I was getting really tired of hearing Bill tell us that Pittsburgh Landing would be right around the next bend. Each time we rounded the bend, we'd just see more endless gray river.

Twilight comes very early at the bottom of Hells Canyon in November. The snow gradually lost its brightness, and a dull gray began creeping in upon us. I had a gnawing fear that we might have floated past Pittsburgh Landing without seeing our vehicles, or that the road into the landing might be closed by snow. The near total lack of conversation hinted that the others were thinking the same things. We were on the verge of stopping, when at last, we spotted our snow-covered rigs sitting alone next to the boat ramp.

Photo in Kirkwood Ranch Museum

The first rubber raft in Hells Canyon, 1927 – Mart and Earl Hibbs.

Chapter Twenty-Two

Hells Canyon Now

Nine years passed, most of which I spent in the Navy and college, before I took my second whitewater river trip. My friend Dave invited my wife and me on a two-hour raft trip on the Clackamas River. We had a great time, and did several more trips with him over the next couple of years. In 1975, we bought our own raft, and did a three-day trip on the Rogue River. That's when I really caught the bug.

Now, after another forty-six years, I left Heller Bar, pondering the best route to Hells Canyon. But first things first. In Asotin, I ran my pickup through a car wash, removing several pounds of caked-on dirt and dust. Then, I stopped at the Scat Machine and cleaned my ScatPacker.

I got a motel room in Clarkston, had a pizza delivered, and logged-on to the motel's WiFi to catch up on e-mail and make a perfunctory check for any permits available for the Snake. As expected, nothing was available, so if I was to float Hells Canyon, I'd probably have to revert to my life of crime. Or maybe I could get lucky again.

I called Linda, and we exchanged stories about things that had taken place during the eight days since we last talked. She commented that I sounded tired, and she wasn't wrong. I hadn't slept well during the four nights I spent in the fire zone. My throat was sore, and it had been a long day. The temptation to drive home was strong.

But I slept well that night, despite the strangeness of being indoors, in a real bed, and after breakfast at a pancake house next to the motel, I found a laundromat close to a grocery store. While my clothes were in the washer, I bought supplies for another week on the river.

When my clothes were dry, I re-packed my bag, went and got a Big Mac, and then headed south on US-95. I spent the night at the Slate Creek landing, where the old Tahiti still protruded from the dumpster.

I got up early, made a thermos of coffee, and was on the road by 6:00. With my coffee and a box of donuts, I made the drive to the Hells Canyon launch site in just over three hours, including a brief stop at Scotty's in Homestead, Oregon to set up my shuttle.

I bypassed the Hells Canyon visitors center and went straight to the boat ramp, where I took my place in the queue. There was a van and trailer on the ramp and another rig in line ahead of me. The people on the ramp seemed to be disorganized and in no particular hurry. After watching them for a while, I walked down to see what I could do to help speed things up.

There were three couples who appeared to be in their thirties and forties, with three rented fourteen-foot Hyside rafts. The ladies were standing in the water at the bottom of the boat ramp, while the guys took turns pumping-up the first of the rafts using a squeaky cylinder pump.

Photo by Jerry Baysinger

The Hells Canyon boat ramp is narrow and has no staging area for rafts. A large group can cause a serious back-up.

"You guys want to use my electric pump? It'll be quicker, and a hell of a lot easier."

They looked at each other and reached a silent consensus.

"Yeah, that'd be great."

"Okay, move the rafts up to the front of your van, and I'll go up and get my pump."

One guy took my pump and started airing-up the first raft, so I went around to the back of the trailer to assess the rest of the situation. There were three one-piece steel frames, each made to carry a dry box and an ice chest. We moved the frames down to the end of the ramp and placed them side-by-side to await the arrival of the inflated rafts. Then we carried the coolers and boxes down and figured out which went with which frame.

Meanwhile, I looked over the heap of personal gear and small items, including a bag of straps, tangled in a spaghetti-like mass. I caught the eye of one of the ladies and suggested that she could help by sorting the straps by length and laying them out on the rocks next to the ramp.

"As soon as we get the basic rigging done on the rafts, we'll move them off the boat ramp." I pointed to an area off to the left-hand side of the ramp.

"Start by staging all of your personal gear on the rocks over there. Sort it according to which raft it goes on."

When the first of the rafts was inflated, I helped the guys carry it down to the water. Two went to work on rigging that raft while the other started inflating the next one. in about fifteen minutes, we had the frames, coolers, and dry boxes tied-down on all three rafts.

"Now, let's move them out of the way and clear the boat ramp for the next people in line," I said, while coiling the cables for my pump.

I was doing my best to convey a sense of urgency about the line of people waiting for the single-lane boat ramp, trying to keep everyone motivated. Carrying my pump back up to my rig, I passed the truck that was ahead of me in line.

"Are you part of that group?" asked a member of the party.

"No. I just let them use my pump to speed them up."

"Good plan. I was afraid they'd be there all day. How long do you think they'll keep the ramp tied-up?"

"I hope they're about done with it. I'm going to go back down and coach them. I think they're all rookies, and they don't seem to understand what they're supposed to do," I said.

"Hey, thanks for doing that."

When the Hyside group finally got everything unloaded from the van and trailer, the group leader (at my suggestion) drove up to a temporary parking area and cleared the ramp. The queue moved forward, and the next group moved to the launch ramp.

That group consisted of three guys on two rafts. I asked the guy I'd talked with before if there was anything I could do to help.

"No, thanks. We've got this," he said.

As I turned to go back up to wait in my pickup, the leader of the Hyside group waved me over.

"You've been down this river before, right?" he asked.

"Yeah. Maybe a dozen times," I said.

"Can you give us any advice on the big rapids?"

"The biggest are Wild Sheep, Granite, and Waterspout. They're not the only ones that can flip you, but they're the most likely ones."

"Yeah? When will we come to them?"

"Don't you have a guidebook or map?"

"We have an article out of Sunset Magazine, but it doesn't say much about the rapids."

I said, "You should go back up to the Visitor's Center and get a map. They might even have one that's free. But they definitely have some good guidebooks for sale."

One of the women in the group said, "That sounds like something we ought to do, Gary."

"Yeah, I'll go up there when I take the van to the parking lot." He turned to me and said, "Thanks for the advice."

"Be sure to stop and scout Wild Sheep and Granite—Wild Sheep on the left, Granite on the right," I said.

He nodded and asked, "So, how many people are in your group?"

"Just me. Solo."

"Yeah? The permit gods must really favor you. We put in ten entries, and felt pretty lucky when one was drawn."

"Actually, I didn't win the lottery."

"Oh, so you picked up a cancellation?"

"No, I came here hoping someone would share a permit with me."

"Oh. Well, did you want to join our group?"

"I'm not looking to actually join the group except on paper. I mean, I have all my own gear and supplies. But if you could add me to your group and get me a tag, I'll just follow along behind you and stay out of your way."

Gary contemplated that briefly, and then said, "I'll tell you what. If you'll stay with us and show us what to do at those

Photo by Jan Brandvold
Minutes after launch, looking back at Hells Canyon Dam

first two big rapids, I'll add you to our permit when I go back up to the Visitor's Center."

And just like that, my permit problem went away.

Gary's group was still rigging their rafts when the second group cleared the boat ramp. I backed down, pushed my raft off the trailer, and tied it up next to the three Hysides. My total time on the boat ramp was less than five minutes.

I made myself a couple of sandwiches while waiting for Gary and his group to finish rigging their boats. It was about 1:00 when they finally were ready to go. I went with Gary to the Visitor's Center, got a tag for my raft, and recommended a guidebook.

As she handed me my tag, the ranger said, "You probably already know that, because of the fires, the river is closed to boating downstream from Pittsburg Landing."

Actually, I *didn't* know that.

She continued, "The fire managers have been hinting that they're going to re-open the river, but they haven't done it yet.

I'd set up my shuttle to go all the way to Heller Bar, on the assurance of the shuttle operator that the river was open. So, whose information was correct? One had to assume that the authorities would have the better information, right?

To cover my bets, I left a note in my pickup instructing the driver to take it to Pittsburg Landing if the river was still closed on August 6th.

"I never asked about your schedule," I said while we walked back down to the rafts.

"We're planning to takeout at Heller Bar next Wednesday," he said. "But I'm going to leave a note, like you did, in case the river is closed."

I nodded. I was confident that the river would be open, so six days was a good leisurely pace, even for a group of rookies.

"Okay. I have a suggestion for you. Make today a short float day. Camp before you get to Wild Sheep Rapid. That

Photo by Jerry Baysinger
Camped at Battle Creek on a trip in 2008.

Photo by Christine Moon
Scouting Wild Sheep Rapid

way, you can run it in the morning when the river flow is lower and your folks will be fresh."

"That sounds like good advice. I'll see what everyone else thinks."

The upshot was that we finally pushed off at 2:00 and floated only an hour before reaching Battle Creek. There's a nice campsite on the beach, and some sightseeing at an old miner's cabin. I set up my camp about twenty yards from the rest of the group, calling it "social distancing," using the language of the day.

In the morning, we carefully scouted Wild Sheep Rapid and identified the entry point to the left of a mid-river boulder. From there, a strong move to the right was needed to avoid a powerful back-rolling wave at the bottom of the rapid. Not everybody was able to follow the planned course, but nobody flipped.

Photo by Joni Scott
Running Wild Sheep Rapid

At about noon, we arrived at the scouting beach for Granite Falls. Looking down on the intimidating rapid, I pointed out a safe course down the left side, and then we watched an outfitter's gear raft make the run exactly as I'd explained: Approach the rapid close to the huge boulder on the left, and then pull further left beneath the boulder.

Everyone came through with the black side down, although some of the runs, were pretty sloppy, including mine. Leading the group of novices had taken a couple of hours longer than I'd have taken by myself, but that was a small price to pay for the tag that gave me the appearance of being legal.

A mile below Granite Rapid, I pulled ashore at what used to be called Oregon Hole. Most maps now call it Two Bars. I'd fulfilled my part of the bargain with Gary, and had gotten his group safely through the two big rapids. We said farewell, and his group continued downstream.

As soon as Gary disappeared around the next bend, I resumed my life of crime. Groups are required to stay together. But I had a permit tag, so it was unlikely that anyone would challenge me. But if they did, I had a story ready: I'd had to stop to make repairs, and would catch up by evening.

I set up for a leisurely lunch and a beer. On all of my raft trips in Hells Canyon, I'd tried to identify the spot where we'd set-up our basecamp on our ill-fated hunting trip in 1964. I'd long ago concluded that it had to have been at Oregon Hole, even though it looked nothing like it had then. The huge sand beach was entirely gone, leaving only a pair of rock bars.

Photo by Jerry Baysinger
Watching a professional boatman make a proper run at Granite Falls

Photo by Jan Brandvold
Oregon Hole – Bill's Paradise looks nothing like it did in November 1964.

Sitting there on a hot August afternoon, I tried to recognize anything familiar in the views up, down, and across the river, but it was impossible to do that. Back then, everything had been buried in snow, and we'd spent most of our time inside the tents.

Late in the afternoon, when the whole west side of the canyon was in shade, I took an exploratory hike up a game trail onto the bench above the rock bars. The dry cheat grass seeds poked into the heavy fabric on my sandals as I made my way toward a cluster of tall Ponderosa pine trees.

The trees where we'd collected pitch for patching Carl's boat had been deeply scarred, both by fire and by people chopping branches for firewood. But if these were the same trees, they'd healed, and there was no sign of the globs of pitch that had saved us. I was beginning to doubt that this was the right place, when I spotted something near the base of one of the trees.

It was a rusty steel-handled hatchet. The rubber grip that it once had was gone, but I recognized the tool. During my Boy Scout days, my brother and I had bought identical hatchets from our favorite military surplus store, Two Swabbies, in Spokane. The last time I saw mine was the day we were foraging for pitch in November, 1964. How very strange it felt to hold that artifact of my youth and realize that I'd be violating the Antiquities Act if I took it from this site. To hell with that. It was mine.

I seriously considered taking it home and restoring it—I'm sure I'd be able to find a new rubber grip somewhere online. But then what? Maybe it was worth more left where I'd found it, a monument to the folly of that ill-conceived adventure. I wondered if anyone else who'd been on that trip was even still alive. All of them had been at least ten years older than I was, so there's a high probability that I'm the only one left.

So, the hatchet is still there. And now I am certain where Bill's Paradise actually was. The sand beach washed away with the big daily fluctuations in flow caused by the demand for electricity from Hells Canyon Dam. And all of the sand that might have replenished the beaches is now impounded in the reservoirs upstream. Bill's Paradise is gone forever—or at least for as long as the dams exist.

Photo by Joni Scott
Jan Brandvold at the McGaffee cabin

There was still smoke in the air, but at a level far more tolerable than what I'd had a week earlier. In the morning, I ran five or six fun Class II rapids in the first two miles. Then, I stopped at Bernard Creek and hiked up to the McGaffee Cabin. It is a well-preserved glimpse of life in Hells Canyon a century ago. The cabin is on the National Register of Historic Places.

There is a very good pictograph display along the trail up to the cabin. I wonder if the Indians who created them were regarded as artists or vandals in their time. Graffiti is not my chosen form of criminal activity, but I wouldn't want to try convincing a judge that contemporary graffiti on rocks in a wilderness area is actually valuable artwork.

Immediately after leaving Bernard Beach, I entered two healthy rapids individually rated Class II+ and Class III+. Taken collectively, Upper and Lower Bernard Creek Rapids might be worthy of a Class IV rating.

Waterspout Rapid a mile downstream is another Class III rapid, and it is followed by a pair of Class II rapids. This area is the Snake River at its best. The rapid at Rush Creek carries a Class IV rating, but at water levels I've seen, it is easier than that. I'm guessing the higher rating comes at higher water levels.

Johnson Bar Landing at River Mile 229.8 marks the end of the really busy stretch of the river. I stopped for lunch and a swim. Late in the afternoon and seven miles downstream, I arrived beneath the high rock outcropping called Suicide Point. I labored in the afternoon heat to hike up to the viewpoint 400 feet above river level.

Photo by Jerry Baysinger
The author at Suicide Point

Gasping and wheezing from smoke inhalation, I sat on a rock wishing I had a beer. The view is spectacular, and well worth the hike. The walk back down is considerably easier, and beer in my cooler provided motivation.

I set up camp on Hominy Bar, directly below Suicide Point. I saw three other groups on the river that day, and all of them had gone past without meaningful conversation.

The evening brought dark clouds, so I set up my tent and kitchen shelter. I went to sleep that night with the pleasant sound of raindrops pattering on my rainfly. In the middle of the night, when I got up and went outside, I was surprised to find everything perfectly dry. The rain had evaporated as soon as it hit.

Because I had to take-down my pop-up shelter and tent, I didn't get out of camp until 8:30. Half an hour later, I arrived at Kirkwood Ranch, two miles down from Hominy

Photo by Jan Brandvold
Museum at Kirkwood Ranch

Bar. There is a museum there, with relics on display in and around the old log cabins.

Photo by Jan Brandvold
Pittsburgh Landing

After spending about an hour browsing Kirkwood Ranch, I continued my voyage, arriving at Pittsburgh Landing at lunch time. I checked the message board for any word about river closure, but found nothing. To be safe, I walked through the parking lot and satisfied myself that my rig wasn't there, meaning that the shuttle service knew that the river was open.

In the middle of the afternoon, and four more miles downstream, I stopped at Canyon Creek. Low on drinking water, I needed to camp there, so that I could run creek water through my gravity-fed ceramic filter.

That gave me a leisurely afternoon and evening to conclude the Grand Canyon part of this story, and start on the Grande Ronde. After dinner, I hung up my solar shower. Travelling solo again, I had no need to keep my shorts on, so I was standing there bare-ass under the shower when a jet boat appeared, heading downstream.

The combined effect of water in my ears, creek noise, and my general deafness kept me from hearing it until it was too late to save any dignity. So, there I stood, trying to rinse shampoo from my eyes, while the jet boat horn assured me that I had entertained everyone aboard.

A lazy float the next day took me about twelve miles, to Deep Creek (formerly called Deadline Creek), where in 1887, a gang of rustlers gunned-down 34 Chinese gold miners. They threw the bodies into the river and stole all the gold they could find. History knows who did it, but nobody knows what became of the gold.

Photo by Jerry Baysinger
Dual compressor, used to power pneumatic tools during the mining era.

People with metal detectors still search this site in hopes of finding something.

I walked up the creek to the remains of a small stone house, where there are some artifacts and Chinese inscriptions. From there, I went up to a point overlooking the massacre site, where a monument has been placed to honor the victims.

Photo by Jerry Baysinger
Slate Creek—site of the 1887 massacre of 34 Chinese gold miners by a gang of cattle rustlers.

Clouds were quickly gathering overhead, so I found a small beach just downstream. The storm front was so blustery that I couldn't set up-camp. Amid lightning and thunder, hail started coming down, and I had to take shelter under an overhanging ledge.

Coming in waves, the hail stones were sometimes as big as golf balls. By the time the storm tapered-off, the beach was completely covered. But the ice melted quickly, and I got my camp set-up without further drama.

I floated seven miles in my first two hours the next day, and arrived at the east entrance to the Mountain Chief Mine tunnel, which cuts completely through the ridge separating the Snake River from the Imnaha River. The tunnel is about a quarter-mile long, but no usable ore was ever extracted, and the smelter was never used. Apparently, the whole enterprise was a fraud, and the promoters of the mine absconded with all of their investors' money.

It used to be a fun hike through the tunnel, but alas, it is now blocked—as are all of the other mine tunnels in the Snake River Canyon. Bats are more important than your adventure.

Back on the river, the daily headwind was picking-up—gentle at first, but the next three and a half miles took ninety minutes. I stopped for lunch at the mouth of the Salmon River, where I'd been

Photo by Jerry Baysinger
Entrance of the Mountain Chief Mine tune

just nine days earlier. The air was clear of smoke, and the commercial jet boats were back in at least limited operation.

Photo by Jerry Baysinger
The west entrance of the tunnel

The first quarter-mile down-stream from the Salmon River confluence is a long, easy rapid with nice waves—when the wind isn't blowing. But as I tried to hold my position in the current, the wind constantly tried to blow the *Vanguard* off course. Whitecaps formed on the standing waves, and I reached a point where I had to swing the raft around and pull against the wind.

I worked for an hour to go two miles, before giving up and pulling to the left bank at Cave Cove. There, a little niche in the canyon wall provides shelter from the upstream wind. It was a strenuous carry to get my gear up the steep sandbar to the mouth of the shallow cave that gives the beach its name. But it was worth it, just to get out of that wind.

I'd covered thirteen miles that day, and I had thirteen more to cover the next day, in order to set up for an early arrival at Heller Bar, the day after that. So, I resolved to get out of camp before 7:30 and try to get to Wild Goose Beach by noon.

Photo by Jan Brandvold
Cave Cove Beach

It was a beautiful morning, and I got the early start that I'd planned. I passed Cherry Creek, this time without stopping, and pushed my way down the Great Snake Lake. With no wind, I was able to cover six flat-water miles in two hours, before reaching Cougar Bar.

There are three Class II rapids in the next mile, and the increased river speed was welcome relief. There are mile posts on shore showing the distance to the end of the Snake River at Pasco, so I could monitor my progress.

At RM 176, I passed the Oregon-Washington state line, and at 1:30, I reached the little cove above Wild Goose Rapid—the same place I'd spent my last night on the Lower Salmon segment of the Great Adventure.

After lunch, I sat down with my laptop and went back to work on this story. Several of the big excursion boats rumbled past, and there were even some private jetboats on the river.

Photo by Jan Brandvold
Cabins along the Snake River

After dinner, I was sipping wine and gazing without purpose at the passing water, when I spotted what I initially thought was an otter. But it wasn't behaving like an otter. It had to be a big fish, maybe a sturgeon. And then I saw the red shorts. Otters and fish don't wear red shorts.

I jumped to my feet and stared at the floating object as it drifted into the eddy directly in front of my camp. It came within five feet of shore, and by then there was no question what it was. It was a human body, face down, probably male, and thoroughly dead.

I quickly looked around and spotted a stick just long enough to reach out and nudge the body to shore. I'm not a sissy-pants, but dragging the body partway out of the water was an extremely unpleasant task. The victim wore no clothing other than the red shorts.

The part of his back that had been above water was mahogany brown, but the rest of his skin was a sickening pale green. He was rapidly ruining the ambiance of my evening.

My phone, of course, had no signal. And I could see no sign of life at the vacation cabins across the river. They had all been evacuated because of the fires. And all of the jet boats I'd seen going upstream during the day had already passed again, going the other way. It was the middle of the week, and I couldn't depend on another jet boat coming by that evening. I was on my own.

My one form of communication was the little Spot II satellite messenger that I used to send a daily "I'm okay" message to Linda. It has an SOS button, but it has no provision for entering a specific message. All it could do was send a distress signal and show my location. I pressed the red button.

I had a five-by-seven reflective mylar emergency "blanket," which I draped over the ghastly sight. I weighted the corners with rocks, thanking God that the wind wasn't blowing. Then I got out the fluorescent orange fabric panels that are required equipment in Grand Canyon, and spread them in the form of a giant X in the middle of the sand bar as a signal for helicopters.

It was 7:00, so there was no more than 90 minutes of daylight left. If a helicopter was coming, it would have to be quick. I dug around in my repair kit and found a couple of ancient road flares. I hoped they would still light.

I moved my chair to the top of the sand bar, fifty feet away from the body, and sat waiting for any sight or sound to indicate a response to my distress call. By 8:00 I was deep in twilight when I heard an engine.

I popped the cap off one of the flares and struck the coarse top of the cap against the tip of the flare. It failed to make a spark. I ran over to my stove and lit a burner. With that, the flare ignited. As the sound became more distinct, I recognized it as helicopter rotor blades beating the air.

When I was sure that the pilot had seen me, I lit the other flare and placed one on each side of the big orange cross. The Life Flight helicopter landed directly in the center of the X.

As soon as the medical technician determined that the victim was beyond help, he used his radio to relay that information to his dispatcher.

"I need to fly out of here and get back to Lewiston before it's too dark to see the canyon walls," the pilot told me. "The sheriff has boats on the way, and they'll be here in ten or twenty minutes."

The flares were still burning when the first jet boat came roaring up Wild Goose Rapid.

"You the one who sent out the distress signal?"

"That's right." I pointed toward the mylar-covered victim. "Body floated into the eddy. I dragged him out and covered him."

"Is it someone you know?"

I said, "No I've never seen him before."

The deputy went back to his boat and made a radio call that I couldn't hear over the sound of another jet boat coming upriver.

The two men from that boat had a quick conversation with the two from the first boat, and then a formidable-looking deputy with a handlebar mustache strode toward me.

"What can you tell me about Bob Green, there?" He gestured toward the covered body.

"Not a thing," I said. "He just floated in. I guess you've been looking for him?"

"Why do you say that?" the deputy asked.

"Well, you mentioned his name—Bob Green. If you know his name, you must have been looking for him."

He gave me a grim smile and shook his head. "Sorry. That's cop humor. When we find an unidentified floater, we call him Bob Green. Bob because that's what he's doing, and Green because…"

"Yeah. I get it. I saw him."

"Otherwise, he'd be John Doe."

Weeks later, I'd learn that he was Nathan Morris. He'd been dumped off his raft at Granite Falls a week earlier. His PFD apparently had been ripped off by the violent water.

"You want your space blanket?" the first deputy asked?

"Uh, no. You can leave it with Mr. Green," I said.

After many photos were taken, the victim was placed in a body bag and loaded aboard one of the jet boats. Meanwhile I signed a hand-written witness statement.

The boats each had an array of overhead floodlights that lit-up the river for a hundred yards ahead, as they pulled out of the eddy, turned downstream and roared to full throttle.

The sound faded away, and I was again alone on the beach. But somehow, I felt more alone than at any other time during my journey.

The next morning, I made a one-hour dash to Heller Bar and had my raft loaded on the trailer before ten o'clock.

Chapter Twenty-Three

The Dependable Deschutes

Statistically speaking, the Deschutes River is Oregon's most popular rafting river. That's because it is relatively close to the state's main population centers, and it is also the last year-round river in the state that is accessible without entering a permit lottery.

But you still need to pay a fee and have a permit, and if you're going to be on the river during a weekend, you are subject to limited access and have to pay an extra fee, on top of the $2 per day recreation fee and $6 reservation fee for each of five segments of river. Is all that clear? I think it's boater suppression through deliberate obfuscation.

I got off the Snake on a Wednesday, and over lunch in Clarkston, I checked the availability of Deschutes permits for the next few days. Friday, Saturday, and Sunday were all booked-up. I'd either have to go on Thursday, or wait until Monday, in order to avoid the limited-access days.

The six-hour drive to the Warm Springs launch site was doable, but I'd need to pick up groceries, ice, and propane along the way. I probably could get there by six. But there's no camping at Warm Springs.

A better idea was to get a motel room in The Dalles, and then make the ninety-minute drive from there to Warm Springs in the morning. That would give me a chance to do my laundry, catch up on emails and phone calls, and have a pizza delivered.

One thing about COVID is that it has made fast food just about non-existent. With inside dining still prohibited at fast food outlets, it is necessary to wait in long lines at the drive-through, thus defeating the whole point of going there in the first place. So, no Egg McMuffins. I got a sit-down breakfast at a restaurant next to the motel, wondering the whole time how the virus knows the difference between someone sitting at a table in McDonald's and someone sitting at a table in Denny's. Pretty amazing virus.

Passing through Maupin, I stopped and filled-out the forms and paid the fees for my Deschutes float, from Warm Springs to the Columbia River, except for a two-mile portage around Sherars Falls. I also arranged to have my rig shuttled from Warm Springs to Sandy Beach, just downstream from Maupin, on Monday the sixteenth.

That gave me five days to go fifty-two miles. The trip could easily be done in four days, or even three, but that would have meant dealing with weekend crowds in the day-trip section around Maupin, where the mandatory takeout at Sandy Beach is impossibly congested.

I also set up the shuttle for my run from Buck Hollow, below Sherars Falls, to Deschutes Park near the confluence with the Columbia River.

I got to Warm Springs at 10:15, launched my raft, and got underway at 11:00. The Deschutes is a river I've floated many times, mostly in the day-trip area around Maupin, but it has never been a favorite. Too many people, too many rules, too many fees, too much civilization (including a major railroad line), and too few campsites.

On the positive side, a one-person group can fit just about anywhere. And there are some rapids that are very fun—even challenging. In other words, it sucks, but not too bad, and it's still better than staying home.

I should mention that for about the first thirty miles, the west bank is Warm Springs Indian Reservation land, and it is said that tribal members occasionally shoot at passing rafts. While I' sure that's not true, you still don't want to pull ashore on that side of the river.

Once underway, I contemplated my float plan. The idea was to spend Sunday night near Harpham Flats, where the day-trip section begins. That would give me a clean shot straight through to Sandy Beach on Monday. The run to Harpham Flats could easily be done in three days, but I needed to take four, in order to avoid having to contend with the usual weekend mob of day-trippers in the Maupin area.

This would be essentially the same float plan that I used on my commercial trips for

Photo by Author
Lute Jerstad launching rafts at Trout Creek

Elderhostel, although those trips were always scheduled to launch on Tuesdays, in order to totally avoid weekends.

My first nine miles took only two-and-a-half hours, and as I when I arrived at the Trout Creek recreation area, I pulled ashore and made lunch. In the afternoon, I floated about eight more miles to River Mile 80.2 where there is a decent and popular campsite that my guides called Lone Pine, although the only trees there now are Juniper. I set up my camp at the edge of the flat, leaving a large area open for others.

Photo by Author
First night's camp on the Deschutes

An hour later, four fishermen in drift boats pulled in and asked if I'd mind if they camped there. I've never said no when somebody asked. That evening, I took time to think about how the weekend traffic might affect campsite availability downstream.

Many people over the years have made a weekend trip out of the 35-mile float from Trout Creek to Maupin City Park. The result is that the campsites around the halfway point, between River Miles 68 and 65, are in extremely high demand on Saturday nights.

That is exactly where I was planning to stop on Friday night, so doing my layover there meant that I could expect to have company. People end up camping on every patch of non-reservation flat ground in the area. But getting there early on Friday would probably give me first choice.

On the river early on Friday, I floated six miles before 10:00, encountering no rapids of consequence. Just ahead lay White Horse Rapid, a two-mile long Class IV rock festival that causes trouble for boaters on a regular basis.

Photo by Author
A boater goes directly over Oh Shit Rock, something that doesn't always end well.

Photo by Author

Do not use your oar to pry yourself away from a rock. You'll just break your oar, and still be pinned against the rock.

I navigated the Class II "warning ledge," and then pulled ashore on the right bank to scout White Horse. I followed the well-worn scouting trail to a viewpoint where I could see the first 200 yards of the rapid, where the touchiest part of the run is located.

Three boulders sit in a line just below the surface, making them difficult to see as you approach them. Dodging the first two without knowing that the third one is lurking below almost guarantees that you'll hit it. That's why it's called "Oh Shit Rock," and it's claimed many boats and several lives over the years.

The other hazard at White Horse is becoming so fixated on OSR that you don't pay enough attention to the mile of whitewater that still lies ahead. Frequently, boatmen start celebrating their safe passage of OSR, only to become lodged on one of the many other dangerous rocks, downstream.

The party of fishermen in drift boats ran the rapid neatly while I watched, and then I took my turn. White Horse is great fun, as long as you stay in control of your boat and know where you have to go. Or it can ruin your day.

Right where the river starts to smooth out, there's a great camping beach on the right bank. I stopped there and spent the next hour hiking up to caves in the rimrock above the river. A couple of miles further downstream, in the North Junction area, I spotted a small blue cataraft beached at a popular campsite.

Photo by Author

View of the campsite (upper left) from a cave

In my motel room at The Dalles, I'd seen a Facebook post showing this very raft. A man who lives nearby carries the little boat down to the beach in his pickup truck and ties it up, making it appear as though the campsite is occupied, in effect, reserving it for a friend who is an out-of-state fishing guide.

Ideas that crossed my mind included cutting the raft loose and letting it float downstream; shooting holes through the tubes; or camping there just to be obnoxious, even though it wasn't where I wanted to camp. But I did none of these things. Eventually, karma will catch up with him.

At 2:30, I spotted old railroad tunnel number five above the right bank. Half a mile past there, at River Mile 68.7, I claimed the first in a row of nice campsites below the Two Springs Ranch. The campsites are close together, but separated by thick vegetation, some of which is poison ivy.

As the afternoon progressed, two groups passed me and claimed sites nearby. While typing on this story, a mama mink scuttled through my camp heading upstream carrying a pup. A few minutes later, she came back through camp alone, and shortly returned with another pup. She made three more trips, and apparently completed the family move.

I spent most of my layover day working on my whitewater memoirs and watching rafts go by. Several trains went by on the opposite side of the river, and a few cars went by on the private road behind my camp.

That road is on the abandoned Deschutes Railroad grade, and is owned and maintained by the Deschutes Club, owners of a private riverfront resort. You shouldn't come here expecting solitude.

I took a walk up to the old railroad tunnel, which is now used by cars heading to and from the Deschutes Club properties. The long tunnel is occupied by owls and bats, and it's a cool place to go on a hot afternoon.

On Sunday, exerting only the bare minimum effort, I drifted downstream at four miles an hour, and at 9:30, I arrived at Buckskin Mary Rapid, an easy rollercoaster of high waves. I stopped long enough to shoot phots of a few rafts running the rapid.

As I had anticipated, it was a very busy day on the river, but the current carries everybody along at the same speed, so unless you get caught in a clump of traffic, there isn't much interaction with other boaters. But when I stopped for lunch at Nena Creek, dozens of boats went by in a continuous

Photo by Author
Buckskin Mary, a fun wave-train

Photo by Author
Weekend crowds on the Deschutes

Photo by Author
Boxcar Rapid regularly flips small rafts that challenge the big hole.

Photo by Author
Oak Springs Rapid has a roadside viewpoint where spectators can watch frequent flips and ejections. Basalt ridges in the channel below can be very hard on swimmers.

parade, most carrying people who mentally were already on their way to work Monday morning.

I understand why that's the way things are, but somehow recreation should be liberated from the calendar (said the guy who has been telling you for 260 pages that losing track of time on a river trip is a crime).

In mid-afternoon, I floated past the mostly deserted campsites at Harpham Flats, where most day-trips on the Deschutes are launched. I can't even guess how many day-trips I've run in this section—nearly always as captain of a paddle raft. I can recall only a couple of times I've done it with an oar boat, as I was preparing to do.

I stopped and set-up camp just above Wapinitia Rapid, in order to be staged for the 9.4-mile run down to the Sandy Beach takeout. This stretch is filled with Class II and III rapids, plus two notable Class IV rapids, Boxcar and Oak Springs. This is where I taught my daughter how to command a paddle raft, and she helped me with many of our commercial day-trips.

I spotted my rig parked along the road as I approached

Photo by Jim Anderson

Paddle Captain John Lewis taking Mariah through Oak Springs Rapid in 1987

Sandy Beach around 1:30. By 2:30, I had my raft on the trailer and was on my way to Buck Hollow.

Along the way, I stopped at Sherars Bridge to look at the Class III Upper and Class IV+ Lower Bridge Rapids. In all of my many trips, I'd never taken the time to look at these two rapids, which are rarely run, because Sherars Falls, just upstream, is truly unrunnable (although it *has been* run at least once—by an inner tube menagerie in the 1970s).

Looking down on Upper and Lower Bridge rapids, I thought they looked pretty straight-forward—though tight—with narrow, steep chutes bordered by cube-fractured basalt cliffs. Before giving up on running these rapids, I spent a few minutes looking for a way to actually do it—starting with how to get my raft into the water.

There are parking lots on both sides of the road at the west side of Sherars Bridge. Both are on tribal land and parking is reserved for Indians, but I wasn't thinking of parking. I just wanted to slide my raft down to the river, and nothing said I couldn't do that.

Yes, I know that it was clearly implied, but why would a hardened river criminal like me worry about rules that are not explicitly spelled-out—or, for that matter, ones that are? On the east side of the bridge, there isn't a formal parking area, but there is room for one or two vehicles to park off the edge of the pavement, in an area that I presumed to be public—anyway, there are no signs saying otherwise.

So, I could slide the raft thirty feet down to the river about twenty yards upstream from the bridge and the start of Upper Bridge Rapid. The first thing I had to do was remove

Photo by Author

Sherars Falls. Try running it only if your balls are bigger than your brain.

everything from the raft except the frame, ice chest, and main dry box, which is bolted in place. I locked everything else in the back of my pickup, and then lowered the raft to the water. I parked my pickup on what I hoped was public land on the other side of the bridge.

I crab-walked down to my raft, untied it, and climbed aboard. I was swept into the current before I could even get to my seat. Grabbing the oars, I turned the raft downstream as I sat down. Suddenly, this didn't look like such a great idea.

The river at this point is very narrow, very deep, and is filled with peculiar hydraulics that interfere with control of the raft, so it is necessary to constantly pull and push on the oars to keep pointed downstream. The pool widens briefly and then runs into reefs on both sides of the river.

The first drop is of little consequence, but just ahead, the river plunges steeply—much more so than it had appeared from above. But the seven-foot drop is easy, riding the center of the tongue straight down into a row of orderly standing waves and into calm water that lasts maybe a hundred yards.

Briefly, the canyon widens out. A cluster of rocks protrudes in the middle of the river, and beyond that there is a solid rock island. From my scouting, I knew that the right channel around the island was extremely narrow, and the left channel was completely impassable.

I kept to the right of the protruding rocks and set up to enter the right channel. I entered the main drop sideways, with my stern almost touching the island, and had to keep pulling to hold my position until I reached the narrow main tongue. I pivoted and hit the big drop straight, and almost immediately pivoted again to pull away from rocks on the left side. It's a frightfully tight passage with no margin for error. A brush against the basalt walls on either side could easily cut a raft open. And then I was in calm water for the half-mile glide to the Buck Hollow boat landing.

My heart was still thumping in my ears when I pulled ashore and tied-up. Running those rapids was a stupid thing to do. I walked back and got my pickup, drove it down to Buck Hollow, and started re-rigging my raft. I was in the middle of that when the shuttle driver arrived. I hastily unloaded the rest of my things and sent her on her way with a generous tip. By then, it was 5:00, so I set up camp near the turnaround for the boat landing, despite a sign that said No Camping. It was meant for people in cars, not people in rafts. At least, that's how I interpreted it.

So, the next morning, I started down the Lower Deschutes. Back when I owned my rafting business, I'd explored the lower canyon from the access road, looking for off-river activities for Elderhostel trips there. But I had never actually floated this stretch of river, so in making my shuttle arrangements, I'd allowed myself extra time in case I felt the need to scout some of the rapids.

The first rapid of significance is Wreck Rapid, just over two miles from Buck Hollow. It gets its name from a head-on collision between two trains in 1949. I stopped and hiked down the left bank, not so much to scout the rapid, but to look for artifacts from the train wreck.

I found a few pieces of scrap metal that may or may not have been from the wreck, and a couple of bones that may or may not have come from horses killed in the wreck. I consider the rapid to be a read-and-run Class III rapid,

Photo by Steve Kernek
Evening in camp around RM 31

although the guidebook insists that scouting is mandatory. So, don't take my word for it.

As I approached a big horseshoe bend to the right near River Mile 35.9, I pulled ashore on the right for a hike up to a petrified forest of tropical trees, including cypress and ginkgo. Looking back across the canyon, I could see a natural bridge in the stone.

In the area known as "the beavertail," I found a decent campsite within sight of Cedar Island. This is one of the very few places where the road is not close at hand. Surprisingly, clouds moved in and a light rain started falling. This prompted me to hastily put up my kitchen shelter, thus causing the rain to stop.

Photo by Steve Kernek
River camp on Left, near RM 14

Some early morning rain validated my decision to put up the shelter, even though it stopped before I got up. My day on the river was uneventful and relaxing. Some would say boring. But I always fall back on the old saying, "the most boring day on the river is better than the most exciting day in the office."

I stopped at a little grove of alders on the left bank at River Mile 19, set up camp, and spent the afternoon writing these memoirs. It had been 118 days since I started this adventure, and the end was in sight. In the back of my mind, I'd always had the idea of ending with a trip down my all-around favorite river, the Rogue, in my favorite season, mid-September. That left time for a Klamath River run, so I pulled out my Quinn guidebook and started developing a float plan.

The next day, Thursday, I could have easily gone all the way to the takeout, but arriving a day before my shuttle would've been pointless. So, I slept late and moved with deliberate lethargy. And I still was on the river by 9:00. Most of the rapids were Class I, so the few Class II rapids were welcome breaks. At 1:00, I found a beach on the left bank about a quarter-mile before Freebridge. Camping there left less than seven miles to my takeout.

Photo by Steve Kernek
Gordon Ridge Rapid, first of three big rapids in the last few miles of the Deschutes

In that seven-mile float, there are three significant rapids, rated Class II+ to Class IV. The descriptions in my guidebooks were pretty good, and I could have run straight through, but I took the conservative step of scouting, just to be comfortable that I knew what I had to do.

At Heritage Landing at Deschutes Park, I trailered my raft, ran my ScatPacker through the Scat Machine, and headed home for the first time in two months. The dog was very happy to see me. The cat demanded that I immediately feed him. Linda offered me a glass of wine on the front porch.

Photo by Steve Kernek
Steve rowing Moody Rapid, the last rapid on the Deschutes

Chapter Twenty-Four

California's Klamath

The Klamath River has sometimes been called "the poor-man's Rogue." There was an outfitter who used to sell Rogue trips that he did not have permits for. He had a staff person work the phones every morning trying to claim permit space out of the "common pool," but sometimes he'd come up short. When that happened, he'd give his guests some kind of concocted excuse—forest fire, flash flood, Indian uprising, whatever—and divert the trip to the Klamath.

There are places where a person brought in blindfolded would have a hard time knowing whether he was on the Klamath or the Rogue. The topography, weather, vegetation, and even the character of the whitewater are all very much alike. But the presence of Highway 96 along most of the run is a detraction that is impossible to ignore.

What the Klamath has going for it is what it doesn't have—a limited-access permit

Photo by Author
Klamath River—the poor man's Rogue

system. The Klamath is always open, and because the flow is dam-controlled (for the time being), there is always enough water for boating. So, like that outfitter back in the 1980s and 1990s, if you strike out on Rogue permits, you can always go to the Klamath instead.

But that's not the reason I made my one and only Klamath trip. Back when my kids were five and six years old, I was looking for a multi-day run that was suitable for little kids—meaning Class II and easy walk-around for anything rougher. I had actually zeroed-in on the Grande Ronde, but as our launch date approached, the weather in that corner of Oregon was atrocious and the river was running very high.

So, at the last minute, I diverted to the Klamath, thus embracing its second-choice status. But it served its purpose. The weather was good, the scenery occasionally spectacular (and at other times, mediocre), the whitewater was manageable for little kids, and most importantly, the kids loved it.

For that trip, I launched at the first access point below Iron Gate Dam and floated 81 miles to Indian Creek in seven days. The kids were hooked for life on rafting, so from that perspective, the Klamath holds a special place in my heart. But I'd never gone back in the succeeding 38 years.

A few times, after we'd been defeated in the permit lotteries, I had unenthusiastically proposed a Klamath float to The Clan of the Nose Hair, but the idea was always met with indifference. So, why should I want to run it now? One reason was the hope that a fresh look at the river might move it up from its last-choice status.

The other reason was simply to fill time. I got off the Deschutes on Friday, August 20th, but I didn't want to run the Rogue until after Labor Day. So, I *had* to run the Klamath—not because I actually wanted to, but rather to give me something to do before my planned Rogue River trip.

Photo by Author
Klamath River 1983 launch. Those two inner tubes belonged to someone else.

"I see you've been working on your flabs," Linda commented when I returned home after the Deschutes.

"Abs," I corrected.

"No, I think I got it right," she insisted.

Isn't that adorable? That's when I shared my plan for the Klamath.

Linda yawned. "I'm going to walk the dog and go to bed."

The next day, while all of my clothes were in the washing machine, I sat down to make a float plan. I knew that my takeout would be Ti Bar (pronounced with a long I). But I had many options for the put-in. I'd kicked this question around every time I'd proposed a Clan trip on the Klamath, generally leaning toward launching at the town of Klamath River, 25 miles downstream from my 1983 launch site. In that entire 25 miles, there is only one rapid worthy of the name.

I figured that The Clan would find that boring, but for my solo trip, it would be a foray into nostalgia. I could re-visit the places where my kids became rafters. My six-year-old son had his own little vinyl raft all rigged for rowing, and my daughter pulled the rest of us into an endless game of Animal Alphabet—each person in rotation names an animal that start with A. Then B. And so on. If it was your turn and you couldn't think of one, you'd get a point. Fewest points at the end of the alphabet made a winner.

I had used *Vanguard* on the Lower Salmon and Deschutes, but for the Klamath and Rogue, the smaller *Miwok* would be the better choice. I swapped everything around again, and then went shopping, once again using the shopping list that I'd used all summer.

On Sunday, with everything cleaned-up, re-stocked, and re-packed, I drove down to the little town of Happy Camp. I found the shuttle service, and arranged to take a driver along the next morning, when I drove back upriver to the launch site.

I camped in the back of my pickup, and after breakfast at a small café, I picked up the shuttle driver and went upstream past I-5 to the private boat ramp at the Fish Hook restaurant (River Mile 148). It took about five minutes to launch my raft and send the driver on her way with my rig. By 11:00 I was on my way, passing Deer Island, where we'd camped in 1983.

The island had been populated by a herd of deer who wandered through our camp all evening. The infrequent Class I "rapids" provided little relief from the slow pace of the first ten miles. But the

Photo by Author
Deer Island, adjacent to R-Ranch

scenery improved greatly after I passed under I-5, and the river gradient increased just enough to make it feel like a river, not a string of ponds.

I floated about fifteen miles and camped under ponderosa pines on a sandy bench at Garvey Bar, above the left bank. I'm pretty sure it's the same place we camped on the second night of our family trip.

Underway by 8:00 the next morning, I covered ten easy miles by noon, and arrived at Schoolhouse Rapid. In 1983 I pulled ashore above the Class III rapid and walked the kids and wife down the road to a river access point a quarter-mile downstream. On my way back to the raft, I spoke to an old guy who lived next to the rapid.

"What can you tell me about the rapid?" I asked.

"Well, if you keep to the right of the island, you'll avoid the bad rock that gives people trouble on the other side." He scratched his sagging belly and took a pull on his Burgie beer.

On his word, I stayed right. Even before I reached the first drop, I knew it was a bad decision. But it was too late to go back and run the left side. I skidded over shallow rocks on the brink of a three-foot drop and picked my way through a narrow slalom below. At some point, I thumped hard on a shallow rock, cutting the first holes in *Mariah's* previously pristine floor.

So, seeking redemption, this time I went left, and found a clearly identifiable channel. As for the "bad rock," any rock is bad if you hit it. I found no rocks that weren't easily avoided. Be skeptical of anything said by a fat old guy drinking Burgie beer.

After a leisurely lunch stop, I floated another five miles. Opposite Beaver Creek, I spotted a decent-looking campsite on the left. Knowing that the great challenge on this stretch of river is finding good campsites, I grabbed it.

Photo by Author
Morning at Horse Creek campsite

My third day on the Klamath was slow. The occasional Class I riffles were welcome relief from the generally slack water. I passed through the small town of Klamath River and identified a usable launch site at the Community Hall. In mid-afternoon, I pulled into a large eddy in the mouth of Horse Creek and made camp on a flat gravel bar.

Four miles downstream from there, shortly after passing the mouth of Scotts River, I came to a Class III rapid at Martin Creek. Two more miles brought me to Hamburg Rapid. This Class IV rapid is difficult to scout, but the run is on the far right, where the greatest threat comes from the willows hanging out over the river.

The afternoon got me to RM 90.7, where the highway crosses the river. The Pacific Crest Trail crosses on that bridge and then follows the highway a mile into the town of Seiad Valley, before heading back into the wilderness. I found a shady spot shortly after the bridge and set up camp.

Photo by Jackie L. Baysinger
Hamburg Rapid, Class IV

My fifth float day took me through the heavily-mined Seiad Valley area, where huge dredges tore up the riverbed and deposited massive piles of rock in their wakes. At RM 83.5 the river makes a sharp right turn in a Class II rapid, and then half a mile later makes another right turn heading into Class IV Savage Rapid. The channel at the extreme right will give you an exciting ride as you pass the jumble of boulders that block most of the river.

Photo by Jackie L. Baysinger
Savage Rapid, Class IV

It was Friday afternoon, and the expected weekend crowds were starting to show up, mostly running day-trips in this stretch of river. In the next mile there is Lower Savage Rapid (Class II+), Otter's Playpen (Class III), and Fort

Photo by Jackie L. Baysinger
Lower Savage Rapid

Photo by Jackie L. Baysinger
Otter's Playpen

Goff Falls (Class II+). These are fun read-and-run rapids followed by four more miles of easy boating.

At China Point, the highway climbs up and away from the river, and for the first time on this trip there is some sense of wilderness. I found a good camping spot at River Mile 74.4, and pulled in to spend the afternoon catching up on my writing.

The eleven-mile Class I run to Happy Camp was less than inspirational. In places, old cars have been deliberately stacked along the riverbank, ostensibly to control erosion, resembling a memorable scene from *Deliverance*.

On my way through town, I stopped and phoned the shuttle service, telling them that I'd arrive at Ti Bar on Tuesday, three days hence. Shortly after noon, I passed Indian Creek and the campground where I'd ended my 1983 trip.

There were many other boats on the river below Happy Camp, but again, most appeared to be day-trippers. I scouted Class III Rattlesnake Rapid and watched a guided paddle boat blast through the steep chute. I took the same route, and a few minutes later found a very nice campsite at Kanaka Creek.

Monday was the first truly busy whitewater day of this trip, with over a dozen Class II and III rapids in the next twelve miles. In mid-afternoon, I stopped to scout Dragon's Tooth Rapid, a difficult Class IV drop that requires precise maneuvering through a narrow chute around a very inconveniently placed mid-stream boulder.

I watched several other boats go through—some making clean runs, and others making it look ugly. One of my gear rafts when I was in the business carried a permanently

Photo by Jackie L. Baysinger
Fort Goff Creek Rapid

twisted frame from an encounter with the Dragon's Tooth, so I gave it my full attention and respect.

I'd been hoping to do a layover day at Ukonom Creek, but in talking with other boaters I'd learned that two different groups were planning to camp there, and both were in front of me. So, when I found a nice campsite above Kings Creek, I took it.

Still wanting to camp at Ukonom Creek, I planned to snag it early, with a one-mile run the next morning. But when I arrived, I found one of the groups I'd talked with the day before doing a layover. So, I stayed on the river and floated seven more miles to Rattlesnake Bar. I could have easily gone the rest of the way to Ti Bar, but my rig wouldn't get there until the next day. That seems to be a recurring theme.

Photo by Author
Klamath River Canyon

I enjoyed a long and leisurely afternoon thinking ahead to the next few days, which included Labor Day weekend. I had no desire to contend with holiday crowds on the Rogue, but it was way too far to go home for the weekend, just to turn around and drive back to run the Rogue. So, I had a few days to burn.

Everything went smoothly the next morning, and once I had my raft trailered, I set out to see for myself why Ti Bar is considered to be a mandatory takeout. Ishi-Pishi Falls fourteen miles down-stream is the real deal. Even though reckless or highly-skilled boaters have successfully run the falls, many less-skilled boaters have met disaster there.

I followed signs to a trail leading to Ishi-Pishi, and walked down to shoot some pictures. From there, I took a drive up the California Salmon, to see the rapids made famous in Gayle Wilson's *Slammin' Salmon* video. The river was way too low to run, and it was difficult to even correlate the rocky creek with the scenes in the video. It was interesting to actually see the rock structures that form the rapids.

Sightseeing done, I headed back up the Klamath River highway to Happy Camp, where I got a motel room with a hot shower and internet. Over dinner, I laid out a plan for my run down the Rogue River.

Chapter Twenty-Five

Rogue River

When people speak of running the Rogue River, they nearly always are referring to the Wild and Scenic stretch—thirty-four miles, from Grave Creek to Foster Bar. I first read about this section of river in *Oregon River Tours* by John Garren. The book came out at about the same time I bought my first raft, early in 1975, and the Rogue immediately captured my imagination.

My raft was the very common, yellow "6-Man" inflatable. I had built a simple plywood frame that provided seating for two and mounting blocks for oarlocks. It was purely a day-trip boat, because it had no provision for carrying any gear beyond a little foam ice chest.

But the Rogue River was tantalizing, and I wanted to go there. With careful (and delusional) study of Garren's river log, I found that the total float time was just over ten and a half hours. To me, that meant I could easily make the run in two days, and conveniently, there was road access to a spot about midway through the trip.

I could drive to that half-way point, at Marial, set up my tent and camping gear, and then drive back to launch my raft at Almeda Bar. I'd float to Marial, spend the night, and then float to Foster Bar the next day. Then, I'd breakdown my raft, and drive back to Marial to retrieve my camping gear. Without having ever seen the Rogue River, I convinced myself that it was a viable plan.

The night before our intended launch (in the days when you didn't need a permit and could launch whenever you wanted to) it rained all night. We decided to postpone our launch a day in hopes of getting better weather, giving us a day to look around the area. On a hike down the trail to Rainie Falls, we watched a raft just like ours get easily flipped at Grave Creek Falls, which our guidebook dismissed as a "minor rapid."

That forced me to re-think the whole thing. I had counted minor rapids as things I wouldn't need to scout—even though I was a total novice. But if a minor rapid could so easily flip our raft, I was going to have to do more scouting than my two-day float plan could accommodate—meaning that I was going to need another day. And that meant carrying camping gear on the raft. But how could our little raft carry everything we'd need?

We could cook over a fire, so we wouldn't need a stove. We could pack a few articles of clothing in plastic bags. We could take only the bare minimum pieces of cookware, and meals would have to be as simple as possible. But one problem was insurmountable. There was no way to accommodate our bulky, old-fashioned, cotton-filled sleeping bags.

We drove out to Grants Pass and bought new, compact sleeping bags, a canvas duffle, some large heavy-duty plastic bags, and nylon cord to tie it all to the raft. I guess straps hadn't yet been invented.

Back at Almeda Bar, I discovered the real limitations of an eleven-foot raft. There were many things that simply wouldn't fit. What *did* fit was the small foam ice chest secured beneath the passenger seat; a "jungle bag" for dry clothes; and our new sleeping bags in a "dry bag" that consisted of black plastic garbage sacks inside a canvas duffle bag, and two ammo boxes containing toiletries, a camera, a flashlight, matches, and a few granola bars.

The rest of our food for the trip consisted mainly of canned goods that could be heated over an open fire. The kitchen set included a couple of small aluminum kettles, two sets of silverware, and a folding backpacker's grill. All of this stuff was crammed into the little foam cooler.

On the day Jimmy Hoffa disappeared from the Red Fox Restaurant outside Detroit, we launched from Almeda Bar, with provisions for a two-and-a-half-day trip. Three days later, we reached Foster Bar, burned-out, half-starved, and totally hooked on rafting.

Ever since then, the Rogue has been a special place for me. I made several more runs in the days before permits, but once the permit system was put into place, the key to running the Wild and Scenic section of the Rogue has been getting a permit.

One of the ongoing follies of river permit systems is that over half of the permits issued in the lotteries are not used. Most of those are cancelled, for any number of reasons, and are put into a "common pool" to be claimed by others in a daily telephone stampede. But despite all efforts to have every available space on the river filled, there still are no-shows nearly every day.

So, my intention for the finale of my Whitewater Summer was to claim one of those, by being at the Rogue River Visitor's Center first thing in the morning on the day I would enter the permit corridor. But what day that would be depended on when and where I started my trip.

On several prior trips, I'd extended my float, which normally is four or five days, by launching further upstream—at Hog Creek, Schroeder Park, or Chinook Park just below Savage Rapids Dam in Grants Pass. And on one of my recent trips, I'd gone past Foster Bar to add two more days to that end of the trip. Not many people extend their Rogue trips this way, because there really isn't much whitewater in these stretches of river, and there is a shortage of good camping beaches.

During the last ten or fifteen years, three old dams have been removed from the Rogue—Savage Rapids Dam, Gold Hill Dam, and Gold Ray Dam—potentially allowing a run from Lost Creek Dam (which *will not* be removed) all the way to Gold Beach.

In the area between Gold Ray and Gold Hill, the removal of the dams has brought back some fairly challenging rapids, and a number of day-trip operators have sprung up in the area. I watched YouTube videos of people running the newly resurrected rapids, and did some preliminary work on a float plan. But I'd never been able to get anybody else interested, given the long stretches of flat water we'd encounter.

Now, however, I had nothing but time, and I couldn't escape the notion that this might be my only opportunity to make this run. Unfortunately, sitting in a motel room in Happy Camp, I didn't have any of the notes I'd made regarding a run where the dams had been.

So, the next morning, I made the three-hour drive to Gold Hill, where I got a campsite in Valley of the Rogue State Park, which is sandwiched between Interstate Five and the Rogue River. Leaving my trailer and raft in the campground, I drove out to reconnoiter the area and assess the rafting possibilities. Since there are highways close by the river throughout most of this run, I hoped I'd be able to see the rapids I'd encounter.

But I was unable to get a good look at any of the tricky stuff, so I stopped at one of the day-trip outfitters and booked a trip for the next day. I spent the rest of my afternoon doing laundry, shopping, and getting things organized for a long float.

My day-trip took me through some easy riffles and, most importantly, the two big rapids uncovered by the removal of the two upper dams. It was time well-spent, because the approaches to the big drops are not clearly defined. In other words, the read-and-run approach is not a viable option.

Photo by JP Baysinger
There is beautiful scenery but a lot of flat water between Lost Creek and Grants Pass.

Back at the campground, I phoned Galice Resort to set up my shuttle, and they told me that they were completely shut down. After their fire in June, they'd been operating out of a portable office building and an event tent in their parking lot, but when the time came to remove the debris left by the fire, they were forced to shut down in order to clear the site. They referred me to Orange Torpedo Tours in Merlin.

I called them and arranged to pick up a shuttle driver the next morning. They were bewildered by my plans, because nobody had ever asked them to do a shuttle like that. But we worked out a price and a plan, so early on Saturday morning, I drove to Merlin and found a driver waiting.

On our way to my launch site, I stopped at the state park and hitched up my trailer. From there, it was a 40-minute drive to the McGregor launch ramp within sight of the Lost Creek Dam. It is a good concrete boat ramp, so it took only a few minutes to get my raft off the trailer. I sent the shuttle driver on her way with my rig, and I started downriver just before 10:00.

I was 25 miles upstream from where my day-trip had started, so this was unfamiliar water. However, I'd asked my guide what was in that stretch, and she said that it was a smooth-water float with no big rapids, and was very popular with fishermen.

Now, I'm not a fisherman, so that was not a reason to float this section, but neither was the absence of challenging rapids a reason not to. Knowing that the run would take me through several small towns, my expectations were low with regard to scenery. So, the best argument in favor of floating this section was simply to be able to say that I'd done it.

The scenery turned out to be a pleasant surprise. From the river, the occasional intrusions of civilization were tolerable. One thing I noticed right away was that there were not many beaches big enough to accommodate a group campsite. But a one-tent camp doesn't require much real estate, so I figured that campsites would not be a problem. At least, not a *big* problem.

It was Labor Day weekend, and I expected to see crowds of boaters, but except for some fishermen in drift boats, I had the river to myself. I set a restful pace, pushing downstream in the gentle current. At 3:30, I was floating through the little town of Trail, when I spotted a small beach isolated from development on the left bank a quarter-mile below Trail Creek.

With an early start the next morning, Sunday, I continued my lazy run in the scenic canyon. One thing that stood out to me was the relative clarity of the water. It wasn't quite like the Selway or Middle Fork, but it was much better than the Klamath, and noticeably better than what I'd experienced in the Wild and Scenic sections of the Rogue.

All morning, I remained in a populated area with frequent riverside development, as I passed through the Shady Cove area. Population thinned-out in the afternoon, and the scenery again improved. But once again, I found myself in one of the more developed areas when I wanted to camp.

A hundred yards downstream from the old Table Rock diversion canal, I found a usable beach on the right bank, opposite celebrity pot-grower Jim Belushi's farm. In the afternoon heat, when the breeze was just right, the aroma of the crop wafted across the river.

Monday was Labor Day, and as I rowed past the boat ramp at the Table Rock highway bridge, I saw at least a dozen people launching their boats and inner-tubes. I floated past the Gold Ray Dam site, and late in the afternoon found a decent place to camp at the foot of a small rapid called Hardy Riffle. For the rest of the afternoon and into the evening, I watched a procession of day-trippers float past in anything that would float.

Photo by JP Baysinger

This section of the Rogue River can be a busy place on holiday weekends.

Tuesday morning, I envisioned a lot of people back at their desks nursing sunburn and hangovers. It was quiet on the river as I approached Nugget Falls (on some maps it is Dillon Falls), rated Class III or IV (depending on who you talk to). I picked my way down the channel on river left, finding it sometimes difficult to use both oars because of the narrowness of the chute. The falls itself is a steep eight-foot plunge into a violent reversal. It's better suited for paddle boating than rowing. My run was awkward, but successful.

The Class IV Powerhouse Run at Ti'lomikh Falls is a two-part plunge in a slot so narrow that you have to ship your oars to squeeze through. The upper drop runs you into a violent side-breaking wave and reversal that leaves only a couple of seconds to regain control and line-up for the main drop.

As I approached the town of Gold Hill in the early afternoon, I phoned a pizza shop and arranged for delivery at the riverside. With all of the day's whitewater action behind me, I indulged myself with pizza and beer before continuing downstream to a little beach where I pulled in and made camp, just above a rapid exposed by the recent removal of Savage Rapids Dam.

In the middle of the night, I woke up to find a rare spotted skunk licking my hand. The natural reflex would be to jump up and bolt away from the threat. But I know that even rare and endangered skunks have sharp teeth, along with the ability to share an aroma that will make you unwelcome in human company for a week. So, I very slowly and carefully withdrew my hand into my sleeping bag. Stinky quickly lost interest and waddled up into the brush, perhaps happy to have enjoyed a trace of pepperoni flavor lingering on my fingers.

Photo by Author
The Highway 99 bridges in Grants Pass

Wednesday morning, I made the slow float to Chinook Park in Grants Pass, which previously had been the furthest upstream I'd launched for a Rogue trip. The next few miles would take me through the most heavily populated area on the entire run.

I passed under the Highway 99 bridges and the new pedestrian suspension bridge, and in mid-afternoon, I passed Schroeder Park. I went a few more miles and camped on a gravel bar upstream from where the Applegate River joins the Rogue.

The blue jet boats that run from Grants Pass down through Hellgate Canyon and back were the only other boats on the river the next day. I

Photo by Author
Camping at Applegate Delta in 1985

think seven or eight boats passed by, first going downstream, and then coming back up. But except for the jetboats, my float to Zig-Zag Creek in Hellgate Canyon was uneventful. Some would say boring. I found it relaxing, and spent most of the time listening to an audio-book on my i-pod.

Photo by Author
Silver Sieve in Hellgate Canyon, 1985

In camp that night, I thought ahead about my plans for entering the limited-access section of the river. My goal for the next day was to get to the Forest Service office at Rand, where the permits are issued. That was eight miles downstream, so it would be a short float day. Just below Hellgate Canyon is Dunn Riffle, the first real rapid I'd seen in two days. Over the next eight miles, there is a lot of slow water and a couple of semi-challenging rapids.

Photo by Author
A small campsite at Zig Zag Creek

I made a brief stop at Galice to look at the site where the store-restaurant had stood since the 1930s. It had survived the great floods of 1955 and 1964, when waist-deep water flooded the main floor. But all that remains is a hole in the ground. It is unclear whether or not they'll be able to rebuild.

When I got to Rand, I walked up to the Smullin Visitor's Center to see what permits would be up for grabs in the morning, and much to my surprise and disappointment, nothing was available. The ranger did say that there were six spaces available for the day after that, but when I expressed interest in one of them, she told me that I'd have to call-in the next morning.

I reminded her that there is no cell-phone service in the area, so it would not be possible for me to call-in. Could I just be there in person and claim one of the spaces? No. They're available only by phone, so as to be "fair to everybody." Everybody, I guess, except those in an area without cell phone service—like Rand.

That left me with two options. I could hang-out for a day and check back the next afternoon to see if there were any no-shows, or I could revert to my life of crime. I decided to give "the system" one last chance to redeem itself. It was Tuesday afternoon. If I couldn't get a permit by Thursday morning, I'd go without and take my chances.

I rowed across the river and made camp on a shadeless gravel bar. There, I huddled under my little pop-up canopy and spent most of the day catching-up on this story. At 3:00, I crossed the river and checked-in at the visitor's center. There were two no-shows. These would be given out in the morning, on a first-come, first-served basis. All I had to do was be there before anyone else.

After sunset, I took down my canopy and packed-up most of my gear. I woke up at 5:30, while it was still dark, and rowed over to the visitor's center to await their 7:00 opening. As it turned out, I could've slept-in. I was the only one in line, so I got one of the permits. The ranger wanted to inspect my gear and make sure that I was carrying an approved toilet.

"My raft is down below. I'm camped across the river, and my toilet is there."

"Well, I can't give you your permit until I inspect your gear."

"We can walk down to the river. You'll be able to inspect my raft and see my camp. The toilet ought to be visible."

"You'll need to bring it up here."

"I can't possibly carry my raft up here."

"Well, you'll just have to find a way."

"What's all this about?" asked another ranger.

Both the first ranger and I started to speak at once, so the second ranger pointed at me.

"You first," she said.

"My raft is parked down below, in the river. I can't bring it up here to be inspected."

She looked puzzled.

"So, what's the problem?" she asked the first ranger.

"Well, I can hardly inspect the raft from here!"

Looking toward the heavens, the second ranger said, "If you can't spare the time to walk down to look at it, just sign-off and issue the permit."

Photo by Author

The Wild and Scenic section begins with Grave Creek Rapid—Class III.

Permit in hand, I rowed back over to my camp, where I made coffee and pancakes. When I was a kid, we had a family superstition that if you cooked pancakes on a camping trip, you'd get rained on. But my courageous defiance of fate produced no rain, and life went on.

As I floated past Almeda Bar half a mile downstream, I thought about all the times I'd launched there. I'd floated the Rogue about a hundred times, and most of those trips had started at Almeda Bar. Awash in a flood of memories, I pushed my way down the flat water toward Almeda Riffle.

The first time I led a row-yourself commercial trip, I learned how much I didn't know about the river. It's one thing for an experienced boater to read-and-run the rapids—I had done that two dozen times. But it's a whole different challenge to stand up in the lead boat and tell the group following you what to expect in a rapid that hasn't yet come into view.

Instructions had to be accurate and concise—first I'd recite a description of the rapid, then I'd explain how to get through it, and finally, I'd summarize it in a few simple steps. I still go through the mental exercise of trying to recall the instructions for each rapid. The truth is, I'd be hard pressed to lead a row-yourself trip there today, even though the rapids of the Rogue have changed very little since my first trip down the river, way back in 1975.

The run from Almeda Bar to the bridge at Grave Creek is easy and nicely-suited for breaking-in new boatmen. With the low flow on this trip, the channel was well-defined, but offered little margin for error. That would be characteristic of the entire run. But the low flow also slows the

Photo by Author

Most people do not attempt to run the main drop at Rainie Falls velocity of the water, so there is generally more time to position the boat where it needs to be.

Photo by Author
The lining chute at Rainie Falls

At Rainie Falls, I caught up with a group of fishermen in drift boats, waiting their turn to run their boats down the lining chute on river-right. Until I saw them, I'd been planning to take my raft down that chute, but it was a large group, and the delay could be half an hour—longer if a boat got stuck in the very narrow, shallow channel.

So, I opted for the center chute. I've never been tempted to run the main falls on river-left, although people frequently do it. The drop is big and violent, and the chances of getting beaten-up by the savage hydraulics are greater than my tolerance for risk. The center chute takes the fifteen-foot drop in four neatly-spaced steps down a slot that is no more than eight feet wide.

The approach is shallow, and boats frequently get hung-up or wedged at odd angles, so that frequent jostling and jiggling is needed. A few seconds after I committed to the center chute, I spotted a fully-loaded, unmanned raft stuck there. I couldn't go back upstream, and I couldn't squeeze past the raft. So, I jammed my raft into a little niche and tied-up to a scrubby bush.

I waded and climbed over slippery rocks to get to the raft and see what could be done. Looking into the bottom of the raft, I could see that the floor was pushed up about a foot, directly in line with the oar locks. But the floor still held air, so it wasn't damaged, and I wondered why the raft had been abandoned.

I climbed onto the tallest nearby rock to see if I could spot anyone walking around without a raft. The one thing that was certain was that I couldn't go anywhere as long as that boat was there. The back of the raft had a heavy pile of gear, and that's what was keeping it from moving forward off the rock.

The cardinal rule in rafting etiquette is that you never, ever tamper with someone else's raft. But I couldn't go anywhere until that raft was out of my way. It would've been easy enough to unload all of the gear and push the raft loose, but then the current might take it away and leave me with a pile of someone else's gear that I couldn't possibly carry on my raft.

I decided to try pivoting the raft around, to get the heavy end on the downstream side of the hang-up rock.

That sounds easy enough, but in reality, it was a very strenuous and slow process. In water up to my waist, I had to lift and shove on the tail-end of the raft, over and over, gaining a small fraction of an inch on each push. Setting up a rhythm helped, but it was exhausting. I could bounce the raft a dozen times, and then I'd have to stop to catch my breath.

I think it took about twenty-five minutes to get the raft turned around and shifted so that the offending rock was beneath the front tube. I climbed aboard and took the oarsman's seat. It was hard to find enough water for the oar blades, but when I finally coaxed the raft to move, I knew it would go. I tugged on the oars two or three more times, and it sluggishly slid free. Obviously, the only place I could go with it was down the chute.

At the brink of the center chute, the boat has to make a tight ninety-degree left turn, and it is common for rafts to get stuck there and wind up going down the chute backward. I was already backward, so I committed to making the run that way.

But backward or forward, the most important thing to do is get your arms, legs, and oars completely inside your boat. Many oars have been broken there, including one of mine. This time, however, the run went well, and I got flushed down into the turbulent pool beneath the main falls, where I re-installed the oars and rowed down to the bottom of the lining chute. I securely tied the raft there.

Photo by JP Baysinger
A backward ride down the middle chute

Photo by Author
More rafts in the lining chute

The fishing party that I hadn't wanted to wait for was long gone by then, and another group was coming down. I set out to get back up to my own raft. It was a slow and punishing hike back up through the brush, over boulders and across several swift channels.

I drank a quart of water and ate two Mounds bars, which I've found to be pretty effective at quickly restoring depleted energy. But long before they could possibly have any effect, I untied my raft and rowed it out of its little cove. My second run down the chute was more graceful than my first, even though the low water level made the drops far more abrupt and violent than I'd encountered on most prior runs.

A mile downstream, I came to "Experience Beach," on the left bank. On one of my early trips, there was a single tent on this beach as I floated past, but there were no people anywhere in sight. My group was engaged in a rowdy water fight at the time, making a lot of noise and having a good time. Keeping myself out of the battle, I looked to shore just in time to see a very hippy-looking couple emerge from the tent. The guy indignantly demanded that we leave, because we were "unraveling the fabric of his experience." We've called it Experience Beach ever since.

Photo by Author
Camping at Experience Beach in 1986

It was only 3:30, and I'd planned to go a few more miles, but I was feeling weary from my exertions at the falls, so when I found Experience Beach unoccupied, I pulled in and set up camp. An hour or two later, a pair of rafts came downstream. One was a rental from Merlin, and the other was the one from Rainie Falls.

"I see you found your raft," I commented.

"Yeah, someone got it loose and tied it up below the falls."

"That was me. I had to move it so that I could go through," I said. "I hope you don't mind."

He rowed over to the beach.

"Mind? God no, I'm glad you got it loose. How'd you do that, anyway? We tried for an hour yesterday, and couldn't budge it."

I played down the amount of effort involved, saying only that I managed to turn it around, and then rowed it backward off the rock.

"We finally decided that the only way we'd get it loose was to unload it into another raft. But all of our other rafts were downstream, so we had to leave this one where it was. We camped down at Whiskey Creek, and this morning the two of us hiked up to Grave Creek and hitched a ride to Merlin. We rented that raft and came back, all set to transfer the gear into it. When we found the raft gone, we thought it must've gotten loose by itself, until we got down and found it tied-up below. I owe you big time."

"Buy me a beer sometime, and we'll call it even," I suggested.

"I'd stay and have a beer with you right now, but there's eight people down at Whiskey Creek wondering where I am, because our dinner is on this raft."

I nodded. "Another time, then."

Chalk up another experience to Experience Beach. And that's the way it is for me on the Rogue. There's a memory at every beach, every rapid, and around every bend in the river. This trip was not meant to be an excursion down memory lane, but it was impossible to set aside the sense of nostalgia.

Nor could I dodge the creeping reality that any trip down the Rogue, including this one, might be my last. Sure, this summer's adventure had put me in better condition than I'd been in for at least a decade, but my age was something that I couldn't roll back.

The air was filled with the aroma of bay laurel and manzanita, even though the autumn leaves had barely begun to turn color. It was a scent that always evokes memories of my autumn trips down the Rogue. The best of those were the ones I did with my son and daughter, starting in 1987, when they were nine and ten years old. On that trip, we shared the river with Vice President George Bush and a swarm of Secret Service agents. We never got close enough to actually see Mr. Bush; but until this year's fire, a photo of him with Marilou and Gil hung on the fireplace at Galice Resort, another reminder that nothing lasts forever.

The morning fog lying over the river signaled the approach of autumn, and sunrise was coming noticeably later every day. Heavy dew was now a nightly event, and sleeping under the stars was no longer a prudent option. So, my goal of getting out of camp by 8:00 every day had slipped closer to 9:00. Not that it mattered. I was under no time pressure.

Sunshine was just reaching the beach at Whiskey Creek when I floated past and waved to the group whose raft I'd freed at Rainie Falls. They waved me in, and I joined them for a cup of coffee. After re-telling how I'd gotten the raft loose, I hiked the short trail up to the old Whiskey Creek placer mine.

Except for a metal roof installed on the main cabin sometime in the 1980s, little had changed since my first visit. I paused and cleaned a layer of dirt off the grave marker for a cat named Mack, who died in 1964. How sad it is that we humans so often outlive our pets, in whom we invest so much emotion.

Back on the river, I floated past Big Slide. There's a beautiful campsite on the bench up the right bank, but getting equipment up to the camp involves a steep, back-breaking carry through a boulder field. I camped there only once, with one of my commercial groups, on the busiest weekend or the year, right after the end of permit season (which used to be around-September 21st), and that's where we realized that we'd somehow forgotten to buy coffee.

In a perfect illustration of how river karma works, a group came by, begging to borrow an oar, because they'd lost one at Rainie Falls. We lent them one of our spares in exchange for enough coffee to finish our trip. This was only a couple of months after I'd given my emergency coffee supply to the old guys at Almeda Bar. Things tend to balance out.

Tyee Rapid a mile downstream features a violent hole on the left side of the main channel, and a tricky approach around shallow ledges on the right. It's easy to do, but the penalty for doing it wrong is hitting that nasty hole, which is why the rapid is rated Class IV.

Tyee is followed by Wildcat, a Class III rapid that gets more challenging at lower water levels. The trick is to identify and stay to the right of the green rock known as "the alligator," which comes out at levels below 1,500 cfs. On this trip, the flow was even lower than that.

Lots of boats hit the alligator, and many get hung up. Some get damaged. But worse than getting lodged on the alligator is getting washed to the left side of it, a course that leads into a swift current that runs straight onto a mid-river reef. I once spent half a day there freeing a gear boat that one of my guides pinned to the rocks at the top of the reef.

The campsite on the left at the foot of Wildcat Rapid is one of the nicest on the river. I've seldom camped there, however, because its location doesn't fit well with my usual float schedule. But fishing trips move slower, and that's what

Photo by Author
Silver Sieve in Plowshare Rapid, 1985

Photo by Bill Essig

The author Running Upper Black Bar Rapid in *Vanguard*, 2009

has occasionally put me there at the right time of day. This was not such an occasion.

In the next mile, there are six rapids, all rated Class II+, making it one of the busiest, most fun stretches on the whole trip. On my first trip down, I scouted every one of these drops—I had little confidence in my guidebook, and even less in my ability to read the river.

Another three-quarters of a mile brought me to Slim Pickens Rapid, where the guidebooks still tell you to squeeze through the very slim chute against the right bank. Drift boats use that channel, but everyone else runs left, where there are several inconveniently placed submerged rocks, but a lot more room for oars.

Busy water continues, with several more Class II and II+ rapids in the next mile. These are the places where, in my early days of rafting, I honed my technical boating skills, with eddy-turns and precise control. I stopped briefly at Big Windy Creek, but didn't climb up to take a ride down the natural water slide, something I've done many times.

Upper Black Bar Rapid requires a tight squeeze along the right wall during a drop of about six feet. The trick is to avoid bumping the wall, without getting more than a foot from it, which would cause you to hit a large, exposed boulder.

At hundred yards downstream is Lower Black Bar Rapid—often called Black Bar Falls—where the river gets funneled into a steep chute that drops eight feet into a disorderly wave train that diminishes into the Black Bar pool. Above the left bank is Black Bar itself, where one of the oldest lodges on the Rogue is located. I've stayed at Black Bar Lodge a few times on trips with my wife around

Photo by JP Baysinger

Black Bar Lodge, my favorite of all the lodges along the Rogue this same time of year, and love its rustic authenticity, wonderful food, and gracious hospitality. But you can't just drop in. You need to make your reservations long in advance.

A mile and a half of mostly calm water brought me to the three-part Horseshoe Bend Rapid. In part one, the best channel is on the left. Looking ahead, you'd prefer to get to the right-hand side, but part two features shallow rocks that force you toward the center. Once past them, you must pull decisively back to the right, to stay away from a boat-wrecking hole that the main current pours directly into. That was essentially my row-yourself speech, and it still applies.

Photo by Author
Looking back at Kelsey Falls

In 1975, on my first Rogue trip, my wife and I were having lunch after a clean run of Horseshoe Bend, when a *Whitewater Voyages* guided trip floated past. It was past noon on the second day of my three-day trip. I had covered less than half of the forty-mile run, and by all accounts, the most challenging rapids were still ahead.

I knew that I had to do something differently, or I'd have to spend an unplanned extra day on the river, without food. So, to save scouting time, I pulled-out behind the last of the *Whitewater Voyages* rafts, trusting that if I did what the guide did, I'd get safely through the rapids.

That plan got us quickly through the rapids of Kelsey Canyon in a fraction of the time it would have otherwise taken. Then, we made the compulsory tourist stops to see the historic cabins at Battle Bar and Winkle Bar, time-consuming concessions to my desire to see everything and still do the trip in three days.

Photo by Author
The cabin at Battle Bar, where Bob Fox was murdered by his deranged neighbor.

The guided group stopped for the day across from Winkle Bar, but we stayed on the river for another two miles. The next morning, I heated a can of corned-beef hash and scrambled the last of our eggs

Photo by JP Baysinger

Zane Grey's cabin at Winkle Bar is on the National Register of Historic Places.

for breakfast. The last of our food consisted of a few snacks and some dry, flavorless "breakfast bars."

We passed Mule Creek a little after noon, and then stopped at Marial Lodge, hoping to buy more film for our Instamatic. I saw a shelf with a selection of film, but nothing that would fit our camera, and despite calling for someone to come to the desk, I couldn't get anybody's attention. At that moment, I looked out and saw the *Whitewater Voyages* group, coming into view. I rushed back to our raft and got in line behind them heading into Mule Creek Canyon.

The thing that saved my ass on that trip was that my 6-man raft was light and very easy to maneuver. I had no trouble executing the exact maneuvers that the guide ahead of me performed. By then, the guides could see what I was doing, and had to know why—because I was a novice and was in beyond my depth.

So, when we got to Blossom Bar, they invited me to join them in scouting the rapid, and took the time to point-out to me all of the critical moves. And then, when we ran the rapid, they even positioned a safety boat below the critical main drop, to pick up the pieces if I blew the eddy turn. But my run was good, and when they stopped for the day at Gleason Creek, just below Devil's Staircase, we thanked them for their help.

We still had over ten miles to go, and every crumb of food was gone. I rowed into the setting sun across the still waters of Huggins Canyon and Clay Hill Flats, finally arriving at Foster Bar at 7:30 p.m., exhausted and permanently in love with the Rogue River.

Forty-six years later, I set a leisurely pace through Kelsey Canyon and down to Long Gulch, where I found the exact spot where I'd camped on that first trip. There really wasn't a beach or camping spot there. Just a little spring with clean, cold water. Nostalgia demanded that I stay, but without room to put up my tent, I had to pass, camping instead on a sandbar half a mile downstream.

At noon the next day, I landed on the gravel bar at the mouth of Mule Creek and set up camp, allowing myself all afternoon for sightseeing. I put on my hiking shoes and walked down the Rogue River Trail all the way to

Blossom Bar, shooting pictures and studying the rapids. It'd been a few years since I'd last run the Rogue, and I needed to see if anything had changed—including my memory.

Even ten years ago, it had seemed to me that Blossom Bar was changing in the "picket fence" area. The course seemed tighter and less forgiving. From high above the right bank, I could see that the low water had indeed tightened-up the obstacle course, although the path through it was still the same.

Photo by Joni Scott
The author in Mule Creek Canyon, 2009

With that blueprint fresh in mind, I left camp at 8:00 the next morning. My run through Mule Creek Canyon was going great, until I approached the place known as the "Coffee Pot," where powerful hydraulics cause the current to swirl and boil erratically.

Oddly, there were rafts holed-up in little niches in the canyon walls above the Coffee Pot.

One of the boatmen shouted, "You can't get through! There's a drift boat wedged in the entrance to the Coffee Pot."

I looked to my left and saw a sliver of space in a tiny cove that already held three rafts. The boatmen there made room as I jammed my way in. Downstream, I could see an eighteen-foot drift boat lodged sideways in the seventeen-foot-wide entry to the Coffee Pot. The upstream gunwale had gone underwater, allowing the river to pour into the boat and pin it in place. Men on shore had attached lines to the boat and were attempting to pull it free.

Photo by Bill Mulholland
The author taking *Cheyenne* through the Coffee Pot in Mule Creek Canyon, 1989

The boatman who let me into the cove explained, "They got stuck an hour ago. Someone ran back to Marial and borrowed come-along winches and rigging. They're trying to pull one end against the current, hoping the other end will come free."

I said, "They'd better hurry-up. More boats are coming down, and they're not all going to find room to stop."

"Yeah. A guy said that a Forest Service man is bringing dynamite to blow it out if they don't get it clear pretty soon."

By then, about six men were on shore working to get the boat free. One attempt failed when a line snapped, and the next attempt tore loose from the on-shore anchor. We saw two men arrive carrying a wooden box of dynamite. They got into an animated argument with the men trying to salvage the boat. Word came back to us that they'd be allowed one last attempt. Meanwhile, boats kept coming. I counted nine that I could see, and I knew there were more upstream.

I wasn't looking when the boat came loose, but I heard a cheer from the salvage crew. Within minutes, someone shouted for us to start coming through. Because I was the last boat to jam into the last cove, I was first to leave. As I went through the Coffee Pot, I could see no sign of the boat, other than a doubled-up line extending from the depths up to the ledge where the rescue team was. The boat had plunged straight to the bottom the instant they'd pulled it free. They'd try to pull it up after all of the backed-up river traffic got through.

It was noon when I cleared the Coffee Pot and started my run down to Blossom Bar. It was good that I'd scouted it the previous afternoon, because if I'd had to stop now, all of the other boats would've caught up and I'd have been ensnared in another traffic jam. I approached the rapid with complete confidence, based on my many successful runs.

Photo by Dave Peterson
The author rowing *Mariah* past a drift boat wrecked on the Picket Fence in Blossom Bar, 1980. The guys with the ladder were attempting to salvage the drift boat.

My run was neat and clean, although I did notice an apparent shift in the direction of the current pouring around the picket fence. That chute flowed directly at an eight-foot-tall boulder just thirty feet below the end of the tongue. In all of my previous runs, the current had always angled left, past the troublesome boulder.

Photo by JP Baysinger

In 2009, we attempted to free this raft from the Picket Fence, but the line on our Z-drag snapped and we had to abandon the effort.

Photo by Author

Bill Mulholland and Nick Giesch running Devil's Staircase Rapid

The beach at Watson Creek is the last good campsite before Foster Bar. It is also a great place to see Bald Eagles.

By coming down the chute sideways, already set-up to pull to the left of that boulder, I was able to get around it and another cluster of boulders a few yards downstream. From there, I had a hard pull to the right, to get around the "ramp rock," and then back to the left to avoid the "Volkswagen rock," followed by another pull to the right, past the "monolith." A clean run is like a ballet, with every step in perfect time. I acknowledged the cheer from the imaginary crowd with a humble nod.

My long afternoon run took me to a beach on the left, just above Watson Creek, where I set up camp. It was a beautiful September Sunday, and I passed several of the giant jetboats coming upriver from Gold Beach.

After passing Foster Bar the next morning, I ran a few Class II rapids before hitting the flat water starting at Agness. Then, I entered a beautiful forested canyon that took me to a campsite at Tom East Creek. I celebrated the last night of my Whitewater Summer with a spaghetti dinner and a half-liter box of Merlot.

At Quosatana Creek the next morning, September 16th, I loaded my raft onto the trailer and changed into clean, dry clothes. In the last five months, I'd spent

123 days on my raft. I was ready to go home, happy that I had done it.

I drove out to the coast, and turned north on 101. When I got to Port Orford, I got a motel room, took a long, hot shower, and phoned Linda. When I tried to tell her that I'd get home the next day, she asked, "Who is this?" Very funny.

Before leaving Port Orford the next day, I drove around the little town where legendary whitewater pioneer Buzz Holmstrom grew up. There are no monuments to him, and I don't know if he'd recognize the town today. But I felt a kind of connection. He'd started here, and I'd finished here.

My Whitewater Summer was over, and I was ready to go home. I'd floated 1,340 miles on eleven rivers, and had committed an uncounted number of legal infractions. It had been a dream turned real, a unique adventure that may never be duplicated—certainly not by me.

Linda's son Kevin had hiked 1,836 miles on the Pacific Crest Trail in about the same amount of time as my adventure. But there was just one major difference between his adventure and mine. He actually did it.

As I said from the beginning, this story is fiction. Still, it proves that the pen is mightier than the hiking boot, I'll take full credit for what I didn't do, and because this story is fiction, it is now up to you to do it for real. I've told you how to do it. All you need is a six-month summer and a willingness to become a Whitewater Outlaw.

Chapter Twenty-Six

Unexpected Encore

A week later, I drove to Spokane with my sister's raft, all cleaned-up and detailed, with a fresh application of 303 protectant. She tried her best to sell the raft to me, but I've gone far past the age where I need to buy any more rafting equipment. The little *Miwok* had served me well, but the best I could do for her was keep my eyes open for a buyer.

Reacquainting myself with my regular life, I was putting the finishing touches on this story, when I came up with a question regarding the name on the cat's grave at the Whiskey Creek Mine, which we had visited on past Rogue River trips. Using Facebook Messenger, I asked my daughter, Tamara, the question.

She answered, "Not sure. I guess we'll just have to go down there and find out."

"Good idea," I responded, believing this to be idle chat.

After Tamara's first Rogue trip in 1987, we had maintained a tradition of floating the river in October, using the combination of school teacher "in-service" days and/or the Columbus Day

Photo by a Fellow Boater

Tamara and Jim on their first Rogue River trip, in October 1987. This would be a good time to clarify that I have a brother and a son, both named Jim. All prior references to Jim in this book have been my brother, JP Baysinger.

holiday to give us the time. But we hadn't done a late season trip like that since 2005, so the idea was appealing.

"I have time off next weekend," she said.

She explained that she'd been planning to do an equestrian endurance ride, but her horse had a bruised foot. And with that, we hatched a plan. The next morning, Sunday, we played the permit game on the phone, and I scored permits for the following Friday. The only hitch was that she didn't have time to get her raft ready. but that was okay. We could both ride on *Vanguard* and maybe take turns rowing.

I spent the rest of the next three days reorganizing my gear for a two-person trip on *Vanguard,* shopping, and packing. On Thursday, we met at Baldini's Pizza in Merlin, across the street from Orange Torpedo Tours. We had dinner, made shuttle arrangements, and then drove to Almeda Bar.

In the morning, deprived of our traditional breakfast at Galice Resort, we settled for coffee and donuts on a frosty picnic table. Then we found a flat tire on the trailer and had to change it. So much for the 10:00 rule.

With the spare tire installed, we picked up our permit and drove to Grave Creek to launch the raft, finally getting underway at 10:30. I got a gentle wake-up call in Grave Creek Rapid, when I bumped into a large rock just below the foot of the rapid. It was a harmless bump, but it bothered me that I hadn't been able to miss the obvious obstacle.

Then, in the flat water above Rainie Falls, we discussed our options. I was concerned about the low water—even lower than it had been a month before—and worried that *Vanguard* might get wedged if we ran the middle chute. So, I decided to run the lining chute instead. Bad idea. It took a quarter-hour to grind our way down, with multiple stops to dislodge the raft from shallow rocks in the chute. But we made it through without damage, and that was the main thing.

It was a beautiful autumn day, even though the temperature never got up to 70. Reminiscing about past trips and sharing stories about other things made the trip everything I'd hoped it would be. Family bonding. It felt just like the old days, and that's something that we old people cherish.

Photo by JP Baysinger

A good run through the middle chute is always cause for celebration.

Because of our late start, we had to forego our planned stop at Whiskey Creek. But the internet had already answered the question that had instigated this trip. The name on the cat's grave is "Kitty Mack," and he was eighteen years old when he died in 1964, as I had already written in Chapter 25.

All morning, I kept feeling that some things were slightly off. My reflexes and timing were imperfect. Maybe I'd gotten too accustomed to the smaller raft. I got bumped off course in Tyee Rapid, and wound up going backward through the final drop. No harm, but sloppy.

At Wildcat, I ran it the same way I had in September, but after passing to the right of the alligator rock, I dragged bottom on at least three different shallow rocks, turning the raft around and generally looking sloppy. Okay, that happens when the water is extremely low. But still...

Photo by Author

In 1987, we camped just above Washboard Rapid. We employed a new two-room cabin tent, which gave us a built-in kitchen shelter.

The fun section from Russian Rapid to Big Windy Creek went well, and I relaxed, feeling that I'd regained my form and control. But then at Upper Black Bar, I ticked my left oar on a hidden rock and failed to get the raft turned to pull away from the right wall. I bumped the wall, rebounded and broadsided the big rock above the left turn at the bottom. Tam high-sided, and we slipped around the rock and into the calm water. That was beyond sloppy. It was ugly, and it made me feel weak, which was ironic, since I actually was stronger than I'd been in years.

We were getting acquainted with the people around us—two guided groups of fishermen in drift boats, a party with half their group in rafts and the other half hiking the trail, and a couple of other one-raft parties. The rest of the afternoon was pleasant, and all went well. We camped on a nice gravel bar on river left, opposite Meadow Creek.

Friday morning, the canyon was filled with fog, but it burned off to reveal clear, blue sky. Heavy dew had accompanied the fog, so we found ourselves packing our tents damp. The morning went smoothly, and we arrived at Mule Creek at lunch time. We claimed the preferred site at the mouth of the creek, exactly where I'd camped a month before.

Photo by Author
The coveted campsite at Mule Creek, circa October 1987

Everyone we talked to had heard the same weather forecasts that I'd heard—that rain would come in the evening. So, we took the precaution of setting up the Parawing shelter over our kitchen. And sure enough, in the middle of the night, I woke up to a light, but persistent rain. By the time we were ready to break camp, the rain had stopped, but everything we packed was soggy.

Tamara had brought a bag of mini-pumpkins to put in interesting places as we went downstream. Someone ahead of us was also decorating with pumpkins, and some of their placements were pretty bold. As we approached Mule Creek Canyon, Tam mused about the possibility of placing a pumpkin on top of one of the "jaws"—the two boulders that mark the entry to the canyon. Of course, we dismissed the idea as impossible, but when we got there, the other people had actually managed to do it. It was impressive, and it saved me from trying something stupid.

My run through Mule Creek Canyon, the Narrows, and the Coffee Pot went well, with only light, inconsequential contact with the canyon walls. And then we had forty minutes of relaxing, smooth floating before arriving at Blossom Bar.

We made a quick hike up to a place where we could see that there were no boats lodged anywhere in the rapid, something that is fairly common and which occasionally interferes with navigation. Finding our path clear, we returned to the raft to make our run.

Photo by JP Baysinger
Blossom Bar, as seen from the scouting trail.

Starting near the left wall, I rowed against the current to slow the raft as we dropped toward the first critical turn. A perfect eddy turn put us right where I wanted to be, and we squeezed past the picket fence rocks. Then, just as I was starting to position for the big drop, the bow of the raft scraped the big conglomerate rock on the right above the main chute. It wasn't much contact, but the back of the raft swung to my left.

"Okay, I guess we're going down backward," I said to Tam.

That would've been fine, but then I brushed the boulder on the left-hand side of the chute, which bounced us back and turned the bow downstream. In an instant, our backward run changed back into a forward run—straight at the boulder thirty feet ahead.

I'd misjudged something—maybe the size of the raft, maybe the momentum, maybe the speed of the current at that spot. Thirty feet ahead, the eight-foot boulder was directly in my path. There wasn't time to make the pull to the left, around the boulder, so I made a desperate attempt to slow the raft for the inevitable collision.

As we hit, the stern swung left, and the left side of the raft climbed up the rock. Tam jumped to the high side, but it kept going higher. I saw her fall across the raft and out of it, an instant before I too went out. I was certain that the raft

Photo by JP Baysinger

Main chute on the right, Picket Fence on the left. At this higher flow, the current in the chute goes to the left of the boulder in the upper center. But this time, it ran straight at it.

was coming over on top of me. For a few seconds, I was disoriented. Before I even realized that the raft was still right-side-up and moving downstream, I managed to grab a side handle.

And then the raft pushed my back against a rock that lay just below the surface. Next to that was another rock, standing about a foot out of the water. The raft stopped, upright, but holding me against the rock. Tamara appeared above me, having passed underneath the raft and somehow climbing back in.

Odd things can happen in moments like that. I gave her my glasses and hat, to keep from losing them. She tried to pull me up, but the combination of my 190 lbs. and the fact that I was pressed against the rock made it impossible. The bulk of my high-floatation life jacket was a mixed asset. On the one hand, it cushioned my back, but on the other hand, it exacerbated the pinning effect.

We struggled that way for about sixty seconds, while the surging water bounced the raft up and down. My worst moment was when the raft began to free itself. It ratcheted me down as it started to squeeze past the rock that held me. But suddenly, I was free—under the raft, but no longer pinned. I got to the surface and took a much-needed gasp of air. I again grabbed the raft, but was still unable to get in. While grasping my life jacket with one hand, Tamara deployed my boarding ladder with the other. But I couldn't find the first step or get my foot onto it.

Tam asked, "Should I hold onto you or row the raft?"

"Row!" I sputtered.

We were moving downstream, and I saw that we were heading right at the "ramp rock," and I was in position to get pinned again. I let go and pushed myself away from the raft, bumping around the end of the ramp rock and over a submerged rock just below. While Tam scrambled to get the spare oar un-strapped, I watched *Vanguard* go by, no longer a threat to me.

I stroked desperately to get my feet out front to fend off the rocks. I bounced to the right of the Volkswagen rock, over a submerged rock into a reversal that pulled me under. I needed every ounce of my lifejacket's twenty-seven pounds of buoyancy, and wished it had more. My multi-layer raingear was filled with water and acting like an anchor. That's something to re-think in the future.

Backstroking hard against the current and angling to my left, I fought for every gasp of air. My lifejacket was tight, and it seemed to be keeping me from getting a full breath. One wave after another buried me, without any apparent rhythm. Surviving this was not a sure thing.

This could be my last run through Blossom Bar. I may never come back to try it again.

And then I found myself on the edge of a little eddy, ten feet from the left bank. As I was swept around a submerged rock, I planted my feet against it and pushed off toward shore. A second later I touched dry rock and found footing in the shallow water.

By then, Tamara was wrestling the raft to shore about 150 yards downstream. I climbed ashore and unbuckled my lifejacket, trying to catch my breath. Relief was tempered by the fact that in all of my trips down the Rogue, this was the first time I'd ever had trouble at Blossom Bar. As I started my careful climb over, around, and through the boulders, I saw Tam heading my way.

"You need help?" she asked.

"No. I'm okay. Just out of breath."

About the time I got down to *Vanguard*, another raft went past, and we asked them to be on the lookout for the oar that we'd lost. They answered that they'd lost one too. We never saw theirs or ours. I love Cataract oars, but floating is something that they aren't very good at doing.

Tam rowed us down to the big sun-drenched rock beach opposite Halfmoon Bar, where we peeled off water-logged clothing and soaked-up the warmth. The water hadn't been very cold—around sixty degrees—so hypothermia wasn't the issue. Exhaustion was the issue. Adrenaline consumes a lot of energy.

We ate lunch, and didn't feel like continuing downstream until clouds formed and started blotting-out the sunshine. It had been great while it lasted. Tam rowed us through the still water of Huggins Canyon, past Brushy Bar and Solitude, to Tate Creek and Tacoma Camp.

Feeling that more rain was imminent, we set up our canopy before building the kitchen under it. And the rain did come—just sprinkles in the evening, but for real throughout the night. During a brief lull in the rain, at 1:15 a.m., I heard four loud, distinctive yells.

The voice was human-like, but didn't form words. It sounded exactly like recordings of Sasquatch yells that I'd heard on a recent episode of *Finding Bigfoot* on the Travel Channel. I can think of no earthly reason why a person would be out in the wilderness in the middle of a rainy night, yelling loudly with no clear message. I'm certain that I heard Sasquatch.

Photo by Author

Jim and Tamara always wanted to camp in this cave in Clay Hill Flats.

It rained very hard at times during the rest of the night, but had stopped by the time we got up. We compared bruises, finding that Tam's were better than mine, and included a goose egg on her forehead. My arms and shoulders ached from exertion during my attempts to get back into the raft. But all-in-all, we'd gotten off easy. The only thing lost, other than the oar, was my

Photo by Author

For several years, we made our final night's camp on the rocks at Flora Dell.

Photo by Author
My son Jim at Flora Dell Falls in 1987

pride. I'll never know for sure exactly what I could have done differently that would have prevented the accident.

I sat in the passenger seat for the float down to Foster Bar, while Tam rowed us neatly through Tacoma rapid and Clay Hill Rapid. She made a comment about how unexpectedly sluggish *Vanguard* was in comparison with her *Cheyenne*. Yeah. I knew that. I'd gotten *Vanguard* before our first Grand Canyon run, and I passed *Cheyenne* down to Tam. I was glad to have the larger boat in the canyon, but have always missed *Cheyenne's* relative nimbleness.

We floated the raft onto the trailer at Foster Bar, and then went up and made lunch outside the new building with changing rooms and real indoor plumbing. I asked others if they'd picked up my oar, and one group showed me half an oar that they'd recovered—it was a blue Cataract oar, but it wasn't mine. It had been a bad day for Cataract oars at Blossom Bar.

On our drive back over Bear Camp Road, we ran into fresh snow at the highest elevations. After a fuel stop in Merlin, I made the non-stop drive home, arriving shortly after dark. In the following week, I got all of my gear cleaned-up, dried-out, and put away.

Throughout the entire process, I pondered whether I was doing it for the last time. My Blossom Bar accident had cast a shadow over my future. Maybe it was time to hang up my oars for good

But like the aging quarterback on a football team, I didn't want to go out on a low note. So, when the permit lotteries started accepting applications for the 2022 season, I joined The Clan discussion, as though I would be there.

Naturally, we all struck out in the lottery, so we settled on the Lower Salmon. That trip went well, and in the next lottery we won a permit to float the Main Salmon in 2023. But massive forest fires in the Salmon River canyon closed the river, so at the last minute, we switched to the Lower Salmon, deferring our permit until the same date in 2024.

We made the run from Spring Creek (near Shoup, Idaho) to Spring Bar (upstream from Riggins) in August, 2024. We had a great trip, but I find myself again wondering if it was my swan song.

Members of The Clan are talking about going for a Hells Canyon permit in the lottery for 2025. I know I'm capable of doing it, but I also know that I can't keep rafting forever, so, stay tuned.

Also by Ken Baysinger
El Camino

A Chevrolet El Camino pulled from Oregon's Willamette River brings new life to a 30-year-old mystery. The disappearance of Jessie Devonshire and Randy Mendelson had been big news in 1980, and it remained the area's most notorious unsolved case. It couldn't even be properly called an unsolved crime, because it had never been proven that a crime had been committed. All that was known was that fifteen-year-old Jessie Devonshire had vanished without a trace and that Randy Mendelson, a twenty-year-old landscaper, had disappeared at the same time.

In the apparent absence of evidence, officials concluded that the two young people had eloped, and the news media quickly lost interest. But the discovery of Randy's El Camino changed everything. Everything, that is, except the fact that Jessie Devonshire was the stepdaughter of Wilson Landis Devonshire, who was an official in the Portland Mayor's office and a rising star among Oregon's political elite.

Within the Clackamas County law-enforcement community, the Mendelson-Devonshire case had been a hot potato for at least ten years following the disappearances. Careers and lives had ended because detectives were unable to provide the answers that the politically powerful principals in the case demanded.

A private investigator by the name of Corrigan can change everything—if he can stay alive and prove the corruption behind the case and cover-up.

ISBN: 978-1-947491-98-4 © 2017

Yorkshire Publishing 392 pages $24.99

www.kenbaysinger.com

Also by Ken Baysinger
Deadly Gold

A tugboat captain salvaging logs from Oregon's Willamette River snags a roll of old carpet containing the skeletal remains of a long-missing young woman, weighted down by a cast iron anchor. The private investigator called Corrigan, having just solved the notorious Mendelson-Devonshire murders, once again finds himself trying to unravel the mystery of a murder victim whose body was pulled from the river many years after her death. The investigation takes Corrigan a hundred twenty-five years back in Oregon history.

In the afternoon of May 25, 1887, thirty-four gold miners lay dead on a gravel bar where Deadline Creek flowed into the Snake River in the depths of Hells Canyon. From the surrounding bluffs, a small gang of cattle rustlers had poured gunfire down on the defenseless miners, who had committed two cardinal sins: they were Chinese, and they had found gold.

In the course of his year-long investigation into the death of Tara Foster, Corrigan learns that there is no limit to the mayhem that is triggered by lust for the Deadly Gold.

ISBN: 978-1-947491-99-1 © 2017

Yorkshire Publishing 402 pages $24.99

www.kenbaysinger.com

Also by Ken Baysinger
Missing and Exploited

A car collector looking for a place to store his vintage Studebakers stumbles across a name carved in a wooden beam from a century-old building. Just a quarter-mile away, the skeletal remains of a young woman are found outside a homeless camp. The investigation that Corrigan starts as a favor to his old friend quickly becomes a nightmare beyond anything he could have imagined. As the body count rises, the mystery becomes ever deeper, until it takes on a life of its own.

For three decades children have been vanishing without a trace, until Corrigan uncovers the terrible truth. And nothing comes without a cost. Relationships are torn apart, and at times even nature works against Corrigan and his small team of investigators as they chase down obscure clues from the cold case files. Chasing leads across five states over six months, Corrigan faces the greatest challenges of his investigative career.

ISBN: 978-1-5245-5269-5 © 2016

Xlibris   390 pages $24.99

www.kenbaysinger.com

Also by Ken Baysinger
Confluence
Second Edition

Frustrated that their "people's revolution" never materialized, a cadre of geriatric radicals hatches a plot to blow up hydropower dams in the Pacific Northwest and replicate the great ice-age floods that carved the Columbia River Gorge.

They get support through an unexpected alliance with old-line communists, the new incarnation of Russia's KGB, the government of Iran, and a would-be terrorist in Key West who has possession of a cold war era hydrogen bomb.

Undetected by Homeland Security, the plot is uncovered by "Swede" Larsson, Town Marshal in Riggins, Idaho (population 406), while investigating the seemingly accidental drowning of a young man in the Salmon River. As the scope of the conspiracy becomes apparent, Swede is joined by his river guide friend Cassidy Pierce and former Vietnam combat pilot Terry Caldwell in a desperate race to prevent a cataclysmic flood.

ISBN: 979-8-218-00779-9 © 2022

Ingram Spark   670 pages $29.99

www.kenbaysinger.com

Also by Ken Baysinger
Identities

By the time he was 77 years old, David Adelman knew that his body was failing. When he read about a seminar that would explore the medical possibilities for getting a fresh chance at being young, David's curiosity was more than just academic. Despite his skepticism, he bought a $25,000 membership in the Human Transmigration Project.

A decade later, barely clinging to life, he learns that he holds the winning ticket in mankind's greatest lottery. And this isn't a simple game of chance. It is cutting-edge medical technology, and David becomes the subject of history's first human transmigration. But his new life holds a shocking surprise that forces him to question some of his life-long beliefs about human nature. Even as he makes the unexpectedly difficult transition into his new life, he finds himself in the center of a mystery that escalates into a desperate fight for the life of a girl he knows only through a strangely vivid recurring dream. And when questionable accidents start taking lives in the small college town of Arcata, California, evidence stacks up against one young man whose motives are as sinister as his actions are devious, leading to a deadly showdown.

ISBN: 979-8-218-01586-2 © 2022

Ingram Spark 360 pages $24.99

www.kenbaysinger.com

Also by Ken Baysinger
Lilac City
the end of innocence

In the spring of 1960, residents of Spokane, in eastern Washington state were trying to understand what was happening to their city. Just a year earlier, a nine-year-old girl selling Campfire mints was abducted, raped, and murdered. The case remained unsolved. Then, on March 20, 1960, Lisa and Gail Draper, high school girls from Spokane Valley vanished while returning home from Seattle, where they had attended the state basketball tournament. Lisa's new Ford Falcon was found abandoned at a roadside café in Ritzville, seventy miles from the girls' home.

Connie Pratt, a second-generation radio and TV repairman, had begun a second career as a private investigator. He will find himself working on behalf of a man who has been convicted of killing the Draper sisters. It is an uphill fight, as the clock ticks toward the execution date.

Pratt puts his life on the line to back up his belief that the man on death row was innocent of the crime. And he gets no help from the authorities, who are convinced that they got the right man. It's a nail-biting race to beat the hangman to the gallows.

ISBN: 979-8-218-45714-3 © 2024

Ingram Spark 386 pages $24.99

www.kenbaysinger.com

www.ingramcontent.com/pod-product-compliance
Lightning Source LLC
La Vergne TN
LVHW021759060526
838201LV00058B/3159